Apple Training Series

Mac OS X
Deployment v10.6

Kevin M. White

Apple Training Series: Mac OS X Deployment v10.6
Kevin M. White

Published by Peachpit Press. For information on Peachpit Press books, contact:
Peachpit Press
1249 Eighth Street
Berkeley, CA 94710
510/524-2178
510/524-2221 (fax)

Find us on the Web at: www.peachpit.com
To report errors, please send a note to errata@peachpit.com
Peachpit Press is a division of Pearson Education

Copyright © 2010 by Apple Inc.

Apple Training Series Editor: Rebecca Freed
Production Editor: Danielle Foster
Copyeditor: Peggy Nauts
Tech Editors: John Signa, Paul Suh
Proofreader: Whitney Walker
Compositor: Danielle Foster
Indexer: Valerie Perry
Cover Illustrator: Kent Oberheu
Cover Production: Happenstance Type-O-Rama

ISBN 13: 978-0-321-63531-0
ISBN 10: 0-321-63531-0

9 8 7 6 5 4 3 2 1

Printed and bound in the United States of America

Acknowledgments

In addition to the amazing staff at Peachpit who were instrumental in completing this work, I would also like to thank the development team for their hard work: John Signa, Simon Wheatley, and Paul Suh. Additional thanks go out to John DeTroye, Jussi-Pekka Mantere, Brian Nesse, Armin Briegel, Arek Dreyer, Schoun Regan, Josh Wisenbaker, Shane Ross, Brian Gupton, the MMR List, and the Blue Man Guild. Finally, I could not have made this journey without the support of my friends and family.

This book is dedicated to my best friend and lovely wife, Michelle.

Table of Contents

Getting Started

This book is based on the same objectives covered in Apple's official training course, Mac OS X Deployment 10.6. This book focuses on solutions for deploying software, ranging from the installation of individual files to the deployment of complete system images to multiple computers. You will learn what you need to create a full deployment plan that includes testing, hardware and software deployment, auditing, and maintenance.

You will also obtain the skills necessary to create a tiered Software Update server solution, as well as learn about third-party solutions to supplement tools provided by Apple. You will get step-by-step instructions for using tools such as Apple Remote Desktop, Disk Utility, PackageMaker, and System Image Utility, and become acquainted with the pros and cons of each for different deployment situations.

This book refers to Apple Knowledge Base documents throughout the chapters, and it closes each chapter with a list of recommended documents related to the topic of the chapter. The Knowledge Base is a free online resource (www.apple.com/support) containing the very latest technical information on all Apple hardware and software products. You are strongly encouraged to read the suggested documents and search the Knowledge Base for answers to any problems you encounter.

You'll also find "More Info" resources that provide ancillary information throughout the chapters and are summarized at the end of each chapter. These resources are merely for your edification and are not considered essential for the coursework or certification.

At the end of each chapter is a short chapter review and quiz that recaps the material you've learned. You can refer to various Apple resources, such as the Knowledge Base, as well as the chapters themselves, to help you answer these questions.

Apple Certification

After reading this manual, you may wish to take the Mac OS X Deployment 10.6 Exam, which counts toward two certifications: Apple Certified Specialist—Deployment 10.6 and Apple Certified System Administrator 10.6 (ACSA) certification.

> **NOTE** ▶ Although all of the questions in the Mac OS X Deployment 10.6 Exam are based on material in this manual, simply reading this manual will not adequately prepare you for all the specific issues addressed by the exam. Apple recommends that before taking the exam, you spend time actually trying some of the Mac OS X deployment techniques covered in this book. You should also download and review the Skills Assessment Guide for the exam, which lists the exam objectives, the total number of items, the number of items per section, the required score to pass, and how to register. To download the Skills Assessment Guide, visit http://training.apple.com/certification/macosx. There you can also download the Sample Test, where you will find practice questions.

Apple Certified Specialist—Deployment 10.6 certification requires passing two exams: Mac OS X Server Essentials 10.6 and Mac OS X Deployment 10.6.

ACSA 10.6 certification requires passing four exams: Mac OS X Server Essentials 10.6, Mac OS X Directory Services 10.6, Mac OS X Deployment 10.6, and Mac OS X Security and Mobility 10.6.

ACSA certification verifies an in-depth knowledge of Apple technical architecture and an ability to install and configure machines; architect and maintain networks; enable, customize, tune, and troubleshoot a wide range of services; and integrate Mac OS X, Mac OS X Server, and other Apple technologies within a multiplatform, networked environment. The ACSA certification is intended for full-time professional system administrators and engineers who manage medium-to-large networks of systems in complex multiplatform deployments.

About the Apple Training Series

Mac OS X Deployment v10.6 is part of the extensive official training series for Apple products developed by experts in the field and certified by Apple. The chapters are designed to let you learn at your own pace. You can progress through the manual from beginning to end, or you can dive right into the chapters that interest you most.

For those who prefer to learn in an instructor-led setting, Apple also offers training courses at Apple Authorized Training Centers worldwide. These courses are taught by Apple Certified Trainers, and they balance concepts and lectures with hands-on labs and exercises. Apple Authorized Training Centers have been carefully selected and have met Apple's highest standards in all areas, including facilities, instructors, course delivery, and infrastructure. The goal of the program is to offer Apple customers, from beginners to the most seasoned professionals, the highest-quality training experience.

To find an Authorized Training Center near you, please visit http://training.apple.com/locations.

1

Chapter Files	Deployment Planning Template.pdf, available at www.peachpit.com/acsa.deployment
Time	This chapter takes approximately 1 hour to complete.
Goals	Learn the main deployment concepts you will use to formulate a complete deployment solution
	Start using the Deployment Planning Template to help create a deployment plan
	Establish a plan for deploying and securing computer hardware
	Define usage policies and explore policy-enforcement techniques
	Finalize your deployment plan by considering testing methodologies and service-level agreements

Chapter 1
Deployment Planning

Planning is the most important step in your Mac deployment process; judicious planning always pays off later. The primary goal of system deployment, after all, is to efficiently distribute a uniform computing environment, and the amount of time spent planning will no doubt be less than the amount of time spent fixing a problem that has been replicated on all your computers.

No single deployment plan works in all situations. Many deployment technologies and techniques are available, and plans are as varied as the organizations that use them. This book will help you choose the approaches and tools that best fit your needs.

First, this chapter introduces you to the six main deployment concepts that make up a complete solution. Next, this chapter delves into two topics that are not central to deployment of Mac OS X software, yet are an important part of a complete deployment solution: hardware logistics and usage management. Finally, this chapter will cover planning concepts that help avoid future problems, including recommendations for test planning and service-level agreements.

Using the Deployment Planning Template

This book will help you develop a complete deployment solution, and you will learn many deployment tools and techniques, but having this technical knowledge does not necessarily mean that you have a good plan. To help you create a deployment plan, a Deployment Planning Template has been created to accompany this book. This document is provided as a digital file so you can print it out on plain paper, which is an easier format to work with when planning. It's available as a free download at www.peachpit.com/acsa.deployment.

As you learn new deployment techniques reading through this book, you're encouraged to document the techniques that you think will work best in your deployment plan. The Deployment Planning Template is formatted to make it easy for you to plan each deployment step. Each section is organized in table format to help you apply specific techniques and solutions to your particular deployment tasks.

Deployment Planning Template

Chapter 1: Infrastructure Considerations

Use this template to document any hardware infrastructure considerations that arise during the planning stage of your deployment.

Will your new equipment work within your current power infrastructure?

Location	Power Availability	Power Requirements

Will there be any high-performance or high-density situations that require more cooling?

What are the network requirements for your new equipment?

Location	Wired Links	Wireless Clients	Bandwidth

Understanding Deployment Concepts

You certainly could start by identifying specific technical solutions, and then create a plan around those solutions. However, this bottom-up approach yields inflexible solutions because you've already chosen the answers before you've considered the problem as a whole. Instead, this book takes a top-down approach, first identifying the primary elements that make up a complete deployment solution.

You'll find, however, that no matter the size or scope, all deployment solutions consist of one or more of the following main concepts: hardware logistics, usage management, item deployment, system deployment, postimaging tasks, and system maintenance.

Hardware Logistics

How are you going to physically deliver the computers to your users or get them onto their desks or into the lab? And delivery is just one part of the physical deployment. You must also consider your deployment's load on your infrastructure and its physical security and consider the replacement or disposal of your existing system.

The concept of hardware logistics is covered later in this chapter in the "Planning Hardware Logistics" section.

Usage Management

Once your systems have been deployed, how will you maintain a secure and consistent user environment? Your organization's management is likely responsible for creating policy that defines users' access to computing resources. The enforcement of these usage policies must be implemented as part of your deployment plan.

Usage management is also covered later in this chapter in the "Planning Usage Management" section.

Item Deployment

In some instances, deploying individual files, folders, or software items, such as an application or a new driver, to your computers may be all you need to do. How will you efficiently deploy these items to all your computers? A variety of techniques can help you accomplish this task.

Item deployment is covered in Chapter 2, "Deploying Individual Items and Containers," and in Chapter 3, "Deploying with Installation Packages."

System Deployment

How will you ensure that all your computers have the appropriate software and uniform configurations? This concept is what most administrators think of when *deployment* is mentioned. After all, maintaining a uniform computing environment across all your systems is the best way to ensure that things run smoothly. As you can imagine, deploying entire systems is more complex than deploying single items, and there are many approaches you can take to achieving a uniform environment. This topic receives the most attention in this book.

System deployment is covered in Chapter 4, "Creating System Images," and in Chapter 5, "Deploying System Images."

Postimaging Tasks

What individual configuration needs to occur on each Mac after they have all received identical systems? Although maintaining system uniformity is a primary deployment goal, some settings must be unique to each computer—for example, each computer must have a unique network configuration. The challenge is to deploy these unique settings on multiple Macs as efficiently as possible.

Postimaging tasks are covered in Chapter 6, "Postimaging Deployment Considerations."

System Maintenance

How will you efficiently make administrative changes and monitor activity on all your computers? How will you ensure that licensed software is properly accounted for on all your computers? How will you keep the software on all your computers up-to-date? Solutions that allow you to perform these tasks quickly on multiple computers simultaneously are a necessity for maintaining your deployed systems.

All of these topics are covered in Chapter 7, "System Maintenance."

Planning Hardware Logistics

Hardware logistics may be a simple issue for some, but for larger deployments the logistics of handling the physical hardware can be a major undertaking. This section explores the ramifications of deploying new hardware and guides you through the process of estimating and planning the deployment of new hardware and the disposal of the hardware you are replacing.

Infrastructure Considerations

First, you must determine whether your infrastructure is equipped to handle the new or additional computers you intend to deploy. If, during your rollout, you discover that your infrastructure doesn't have the power, cooling, or bandwidth capacity to support your new computers, you will be faced with an additional costly infrastructure upgrade that you didn't see coming, or your deployment will fail. With proper planning, however, this scenario can be avoided.

Power Infrastructure

Apple and Intel have made great strides toward minimizing the power requirements for Macintosh computers. Nevertheless, the demand for higher-performance equipment is driving power requirements for computers ever higher, and the additional peripherals in your new system will also draw from your power infrastructure. Further, the electrical systems of many older buildings were not designed for modern computing environments. Even if you're using infrastructure that supported your previous computing resources, you should double-check the power requirements for your new hardware and make sure that your infrastructure can handle the load.

> **NOTE** ▶ If you overload a power circuit, in most cases a safety breaker will kill the power to prevent the wiring from overheating and starting a fire. Other times, your equipment may experience low power situations commonly referred to as brownouts. Either situation is generally bad for your computer equipment and should be avoided. Shorts and brownouts are common causes of damaged power supplies and logic boards.

The most accurate method for making sure that your infrastructure meets the power needs of your new system is to test one of your new computers using a pass-through electric monitor. These devices accurately measure the electric usage of your equipment. It's important to understand that the power draw of a computer varies widely between sitting idle and crunching numbers, so you should use an electric monitor that can track peak usage and averages.

You can also estimate the power requirements of your new computers using simple calculations.

Electric power is measured by the watt, and electric current is measured in amperes (or *amps*). Most computer equipment is rated by the amount of power (*watts*) that is used during operation. Most electric outlets and circuits, on the other hand, are rated by the amount of current that runs though the wiring (amps). As long as you know the voltage (*volts*) of an electrical system, you can easily translate between watts and amps. In North America, Japan, some Central and South American countries, and some Pacific islands, standard wall power outlets supply between 100 and 127 volts. Outlets in most of the rest of the countries in the world supply 220 or 240 volts. There are some countries (such as Brazil or Saudi Arabia) where different regions have different voltages within the same country, and even in countries where the standard is 120 volts there are often 220-volt outlets for special purposes. Check your wiring and use the appropriate value in your calculations.

To calculate the power requirements for your new deployment:

1 Find the standard power usage of the equipment you're going to be using in your deployment.

   Vendors are required to list power usage on the outside of the equipment or in the documentation. The power requirements for Apple hardware is listed on the Apple website. Each Mac model has its own set of web pages, and the power requirements are located on the Technical Specifications page.

2 Calculate the number of amps required. Vendors list the power requirements in watts, so to calculate the amps, divide the watts by the circuit volts (watts ÷ volts = amps).

   For example, if you were deploying 21.5-inch iMac computers, according to the Apple website, they would draw a maximum of 241 watts. Assuming standard voltage of 120 volts, the maximum current that a 21.5-inch iMac requires is roughly 2 amps (241W ÷ 120 V = 2.01A).

3 Calculate the power requirements that your infrastructure can support. Standard wall power circuits are generally 15 or 20 amps per circuit.

   Some simple division enables you to figure that a 15-amp circuit will support seven 21.5-inch iMac systems (15A ÷ 2A = 7.5), and a 20-amp circuit will support ten 21.5-inch iMac systems (20A ÷ 2A = 10).

Note that these are maximum-rated loads; in typical usage it is rare for computers to draw anything even close to this level of power. Using this method will likely significantly overestimate the power usage of your systems. Because of this, it is always better to use a meter to determine the power usage of your equipment.

Beyond the computers themselves, you should also consider the power requirements of peripheral equipment such as USB hubs, Ethernet switches and routers, and laser printers. These can add a significant additional load.

Another factor that you will need to consider is which outlets are tied into individual circuits. Especially in older buildings or areas not designed for computer systems, multiple individual wall outlets (even in separate rooms) may be part of a single circuit and may even be tied to the lighting. Be sure to verify the capacity of your power infrastructure with someone who understands the issues, such as an electrician who specializes in infrastructure for computer systems.

> **TIP** Ideally, your computing equipment should be supplied power from sources behind power conditioners or uninterruptible power supplies that provide a steady stream of power should there be any external interruptions to your power source. These solutions range from support for a single computer to support for entire office complexes, and they are available from a variety of vendors.

Cooling Infrastructure

Computers, like humans, prefer to operate within a comfortable temperature range. If you navigate to the Apple Technical Specifications webpages, you'll note that most Apple computers are designed to operate in an environment with ambient temperatures between 50° to 95° F (10° to 35° C). Generally, keeping the ambient temperature cool enough is the focus for most administrators, as modern computer hardware can give off quite a bit of heat.

All modern Macintosh computers have thermostats and cooling systems that will try to prevent them from overheating. Nevertheless, if the ambient temperature is too high, the computer is very likely to fail and even be seriously damaged.

There is no specific rule to follow when it comes to gauging cooling infrastructure requirements, and for many deployments no adjustment is necessary. However, if you are deploying high-power Macintosh hardware (Mac Pro or Xserve computers) or your environment is especially dense, like that found in computer labs or server closets, you may need to reevaluate your cooling infrastructure. A general rule of thumb for high-power and high-density deployments is that every amp used to power the computing equipment should be matched by another amp used to provide cooling. Again, though, there are many variables to consider, and you should consult a heating, ventilating, and air conditioning (HVAC) specialist.

MORE INFO ▶ Apple lists the specific heat output of nonportable Mac hardware in the following Knowledge Base articles: HT3468, Mac mini; HT3559, iMac; HT2836, Mac Pro; and HT3513, Xserve.

Network Infrastructure

Scoping an appropriate network infrastructure is a book unto itself, but at the very least you need to estimate the network link and bandwidth requirements for your new deployment.

From a network link perspective, it's simple to estimate wired network requirements. Generally, you need as many available Ethernet ports as you have computers or network devices to deploy. Planning an appropriate wireless network, on the other hand, is much more complicated. The availability of these networks is affected by interference variables you may have little control over. In any case, you will need to define a few primary specifications for your wireless network, including the expected number of simultaneous users, the required coverage area, and the minimum required bandwidth.

You should also take into consideration the bandwidth and architecture required by any network-based deployment tools you plan to use. Some of the deployment methodologies covered in this book can require a lot of network bandwidth. You will be well served to do some preliminary bandwidth testing using your chosen deployment tools.

Hardware Security

It's no secret that Mac computers are very desirable and valuable objects, thus making them high-priority targets for thieves. Further, the svelte design of many Mac systems makes them even easier pickings because they are so compact and easy to transport. Consequently, protecting your Apple hardware from theft should be a fundamental part of your deployment plan.

The physical security required will vary based on the location, mobility, and purpose of your deployed computers. Additional security should always be considered in open environments such as computer labs and conference areas. Office environments and equipment rooms are already generally secure and probably don't require any additional security measures. Portable computers pose a more complex security problem because physical security is often left to the computer's user. Fortunately there are a wide variety of third-party security options available for Macintosh computers.

MORE INFO ▶ To learn more about data and network security, please refer to *Apple Training Series: Mac OS X Security and Mobility v10.6* (Peachpit Press, 2010).

Secure Location

Security starts with the actual location of your deployed computers. If your computers are located in a highly secure environment, then you probably don't need to consider additional measures. For this reason, you should make every attempt to secure the location where your computers reside. Solutions include any method you would normally use to secure a room, including door locks, alarm systems, and surveillance systems. For open lab environments, simply having full-time lab attendant staff in the area is usually pretty good theft deterrence. If you want to protect the computers from the staff as well, you should consider implementing additional physical security mechanisms.

Physical Security Mechanisms

If you don't have an adequately secure location, you can choose from a variety of locking mechanisms to physically secure your Macintosh computers. All modern Macintosh portable computers (excluding MacBook Air) and desktop systems feature some sort of interface that allows an external lock mechanism. Most Mac computers feature the Kensington security slot as part of their external housing. This is a small slot that allows you to attach a compatible security lock without having to modify your computer's case. Kensington and other third-party manufacturers sell a wide range of security solutions that work with the built-in security slot.

Recent desktop tower Mac systems also feature a more traditional locking mechanism to restrict access to the internal components. You may find that common padlock-style locking mechanisms are a viable option for securing this type of Mac. The company Noble sells a line of custom Mac locks that work well in this situation.

If you want to secure only smaller items, such as portable computers and iPods when they aren't in use, you should consider storage carts. Secure storage carts also come in many shapes and sizes, but one vendor, Bretford, has partnered with Apple to create security carts that specifically fit portable Macintosh computers. Bretford also manufactures security carts for iPod deployments.

Theft-Recovery Solutions

Portable computers aren't nearly as convenient when they are locked to a desk, so at some point you may have portables that are destined to leave your secure facilities. Even if you trust the user who is taking the portable on the road, you simply have no way to ensure the physical security of the computer when it's outside your secure location. You can provide your user with a locking mechanism, but you still can't guarantee that it will be used.

In this case, you may want to invest in a portable theft-recovery solution. Third-party theft recovery solutions include; Computrace LoJack for Laptops by AbsoluteSoftware, MacTrak by GadgetTrak, and Undercover by Orbicule. These third-party solutions install hidden background software on your Mac OS X computers that will help law enforcement officials locate your portable should it be stolen. The software works by "phoning home" via the Internet during regular intervals. If you report your portable as stolen, the solution's vendor will help you track the computer if it becomes active on the Internet.

Hardware Handling Logistics

The delivery person is here with a truck full of new computers. Now what? If your deployment plan includes detailed handling logistics, you will be well prepared for this moment. But what are you going to do with all your old computers? Your deployment plan should also include handling logistics regarding movement or disposal of old equipment. Finally, at some point you will likely have to deal with hardware failure. How do you plan to quickly resolve hardware replacement issues?

Hardware Installation

For most technophiles, unboxing new hardware is a joyous occasion, but if you have a building or campus full of new computers to deploy, it becomes another logistical hurdle you must overcome. You should plan a workflow that takes into account all the stages from delivery to deployment. Typical installation workflows include these steps:

1   Receive delivery. Make sure your receiving staff is ready for your order and that the location is equipped to securely receive and temporarily store your new equipment in its packaging.

2   Unbox equipment. Large deployments usually require a staging area where the equipment is unboxed and sorted. The packaging materials will also need to be sorted and moved to the proper location for disposal or recycling. You may want to save some of the packaging in case you need to store or return equipment.

3   Record or tag assets. Most organizations require that physical assets, such as computers, be tracked and possibly tagged for accounting purposes.

4   Perform initial configuration. It's best to configure your computers before they are physically deployed. It's common to set up a specific system imaging area where you load your preconfigured image onto the new computers.

5   Test equipment. You may want to test your new computers prior to deployment so that you can immediately repair or replace bad equipment before it has a chance to affect your users. Testing routines vary, but for mission-critical applications, you will want to perform a "burn in" of your new equipment by letting it run continuously for several hours or days before it is deployed.

6   Deploy equipment to user or location. You must actually deploy the new computers to the locations where they will be used. Someone from your staff will likely also have to connect any cables and secure the new computers.

To properly manage these installation tasks, you will need to estimate the amount of time, workspace, and manpower required for each stage. Everyone involved will want to know when the computers will be deployed, so you should try to stick to a schedule. To successfully meet that schedule, you will need to procure an appropriate amount of deployment workspace and staff to complete the installation job.

> **TIP** ▸ When purchasing new computers, Apple can provide your organization with a custom software solution or a professional services solution that can take care of many of these installation logistic issues. Your Apple account executive will help to find the installation solution that is right for your organization.

Disposal and Recycling

There are many logistic similarities between the disposal of obsolete computers and the installation of new ones. Both require adequate planning and accurate estimation of time, workspace, and manpower to be successful. A typical disposal workflow includes these steps:

1   Back up or transfer user data. There is a very good chance that your users will have data that they want to save or move to the new computers. Your current installation should already have a backup system in place, but it may be faster to directly transfer user data to the new computers as part of your deployment plan.

2 Securely erase data. Some of your computers may store sensitive data. If this is the case, and your old computers' hard drives aren't destined to be destroyed during disposal, then you will need to securely erase the data from those drives.

> **MORE INFO** ▶ To learn more about securely erasing hard drives, please refer to *Apple Training Series: Mac OS X Support Essentials v10.6* (Peachpit Press, 2010).

3 Take inventory. Identify the computers slated for replacement or disposal. This inventory may be required for both internal accounting and for the records of whomever is receiving your old computers.

4 Collect the equipment. Someone will have to collect the old computers and transport them to the disposal destination. Often this task is handled by the same staff that delivers the replacement computers.

5 Dispose of the equipment. In most cases, the company or individual who will be receiving your old computers will be picking them up at your location, but you will have to define a location to temporarily store the old computers until they leave your facility.

> **NOTE** ▶ All local waste or recycling services require special handling for any type of battery. You should always check with your waste service provider when disposing of any electronic equipment.

Computer equipment is both highly desirable for recyclers and highly toxic in traditional waste streams. Many localities require special handling for the disposal of electronic equipment. Even if you're not sure what your local regulations are, attempting to find a service that will recycle or resell your old computers is the right thing to do.

> **TIP** ▶ When purchasing new computers, Apple can provide your organization with a disposal or recycling solution that may actually net your organization some monetary return. Your Apple account executive will help to find the disposal solution that is right for your organization.

Repair and Replacement

It's inevitable that at some point hardware equipment will either malfunction or break from misuse. The more equipment you have the more likely you will have to deal with repair or replacement issues. Apple has a wide network of Apple Authorized Service Providers (AASPs) that can perform in- or out-of-warranty service for your Apple equipment.

> **MORE INFO** ▶ You can find your local Apple Authorized Service Provider from Apple's service site, www.apple.com/support.

However, if you are deploying a large number of systems, relying solely on a third-party source for your equipment repair may not be the best solution. Many Apple customers with large numbers of Macs are better served by implementing local repair and replacement techniques. This allows the customer to receive a much quicker turnaround for hardware repair and replacement procedures than through an AASP. As part of your deployment plan, consider implementing the following techniques for dealing with hardware repair and replacement:

▶ Apple's Self-Service Account program. As the name implies, this allows customers to perform their own repairs for in- or out-of-warranty Apple hardware. This program includes access to Apple's online service system and next-day shipment for many replacement parts. You can find out more about this program at www.apple.com/support/programs/ssa.

▶ Purchasing spare accessories or systems for immediate hardware replacement. Budgeting for this varies widely based on need and size of deployment, but the best solution for the user is to simply have another one available when they need it. For smaller deployments you may need only a few spare accessories like power adapters, batteries, and cable adapters. For larger deployments, however, you should carry several spare systems as you are also likely to have a larger number of failures over time.

▶ Stocking replacement parts through third-party vendors if your equipment includes older and out-of-warranty Apple hardware. Common hardware parts supplied by third-party vendors, such as system memory and hard drives, are often compatible with Apple hardware.

Planning Usage Management

You can spend weeks perfecting your deployment system configuration, but without a proper usage management plan all that work will be in vain. Unavoidably, users will attempt to make changes to your deployed computers, or they may unintentionally install software that can negatively affect your systems. To ensure the continued health of your deployed computers, you should develop usage policies and a plan to enforce those policies.

Usage Policies

Computer usage policies vary from nonexistent to draconian. The level of detail and restriction defined in a usage policy has more to do with the type and size of the organization than with technical details. The larger the number of deployed systems, the more rules need to be in place to keep problems under control. Thus, smaller organizations tend to have more liberal usage policies, and larger organizations tend to require more control. Also, different types of users often require different usage policies. For example, the policies for an open computer lab will probably be much stricter than the policies for individual faculty and staff computers. As a result, you will most likely have separate usage policies for different situations.

If your organization already has usage policies, you should take time to evaluate those policies for your new deployment. As technology changes, new features are introduced that your previous policies may not address. For instance, all new Macs come standard with wireless networking and Bluetooth; will you allow all your users to have access to these new features?

There is no best plan for defining usage policies, but the following list presents main categories that you will need to consider when creating or updating your computer usage policies:

▶ Computer access—Policies should define acceptable use of computing resources, including who has access to which computers.

▶ Software—Policies should define which applications are required and allowed. Many policies also restrict usage to an approved list of applications.

▶ Peripherals—Policies should define acceptable use of peripherals, including which peripherals are allowed. Many organizations require strict policies when it comes to the use of shared printers in order to minimize costs.

▶ Storage—Policies should define acceptable use of storage, including storage permissions and usage quotas. Your storage policies should also dictate where the users' home folders will reside. Storage security is also something that should be part of your usage policies.

▶ Network access—Policies should define acceptable use of network access, including which users and computers have access to your network resources and access to wireless networks or secure networks via VPN connections. Policies should also define regulations regarding how to deal with rogue network activity.

▶ Shared network resources—Policies should define acceptable use of shared network resources such as file servers, internal websites, and network printers. Many organizations have strict policies regarding the use of communication systems in particular.

The point of creating comprehensive usage policies is to define enforceable rules that must be followed by the computer users, so it's vital that management agree on and support them so they can be enforced.

Policy Distribution

It's also important that users be made aware of and agree to your usage policies, so you must have a plan to distribute those policies to the users. Laws differ from region to region, but having users agree to the usage policies may give management more power to enforce those policies.

> **NOTE** ▶ In educational environments, many users are not old enough to be legally bound to usage policies. In these cases, the techniques covered in the following section, "Policy Enforcement," are a more appropriate choice.

One option is to have users actually sign a paper contract before they are allowed to use your computer equipment. Although this provides an easily enforceable document, it also creates paperwork. Further, any time you change the usage policies, you will have to have users sign new paper contracts.

A popular trend in recent years is to have users agree to usage policies electronically. For example, nearly every web-based service uses an electronic agreement system during the sign-up process. The service provider can then easily update its usage policies at any time, making the system redisplay the usage agreement for the user the next time the user wants access to the service. There are many ways to implement this sort of scheme using different authentication systems. Perhaps the most popular method when using Mac OS X is to modify the login window using managed preference settings as described in the following section, "Policy Enforcement."

Policy Enforcement

Just because users have agreed to your usage policies doesn't mean they will follow them. Fortunately, Mac OS X includes several built-in technologies that allow you to enforce usage policies at the system level. Planning and configuring these usage enforcement technologies will be a major part of your system deployment. Mac OS X offers five primary technologies that can be used to enforce usage policies: user account management, home folder management, file system permissions, authorization management, and managed preferences.

User Account Management

Even if you don't want to enforce strict usage policies, you will still create accounts on Mac OS X for your users. The choices you make regarding user account types are fundamental decisions that have far-reaching implications for the rest of your system deployment because a user's capability to do things on Mac OS X is directly related to the account type.

In fact, the most basic form of usage management is the "standard" user account type. Users with standard accounts, unlike those with administrator accounts, cannot make substantial changes to the system without administrator authorization. You can exert even more control over your users by using network-based accounts or client management techniques.

MORE INFO ▶ To learn more about user account types, please refer to *Apple Training Series: Mac OS X Support Essentials v10.6* (Peachpit Press, 2010).

Home Folder Management

To log in and use the Mac OS X interface, a user must have a read/write home folder. The system must have a location to store user items while the user is logged in to the computer. Therefore, all users, even guest users, must have a home folder where they can store their personal items. Just as the choices you make regarding user account types have far-reaching implications, so do your choices for home folder management. In many full-system deployments, the contents of the users' home folders are the only items that vary from system to system and the only items that the users are allowed to modify.

Because of the inherent variability in the users' home folders, a specific management strategy is needed. Mac OS X v10.5 supports home folders stored on the local system drive, on an external storage device, on a mounted network volume, and on a local system and network hybrid known as a synchronized mobile home folder. All these home folder storage options, except for storage on the local system drive, require you to use network-based user accounts and client management techniques.

MORE INFO ▶ To learn more about local home folders, please refer to *Apple Training Series: Mac OS X Support Essentials v10.6* (Peachpit Press, 2010). To learn more about network-based home folders, please refer to *Apple Training Series: Mac OS X Server Essentials v10.6* (Peachpit Press, 2010).

File System Permissions

Mac OS X uses file system permissions as the primary mechanism for controlling access to files and folders. The default permissions already provide a very secure storage environment. However, you can further restrict user access by adjusting file system permissions to better suit your needs. It's not uncommon to configure custom permissions as part of a system deployment.

> **MORE INFO** ▶ To learn more about configuring file system permissions, please refer to *Apple Training Series: Mac OS X Support Essentials v10.6* (Peachpit Press, 2010).

Authorization Management

Mac OS X uses a combination of technologies to manage authorization rights. These systems allow a user to bypass certain file system permissions to perform various administrative tasks. These technologies include the /etc/authorization database, the /etc/sudoers file, and application of the suid and guid permission settings. Again, the Mac OS X default settings provide a very secure environment, but you can tweak these settings for your system deployment if your needs require.

> **MORE INFO** ▶ To learn more about advanced authorization management, please refer to *Apple Training Series: Mac OS X Security and Mobility v10.6* (Peachpit Press, 2010).

Managed Preferences

When administrators need to restrict a user's ability to access features on a computer, their typical approach is client system management. Mac OS X includes a sophisticated management architecture for Mac OS X preferences, also known as MCX. With this technology an administrator can centrally manage a wide range of application preferences and system configurations, including the ability to restrict access to applications and hardware resources. Further, these settings can be applied locally or hosted from a shared network directory service.

MORE INFO ▶ An introduction to Mac OS X managed preferences is provided in *Apple Training Series: Mac OS X Server Essentials v10.6* (Peachpit Press, 2010). However, advanced Mac OS X managed preference techniques are also detailed in this guide in Chapter 4, "Creating System Images."

Developing a Testing Plan

Rolling out a new system only to find that a minor problem on one computer is quickly escalating into a major issue on all your computers can be catastrophic. This situation can be avoided with thorough testing. A customized Mac OS X system deployment can contain thousands of points of failure. Thus, it's best to establish your criteria for success and determine how to remedy failures by examining distinct components. A *test plan* helps ensure that your deployment techniques are accurate and error-free.

Plans may include discrete testing for the following components:

▶   Mac OS X components

▶   User/custom components

- ▶ Mac OS X application workflows
- ▶ User/custom application workflows
- ▶ Network connectivity and services
- ▶ Peripherals or additional hardware components

To track the progress for each testing category, create a checklist for the tasks that you will perform to verify that a mechanism works or does not work. A common deployment testing methodology employs a comprehensive checklist, or *click matrix,* that includes all the configurations and tasks that must be completed and validated before the system is deployed. Each task should simulate your users' workflow.

If you think something might make a difference in how the computers are used, that thing should be tested. Each test should also be documented, recording which files changed, where temporary files are stored, whether permissions or ownership changes, and so on.

The figure here shows the click matrix format for the testing of a single task.

Example Task: Open a Pages document and save it to the user's Documents folder.

	Local	Network	Network (Mobile)
Base OS	☐	☑	☐
Custom OS— Dept1	☑	☐	☑
Custom OS— Dept2	☑	☑	☑

Action required: Investigate why network Home does not work

As you can see, this format provides a clear picture of what software works for which deployed image. Having a thoroughly documented click matrix will help ensure that nothing is missed and that client systems are highly reliable. Be sure to archive your click matrix for the next time you need to rebuild your system image.

Performing Network and Server Testing

Basic network and server functionality testing should be part of your standard routine. You should be sure to test access to all relevant network services, applications, and peripherals on both wired and wireless connections.

You should also consider testing network resources based on performance measurements to make sure that your network resources can support the increased load of deployment and support for your new systems. Some specific network services that are susceptible to usability issues caused by overtaxed resources include file services, NetBoot, directory services, wireless services, and network filtering services.

Reliable performance testing can be difficult to achieve before you roll out your systems because, in many cases, you can't test a performance scenario until you actually have all your computers deployed to place a load on the service. Nevertheless, you should try to test at least a small group of network clients. You may find that even a small group provides enough of a load that you can get a general idea of expected performance.

Using Automated Testing Solutions

Thorough testing can be completed manually, but the process is tedious and prone to human error. Automating your testing will greatly improve reliability and reduce the time you have to spend at this task. Mac OS X includes traditional command-line automation via shell scripts, and it includes graphical automation via the AppleScript and Automator systems. Further, you can combine scripting technologies to automate testing in both environments.

> **MORE INFO** ▶ An introduction to the automation technologies built in to Mac OS X can be found in *Apple Training Series: Mac OS X Support Essentials v10.6* (Peachpit Press, 2010). You can also check out the Mac OS X Automation resources website, www.macosxautomation.com.

Although the built-in scripting tools are powerful in the right hands, if you require a more sophisticated automated testing environment, consider a third-party product such as the Eggplant series by TestPlant. Eggplant is a series of tools designed specifically for testing, but they can be used to automate any administrative task.

The Eggplant tools are easy to use for beginners and also feature powerful scripting abilities and test reporting. Eggplant is unique in that it supports any application regardless of its origin and delivers true interoperability testing between applications and system components rather than testing only one item at a time.

Developing a Service-Level Agreement

A *service-level agreement* (SLA) is a document or contract that ensures that the resulting technology solution meets agreed-upon expectations. It defines a target for both the requirements of the users (or clients) and the services that administrators (or implement-ers) are providing. Specifically, the SLA specifies what service is to be provided, how the service is supported, and information about times, locations, costs, performance, and responsibilities of the parties involved.

SLAs can help define details such as the following:

► Services provided

► Performance measures

► Problem management

► User (or client) duties

► Warranties

► Disaster recovery policies

► Termination of agreement

Developing an SLA helps ensure that all parties understand the expected outcomes of a system deployment. This document holds both the administrators (or implementers) and the users (or clients) responsible for their "end" of the solution. The administrators will be expected to provide the agreed-upon services only, regardless of what users may later request.

Typical sections within an SLA

A: Statement of intent	This section states the objectives of the document.
B: Approvals	This section lists who approved the SLA.
C: Review dates	This section contains the track record of the SLA reviews.
D: Time and percent conventions	This section contains the descriptions of what time conventions and metrics are being used.
E: About the service	This section introduces the service addressed by the SLA.
F: Description	This section describes the service in detail.
G: User environment	This section describes the architecture and technologies that are used by the consumers of the service.

H: About service availability	This section introduces the availability concepts used in this SLA.
I: Normal service availability	This section describes what is considered normal schedule service availability.
J: Scheduled events that impact service availability	This section describes what scheduled outages are to be expected.

What You've Learned

▶ For a successful system deployment, you need to create a plan that addresses seven main deployment concepts: hardware logistics, usage management, item deployment, system deployment, remote administration and monitoring, license management, and software maintenance.

▶ This book includes a Deployment Planning Template that will help you plan your complete deployment solution.

▶ For a successful deployment, your deployment plan must address hardware logistics issues, including infrastructure considerations, hardware security, and hardware handling logistics.

▶ To maintain a consistent computing environment after deployment, you must manage system usage, which includes planning, distributing, and enforcing usage policies.

▶ There is no one perfect deployment plan that fits every situation; instead, each plan should be based on the organization's needs.

▶ A deployment plan often requires a variety of tools and techniques.

▶ A complete deployment solution should include a deployment plan, a testing plan, and a service-level agreement.

References

You can check for new and updated Knowledge Base documents at www.apple.com/support.

Power Considerations

▶ HT2346, "Intel-Based Apple Portables: Identifying the right power adapter and power cord—US"

- ▶ HT2999, "Mac mini: How to identify power adapters"
- ▶ HT3468, "Mac mini: Power consumption and thermal output (BTU) information"
- ▶ HT3559, "iMac: Power consumption and thermal output (BTU) information"
- ▶ HT2836, "Mac Pro: Power consumption and thermal output (BTU) information"
- ▶ HT3513. "Xserve (Early 2009): Power consumption and thermal output (BTU) information"
- ▶ TA22755, "Workgroup Cluster: Power Requirements and Considerations"

Enforcing Usage Policies

- ▶ TA26506, "Mac OS X: About working with an administrator account"
- ▶ HT2400, "Mac OS X: How to manage user access to applications, system preferences, and disc burning via 'Capabilities,' 'Limitations,' or 'Parental Controls'"

Web Resources

- ▶ Bretford Mac-specific security carts, http://apple.bretford.com
- ▶ Kensington Security Slot specifications, http://us.kensington.com/html/1356.html
- ▶ BAK2u theft recovery software, www.bak2u.com/mac.php
- ▶ Computrace LoJack for Laptops by AbsoluteSoftware theft recovery software, www.absolute.com/products/lojack
- ▶ iAlertU by SlappingTurtle Software theft prevention software, www.slappingturtle.com/home
- ▶ MacTrak by GadgetTrak theft recovery software, www.gadgettrak.com/products/mac
- ▶ Undercover by Orbicule—theft recovery software, www.orbicule.com/undercover
- ▶ Apple's Self-Servicing Account program www.apple.com/support/programs/ssa
- ▶ Mac OS X automation resources, www.macosxautomation.com
- ▶ Eggplant automated testing solution, www.testplant.com

Review Quiz

1. How do you calculate the total power required to safely operate your deployed computers?
2. How can you identify the appropriate operating temperature range of Apple hardware? What operational temperature range does most Apple hardware support?

3. What key hardware feature included on Mac systems helps you ensure physical security?

4. What are some of the issues that must be addressed when disposing of electronic equipment?

5. What five primary technologies in Mac OS X can be used to enforce usage policies?

6. How does using a shared network directory service actually enforce usage policies?

7. What is a click matrix?

8. What is a service-level agreement (SLA)?

Answers

1. The power requirements for electronic equipment are usually rated in watts, but electric circuits are rated in amps. If you assume the standard of 120 volts, you can calculate the amps drawn by an electronic device when given the wattage by using the following equation: watts ÷ 120 volts = amps. You should check with an electrician to verify the available amps to your power source.

2. Apple lists appropriate operating temperatures on its website under the "Tech Specs" section of each product. Most Apple hardware supports an operation temperature between 50° to 95° F (10° to 35° C).

3. Mac systems include either a Kensington security slot or a physical case lock, which can be used to affix a security device that helps prevent theft.

4. When disposing of electronic equipment, you must consider the following: how to transfer user data, how to safely erase sensitive data, how to inventory your old equipment, and how to dispose of or recycle the equipment within local regulations. Also, all batteries must be properly disposed of.

5. The five primary technologies on Mac OS X that can be used to enforce usage policies are user account management, home folder management, file system permissions, authorization management, and managed preferences.

6. A properly configured shared network directory service can host managed preferences, which can be used to restrict a user's ability to access features on Mac OS X.

7. A click matrix is a testing methodology that includes all the configurations and tasks that must be completed and validated before the system is deployed.

8. A service-level agreement is a document or contract that ensures that the resulting technology solution meets agreed-upon expectations.

2

Chapter Files   Deployment Planning Template.pdf, available at www.peachpit.com/
acsa.deployment

Time   This chapter takes approximately 2 hours to complete.

Goals   Learn why you need to deploy items inside containers

Create compressed archives to deploy files and folders

Use Apple Remote Desktop to deploy items

Create disk images to deploy files and folders

Use advanced disk image deployment features

Chapter **2**

Deploying Individual Items and Containers

The most common and simplest form of software deployment is the deployment of individual items, such as files. However, as you likely know from your own experience downloading applications and drivers from websites, these items aren't usually made available in their original usable formats but instead are stored inside some sort of deployable web-compatible container file. Instead of providing files that you can drag and drop to your computer and use, software vendors must store items in a deployable format, to ensure data integrity and decrease file size.

In this chapter, you will explore options that you can use to deploy collections of files and folders: archive files, disk images, and Apple Remote Desktop 3.3. These options work best for deploying simple items that do not require complex installation routines. For example, if your systems are already deployed, but you need to update a few key files, the techniques covered in this chapter will help you quickly deploy those items. Similarly, if you want to make available a collection of optional applications and software installers, you can use the techniques presented here to prepare those items for easy downloading.

Although this chapter includes techniques that you can use to deploy preexisting installer packages, it does not cover the creation of such packages. If you need to deploy complex items that require installation of items in multiple folders or execution of scripts, you should consider creating a custom installer package, as described in Chapter 3, "Deploying with Installation Packages."

Understanding Mac OS X File Management

Mac OS X uses a unique file system, the Mac OS Extended format, that provides both perceived simplicity and enhanced file-system metadata. These file-system features are responsible for the simplification of the Mac OS X file structure. A prominent example of this simplification is that an entire application can be represented as a single icon to the user in the Finder. The enhanced metadata attributes make advanced technologies such as Spotlight and Time Machine possible.

The downside to these file-system features is the increased complexity of the underlying file system. This complexity affects both compatibility and deployment practices. In this section, you will briefly explore the unique file elements used in Mac OS X and why you need to use file containers to deploy these items.

Unique Mac OS X File Elements

The Mac OS Extended file system uses several unique file elements to hide complexity from the user: file-system metadata, bundles, and packages. These file elements need special attention when using deployment tools.

> **MORE INFO** ▶ File-system metadata, bundles, and packages are covered briefly here, but to learn more about these topics and the Mac OS Extended file system in general, please refer to *Apple Training Series: Mac OS X Support Essentials v10.6* (Peachpit Press, 2010).

File-System Metadata

Every file and folder on a Mac OS Extended volume has additional *file-system metadata* that is not immediately visible to the user but is an essential part of the file system. This includes additional attributes such as creation date, modification date, ownership, permissions, access control lists, Spotlight information, Finder labels, and legacy file type information. This also includes file-system flags, which are used to identify special file types such as aliases and locked files. Some of these attributes and flags are accessed from the Get Info window of the Finder.

Other file systems have similar file attributes and, in general, offer support for common attributes such as ownership and permissions. However, these attributes can change or even be lost when files are copied using traditional methods. Even when items are copied between Mac OS X systems, file ownership is usually modified to match the account of the user who is performing the operation. When files are transferred to third-party file systems that don't support all of the attributes of the Mac OS Extended file system, unsupported attributes are simply stripped away.

Another form of file-system metadata, *resource forks,* have a long history in the Macintosh operating system, dating back to the original Mac OS. To simplify the user experience, Apple created a forked file system to make complex items, such as applications, appear as a single icon, allowing multiple pieces of data to appear as a single item in the file system. For instance, a file will appear as a single item, but it will actually be composed of two separate pieces: a data fork and a resource fork. Mac OS X extends this practice by allowing developers to take advantage of an arbitrary number of forks for any file, adding even more metadata options.

This system makes the user experience much richer, but because most other operating systems don't use such extensive metadata, compatibility is an issue. Only volumes formatted with the Mac OS Extended file system can natively store this additional metadata. However, when using Mac OS X to copy a file to any other third-party file system, the metadata information will be separated and stored as a hidden file. This practice of splitting files is commonly known as the *AppleDouble* format. For example, if you were to copy a Mac OS X–generated file called Report.doc on a Windows FAT32 volume, the Mac file system would automatically split the file and write it as two discrete pieces on the FAT32 volume. The file's data would have the same name as the original, but the metadata would end up in a file called ._Report.doc, which would remain hidden from the user in the Finder. The AppleDouble format can be problematic for non-Apple deployment mechanisms, as the metadata parts are often ignored.

Bundles and Packages

When Apple moved to Mac OS X, it wanted to avoid the use of resource forks while still retaining the ability to make complex items appear as single icons. Instead of creating a new container technology, Apple simply modified an existing file-system container, the common folder. A *bundle* is nothing more than a normal folder that is used to group related resources in one location. *Packages* take this concept a step further: A bundle with the bundle file attribute set appears as single opaque item in the Finder and is known as a package.

This package-based approach allows software developers to easily organize all the resources needed for a complicated product into a single package, while simultaneously making it harder for normal users to interfere with the resources. Where a user sees only a single icon in the Finder representing an application, in reality it is a folder potentially filled with thousands of resources.

If you encounter a folder with a name that appears to be a file extension, you are probably looking at a bundle. For example, /System/Library/Frameworks/Cocoa.framework/ is a bundle that contains multiple items related to that software, but it appears as a normal folder. The contents of a package, on the other hand, are revealed only when you right-click (or Control-click) the package and choose Show Package Contents from the shortcut menu.

From a deployment perspective, the use of bundles and packages in Mac OS X presents another dilemma. On the one hand, bundles and packages simplify deployment because otherwise complex items can be managed as single items. Thus, you can copy an entire application and all its accompanying resources by simply copying a single icon. On the other hand, bundles and packages are treated as normal folders by third-party systems and transfer mechanisms, which in many cases means that the bundle-bit attribute will be stripped away, and the once-opaque package will appear as a folder in the Finder. This will prevent the package from opening as intended. Further, it confuses users because they will see a folder instead of an application icon, which can also lead to accidental partial copies if they don't know to copy all the items.

Understanding File Containers

To work around these several show-stopping issues that prevent you from successfully using many third-party tools to store or transfer items with Mac-specific file elements, you can place items that you intend to deploy inside file *containers*. Containers are special files that can encapsulate other files, folders, or even entire file systems.

From the outside, a container file appears as a simple monolithic data file that is easily stored and transferred via any method. The contents of the container file, however, can be as varied and complicated as your deployment requires. Container file formats can have other features that make them extremely attractive for deployment use. For example, most container file formats use some form of data compression. Throughout this chapter you will be introduced to other benefits of using file containers for deployment.

Mac OS X has two built-in file container technologies that allow you to safely deploy items containing file-system metadata, bundles, and packages:

▶ Archive file—This container file type allows you to store individual or multiple files and folders in a single compressed monolithic file.

▶ Disk image—This container file type allows you to store the contents of an entire file system in a single monolithic file. There are many disk image variations and options.

The container files created by these technologies can be safely stored and transferred using nearly any deployment mechanism.

Choosing the Format for Deploying Items

With the archive and disk image container formats, you have a total of three possible formats for deploying items: traditional drag and drop, archived files, and disk images. Consider the following pros and cons before choosing a deployment format:

Drag-and-Drop Deployment

Pros:

▶ Doesn't require any encoding or decoding.

▶ Doesn't require any special tools on any system.

▶ Simple for inexperienced users.

Cons:

▶ Mac OS X file elements may not be preserved if storing or transporting using third-party mechanisms.

▶ Multiple items may not be transferred properly when using certain third-party mechanisms, as related items may become separated and lost during the transfer.

▶ No default file checksums to verify content.

▶ No default compression, thus no storage or bandwidth savings.

▶ No default encryption to secure content.

Archive File Deployment

Pros:

▶ Mac OS X file elements are retained if encoded and decoded using the correct Mac OS X tools.

▶ Multiple items contained in a single file that is easily transferable using any mechanism.

► Compressed format saves storage space and bandwidth.

► Uses ZIP or .tar.gz format that can be decoded on nearly any system.

Cons:

► Requires additional encoding and decoding steps.

► No file checksums to verify content.

► The Finder doesn't support the creation of encrypted archives.

► The Finder doesn't support modifying existing archives.

Disk Image Deployment

Pros:

► Mac OS X file elements are always retained.

► Multiple items or even entire file systems can be contained in a single file that is easily transferable using any mechanism.

► File checksum helps verify content.

► Optional compressed format saves storage space and bandwidth.

► Optional encrypted format secures items from unauthorized access.

► Optional read/write format allows easy modification and expansion of disk image contents.

► Variety of advanced deployment uses beyond simple items.

Cons:

► Requires additional creation, mounting, and copying steps.

► Most third-party systems are not able to open the Mac OS X disk image format.

► Can be complex for inexperienced users.

Archiving for Deployment

Mac OS X has built-in support for archive files and supports ZIP, the most common file archive format. Files saved in this format use the .zip filename extension as their identifier. This format provides robust lossless compression and is accessible to every modern operating system. In this section, you will learn how to archive items in ZIP files and how to extract items from ZIP files.

Creating ZIP Archives

You can create a ZIP archive file from single or multiple items using the Finder or the command line. By default, creating a ZIP archive file using either method will not delete the original documents you've selected to archive. The Finder cannot create .tar.gz archives, although you can decompress them from the Finder.

Creating ZIP Archives Using the Finder

To create a ZIP archive file in the Finder:

1 In the Finder, select the items you want to archive.

You can hold down the Shift key to quickly select contiguous lists of items, or hold down the Command key to quickly select noncontiguous items.

> **TIP** Put all the items in one folder, and then compress the folder rather than selecting multiple items. This extra step will help keep things orderly later, as the items will end up in the same folder when they are extracted.

2 Choose File > Compress *Items*.

The word *Items* in the menu will be replaced by the name of the item you have selected (if you selected just a single item) or the number of items you have selected (if you selected multiple items).

> **TIP** You can also archive and compress items in the Finder by right-clicking or Control-clicking the selected documents and then choosing Compress Items from the shortcut menu.

If the archival process is going to take more than a few seconds, the Finder will show a progress dialog with the estimated time required to complete the compression task. You can also choose to cancel the archive by clicking the small X button on the far right.

When the archival process has completed, you will be left with a ZIP archive file named either Archive.zip or *Item*.zip, where *Item* is the name of the single item you chose to archive and compress. The ZIP archive file will be placed in the same location as the original items.

Once the archive process is complete, it's always interesting to compare the original items' size with the archive's size using the Get Info or Inspector windows in the Finder. In many cases you can expect a 50 percent decrease in file size. On the other hand, many media formats are already quite compressed in their original form, so you may not see much change when compressing these types of files.

 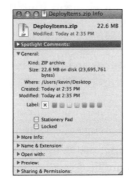

NOTE ▶ When creating ZIP archive files using the Finder, the resource fork, bundle, and package elements are retained. However, the Finder does not preserve certain extended file attributes, such as file access control lists, when creating ZIP archives. The ditto and tar commands in Mac OS X properly retain all file elements.

Creating ZIP Archives Using the Command Line

There are two tools that you can use to create ZIP archives from the command line. The zip command and the ditto command can both create ZIP archives. Both commands attempt to preserve Mac OS X file-system metadata, but currently only the ditto command will preserve the full gamut of Mac OS X file-system metadata elements including ACLs. The zip and ditto commands will place the Mac-specific elements into an

AppleDouble format additional file, __MACOSX or ._Filename. If you need to send the ZIP file to a non-Mac system, use the -X flag on the system to exclude the Mac-specific elements from the archive.

> **TIP** ▶ If you ever want to know more about a particular command, you can access its manual page entry by entering man and then the name of the command. For example, to access the zip manual page, enter man zip in the command line.

Creating .tar.gz Archives Using the Command Line

The tar command will create a .tar.gz archive that preserves all Mac OS X file-system metadata elements. As with a ditto-created ZIP archive, Mac-specific elements will be placed in an AppleDouble format additional file, __MACOSX or ._Filename. If you need to send the .tar.gz file to a non-Mac system, set the environment variable COPYFILE_DISABLE=true to exclude the Mac-specific elements from the archive.

Extracting ZIP or .tar.gz Archives

You can also extract the contents of a ZIP or .tar.gz archive file using the Finder or the command line. By default, extracting the contents of a ZIP archive file using either method will not delete the archive file.

To use the Finder to extract the contents of an archive file, simply double-click the file. By default, the Finder will automatically decompress the items and place them in the same folder as the archive file. The archive file will not be deleted or moved. Extracting files using this method will always retain any Mac OS Extended file elements as long as the archive creation utility also supported those items.

In the command line, extracting ZIP archives can be accomplished with unzip, ditto, and tar. Again, the most capable command here is ditto, which can extract files in a variety of archive formats and still retain Mac OS X file-system metadata elements.

Setting Finder Archive Utility Preferences

The Finder actually passes off the responsibility of both creating and extracting from ZIP archives to the /System/Library/CoreServices/Archive Utility helper application. If you were to open this application by double-clicking on it, it wouldn't appear to do anything. That's because it's normally waiting for file input to perform an archive action upon. In fact, if you drag an uncompressed item on top of the Archive Utility's icon, it will make an archive of it. Conversely, if you drag an archive on top of its icon, it will extract the archive's contents. Most interestingly, you can adjust Archive Utility's behavior from its preferences dialog, accessed by selecting Archive Utility > Preferences from the menu bar.

Further, there is a hidden system preference inside this application, which you can enable in order to set advanced options for handling archive content.

To enable the Archive system preference:

1   In the Finder, navigate to the /System/Library/CoreServices/ folder.

2   Right-click (or Control-click) the Archive Utility and choose Show Package Contents from the shortcut menu.

A second Finder window appears, starting at the root of the Archive Utility package.

3   Navigate to the Contents/Resources/ folder and double-click the Archives.prefPane file.

This opens the System Preferences application, which will ask for whom you want to install the Archives preference pane.

4   Make a selection, and then click Install.

If you select "Install for all users of this computer," you will have to authenticate as an administrative user.

The Archives preference will open, revealing several advanced Finder archiving options.

5   From this preference, you can change how the Archive Utility handles the creation and extraction of ZIP archives. When you have made your changes, close the preference window to save the new configuration.

NOTE ▶ Use caution when changing the "After expanding" and "After archiving" options; these settings may automatically delete items.

Set Up Apple Remote Desktop 3.3 (ARD)

Apple Remote Desktop 3.3 (ARD) is the remote control, management, reporting, and deployment tool for Mac OS X systems. Every Mac OS X version 10.6 system includes the client-side ARD Remote Management software that allows remote administration. However, the tool used by administrators to access the ARD features, the Remote Desktop administrator application, is not included with Mac OS X. Although this software is a separate purchase, it's an indispensable tool for deployment and general Mac administration. Because of this, the ARD system is demonstrated heavily throughout this reference guide.

NOTE ▶ All references to ARD in this guide are based on the version that was available at the time of writing, Apple Remote Desktop 3.3.

Before you can use ARD to deploy items, you must configure the separate components. There are two main processes for setting up the ARD system. First, you must enable the ARD remote management service on all the Mac OS X systems you intend to remotely administrate. Then, using the Remote Desktop administrator application, you must establish a connection to the remote systems.

TIP If you intend to use ARD to administer your deployed systems, you should absolutely make enabling the Remote Management service part of your system deployment plan.

TIP ▸ The Remote Desktop administrator application can create an installer that can be used to set up and enable the Remote Management service on any client Mac. If you already have Remote Desktop installed and open, choose File > Create Client Installer. This opens an assistant that will automatically create the installation package for you.

Enabling ARD Remote Management

The client-side ARD Remote Management service is disabled by default on Mac OS X. The same is true for Mac OS X Server, but because the initial Server Setup Assistant prompts you to enable Remote Management by default, it's more likely that this service is enabled on Mac OS X Servers. In any case, you must ensure that Remote Management is enabled to take advantage of the ARD system.

To enable the ARD Remote Management service:

1 Open the Sharing preference and authenticate as an administrative user to unlock the preference.

2 In the Service list, select the Remote Management checkbox to enable ARD client-side services.

If this is the first time you have enabled remote management, you'll see a dialog that allows you to select the ARD options you want to allow for all nonguest local users. You can individually select options, or you can hold down the Option key and then select any checkbox to enable all options. Click OK once you have made your selections.

3 Optionally, if you want to limit ARD access, select "Only these users" and click the Add (+) button. Then select a standard or administrative local user for whom you want to grant ARD access.

Once you've added the administrative user, an ARD access options dialog appears for this user. This dialog is identical to the access options shown in the previous step, except it's used to define options for a specific user. Select the appropriate ARD access options and click OK.

TIP ▶ You can edit a user's ARD options at any time by double-clicking that user's name in the user access list.

4 To see additional ARD computer options, click the Computer Settings button.

A dialog appears that allows you to enable guest and VNC screen-sharing access, enable the Remote Management menu bar item, and add information to help identify this particular Mac. When you've made your selections, click OK.

MORE INFO ▶ You also can enable the ARD Remote Management service with the `kickstart` command-line utility. Further you can use directory service-based information for managing access to ARD features. You can find out more about the `kickstart` command in Chapter 6, "Postimaging Deployment Considerations," and ARD directory service integration in Chapter 7, "System Maintenance."

Connecting to Remote ARD Systems

Once your Mac OS X v10.6 systems have the ARD Remote Management service enabled, you can connect to them using the Remote Desktop administrator application. Once you establish an initial connection to the remote systems, the Remote Desktop application will automatically remember those systems so you don't have to reestablish the connection.

NOTE ▶ The steps here assume that you have already purchased, installed, and possibly updated the Remote Desktop 3.3 administrator application on a Mac OS X v10.6 computer.

To enable the ARD Remote Management service:

1 Log in as an administrator user. (ARD 3 has a privilege protection scheme that will only allow an administrator user to access all of the features unless you specifically allow non-administrator users to access those features. In addition, setting the license key will only work for an administrator user.)

2 Open the /Applications/Remote Desktop application.

   If you plan on frequently using ARD, you should add the Remote Desktop application to the Dock.

3 If this is the first time the Remote Desktop application was opened on your computer, you will be prompted to enter your ARD 3 serial number and registration information. Enter the appropriate information and click Continue.

   Entering the registration information will authorize the Remote Desktop application for every user on the system.

4   If this is the first time the Remote Desktop application was opened by your current user account, you will be prompted to enter an ARD password and report collection settings. Enter the requested information and click Done.

The password is used to secure the authentication information for the computers that you access via ARD, so you should pick an appropriately secure password. If you are the only user of this computer you may want to save the password to your keychain for safekeeping.

5   The default report collection settings can be left as is and easily changed later from the Remote Desktop preferences. However, it's strongly suggested that you disable the more intensive report collection features and leave only the "System Overview" as the default report collection setting. This will prevent potential overuse of the report collection features on computers that may not benefit from these features, like server computers.

MORE INFO ▶ The report collection features of ARD are detailed in Chapter 7, "System Maintenance."

6 When the Remote Desktop application opens for the first time, it will automatically enable the Scanner list. By default, Remote Desktop will scan the local network using Bonjour to discover any network devices. Any Mac with the ARD Remote Management service enabled will appear with a bright blue computer icon next to its network name. Those without ARD enabled will appear with light blue or gray icons next to their network names.

7 Optionally, you can adjust the scan criteria from the pop-up menu at the top of the Scanner list.

From this pop-up menu, you can scan the entire local network, a specific range of network addresses, or an individual network address. You can also import a computer list file from another Remote Desktop system, an ARD Task Server, or a connected directory server.

8 Once you have found a Mac or range of Macs to remotely administer, select them from the Scanner list and drag them to the All Computers list in the sidebar. You can always add more remote Mac systems later if you are unable to select them all from a single Scanner list.

TIP You can create multiple computer lists by clicking the small Add (+) button at the lower-left corner of the Remote Desktop window. When you drag computers to your custom computer lists, they will also appear in the All Computers list.

9 A dialog appears requiring you to enter the authentication information for a user account on the remote Mac that is allowed to access the ARD service. Enter the requested information and click Add.

Optionally, you can click the small disclosure triangle at the bottom left of the dialog to show the advanced options. If your Mac systems are using different accounts for ARD access, you will have to either add those systems separately or bypass the name and password verification at this point, and then manually add the correct information later.

10 Click All Computers to verify that the Mac computers you selected have been success-fully added.

By default, double-clicking a Mac name in a computer list will bring up a general infor-mation window allowing you to change your ARD connection settings to that Mac.

11 If the computers you're managing are not using the latest version of the ARD software, then you will have to update them. You can do this easily from ARD by selecting the out-of-date computers and then choosing Manage > Upgrade Client Software from the menu bar.

This will open a new dialog allowing you to easily upgrade multiple Mac clients with the latest ARD software.

Once you have established an initial connection to your remote Mac systems, you should explore some of the Remote Desktop features on your own. This book covers a variety of deployment-specific ARD features, but there are many more administrative features that are not covered here that you may find useful.

Using ARD to Deploy Items

ARD features two methods for deploying items to remote clients; drag and drop for simple copies of a few items to a single remote client, or the Copy Items dialog for copying multiple items to multiple remote clients. In this section you will learn how to use both methods.

Item copies using ARD can also be encrypted to provide secure transport between the Remote Desktop administrator application and target Macs. This feature is not turned on by default because it does slow down copy performance. However, if increased security is necessary in your environment, you can choose to always send encrypted ARD copies. The settings can be found in the Security pane of the Remote Desktop preferences.

Deploying Single Items with ARD

If you need to deploy items to only an individual remote Mac, you can quickly and easily accomplish this task using the drag-and-drop copy feature within ARD. One of the benefits of using ARD as a transport mechanism is its full support for Mac OS Extended file elements. You do not have to place any items inside an archive file to use the ARD item deployment mechanism, though you will realize an increase in network transfer speed by compressing any items that you copy to the remote Mac.

> **NOTE ▶** Copying items by dragging and dropping takes advantage of the ARD remote control functionality. To use this feature, your access to it must be enabled in the Remote Management settings of the target Mac. Also, by using this method you will probably interrupt the user currently logged in to the Mac.

To deploy items using drag and drop in ARD:

1 Open the /Applications/Remote Desktop application and authenticate if necessary.

2   From a computer list in the sidebar, locate and select the target Mac that you will be deploying the items to. From the toolbar, click the Control button, or choose Interact > Control.

TIP ▶ If a user is currently logged into the remote Mac you're attempting to control, you can temporarily hide the screen from the user by using the Curtain remote control feature. Curtain remote control can also be accessed from the ARD toolbar or the Interact menu.

A new ARD window appears, allowing you to view and control the graphical user interface of the target Mac.

3   Taking control of the target Mac, use the Finder just as you would normally and navigate to the intended destination of the items you're about to deploy.

4   From the Finder on your local Mac, select any number of files or folders and drag those items to the ARD window that is controlling the target Mac.

Once inside the ARD window, you will have full drag-and-drop Finder access, so make sure you drag the items to the intended destination. Simply letting go of the mouse button while inside the ARD window will initiate the copy process.

5   A dialog appears that allows you to verify the items to be deployed and the target
destination. Click Send if everything appears to be correct.

Another dialog appears showing copy progress. The Remote Desktop application allows
multitasking, so closing the ARD remote control window will not stop the copy process.

If this is a particularly long copy operation, you should close the remote control session
to return control to the user on the target Mac.

If the copy progress appears to stall, you may have experienced a network interruption.
If so, click Cancel to stop the copy operation, and then initiate the copy operation again.

Once the copy operation completes, it will be saved in the ARD History list in the sidebar.
You can verify the copy by retaking control of the target Mac or by looking at the History
list. You can also use the History list to revisit and replay any previous ARD tasks, even the
tasks that may have previously failed. The History list can be a huge time-saver if you perform many repetitive tasks using ARD.

Deploying Multiple Items with ARD

The ARD drag-and-drop technique can be handy, but it's not very useful for mass deployment because it doesn't scale beyond one Mac at a time. However, ARD includes a much
more powerful multi-item and multitarget Copy task. Along with a host of advanced
deployment options, ARD uses a multicast copy system that can greatly reduce the
amount of time it takes to deploy items to multiple Macs. Instead of copying each item

individually to each target Mac, ARD sends out a single multicast stream so all target Macs can receive the items simultaneously.

To deploy items using the Copy task in ARD:

1 Open the /Applications/Remote Desktop application and authenticate if necessary.

2 From a computer list in the sidebar, locate and select the target Macs that you will be deploying the items to. From the toolbar, click the Copy button, or choose Manage > Copy Items.

> **TIP** Remember, you can select multiple computers by holding down the Shift key to select a list of computers or by holding down the Command key to select multiple out-of-order computers.

An untitled ARD copy window appears, allowing you to set item deployment options.

3 Drag items from the Finder to the "Items to copy" list, or click the Add (+) button to open a browser dialog and locate the items.

4 From the "Place items in" pop-up menu, choose the destination on the target Macs for the copied items.

As you can see, this menu offers a number of destination options, including the ability to specify the full path. Use caution when specifying a path because not all target Macs may have the exact same folder structure.

5 Optionally, from the "If an item already exists" pop-up menu, choose how you want to proceed if an item already exists on a target computer.

By default, the Remote Desktop application will open a dialog asking what to do, but you can set another action if you desire a specific behavior.

Use extreme caution with this option, because certain choices will automatically erase items on the target Macs.

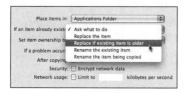

6 Optionally, from the "Set item ownership to" pop-up menu, set ownership information for the copied items on the target Mac.

By default, the ownership will be inherited from the destination folder, which is acceptable in most cases. You need to use this option only if you know for sure that specific ownership is required.

7 Optionally, select other copy settings using their associated checkboxes. The options you pick here are dependent on your situation, so there is no "right" combination.

8 At the bottom of the copy window, check the status of any selected Macs. Your copy operation will not complete on any Macs that are sleeping or otherwise unresponsive.

To resolve unreachable connections, don't close the copy window. Instead, return to the main Remote Desktop window and attempt to wake or reconnect to the unreachable Macs using the tasks in the Manage menu. You may have to physically wake or restart the computer if you are unable to reach it using the ARD tools.

9 When you are satisfied with the copy settings, click Copy.

You will automatically be returned to the Active Tasks list, where you can view the progress of the copy task.

Again, if the copy progress appears to stall, you may have experienced a network interruption. If so, click the Cancel button to the right of the progress bar to stop the copy. You can easily reattempt the copy process by accessing it from the History list.

You may have noticed the Schedule and Save buttons at the bottom of the ARD copy window. These two buttons lead to time-saving ARD features that you should incorporate into your deployment workflow. The Save button allows you to place a shortcut in the Remote Desktop sidebar that links to a saved version of any configured task. This makes frequently performed tasks easy to find and execute. The Schedule button lets you schedule tasks for when they are most convenient. Scheduling automated administration tasks with the ARD is covered in Chapter 7, "System Maintenance."

Understanding Disk Images

Of the two container technologies built into Mac OS X, disk images are more versatile. Along with simple files and folders, disk images can contain entire file systems, allowing you to store the contents of a whole computer system in a single file. Disk images are also used throughout Mac OS X to enable technologies such as FileVault home folder encryption and network Time Machine. Further, the disk image format is the primary deployment mechanism for Mac OS X applications and software installers distributed via the Internet.

In this section, you will first explore general disk image technology concepts. Then you will learn how to create and modify general-use disk images for storing and deploying files, folders, applications, or software installers. You will use both the Disk Utility application in the graphical interface and the hdiutil command in the command line.

Disk Image Volumes and Formats

Although you can create small disk images that contain only a few items, every disk image file is a container that simulates the capabilities of a storage device. You can store multiple partitions and file systems inside a single disk image, just as you would on a standard hard drive. Nearly any volume type for which Mac OS X supports read/write capability can be stored in a disk image file. In general, though, most disk images contain a single partition that is created as a Mac OS Extended volume.

Mac OS X v10.6 supports the following popular volume types inside a disk image:

► Mac OS Standard (HFS)

► Mac OS Extended (HFS+)

► Mac OS Extended and Journaled (HFS+J)

► Mac OS Extended, Case Sensitive, and Journaled (HFSX)

► MS-DOS (FAT 12/16/32)

► Compact Disk File System (ISO 9660)

► Universal Disk Format (UDF)

You also have a choice of disk image format types when creating or converting a disk image. The disk image format type defines the data structure of the disk image file itself—that is, how the data is saved when the disk image is created or modified. It does not, however, define the structure of the contents; no matter what disk image format you choose, the contents will always appear to Mac OS X as they do on a standard storage device.

Mac OS X v10.6 supports the following disk image formats:

▶   Read/write disk image—This is the standard disk image type and is indicated by the .dmg file extension. This type allows you unlimited read and write capability to the contents of the disk image. With all read/write image types, you can create a blank image and add content to it later, or you can create an image with the contents of a folder or another image, which you can modify to suit your needs. A read/write disk image file is saved as a single monolithic file, and its size is set when created. However, you can change the volume size later using disk image management tools.

▶   Read/write sparse image—This is an expandable disk image type and is indicated by the .sparseimage file extension. This type is also read/write capable, but the disk image file will automatically size to fit the disk image contents. Using this type, you still have to define a maximum image size, but the image file itself will be no larger than what's necessary to store the image contents plus some overhead. Again, the disk image file itself is saved as a single monolithic file.

▶   Read/write sparse bundle image—This image type was introduced in Mac OS X v10.5 and is indicated by the .sparsebundle file extension. This type is similar to the sparse image, with the disk image file automatically sized to fit the disk image contents, but the disk image file is saved as a package containing multiple storage bands. These storage bands can vary in size up to 128 MB, but the default size is 8 MB. As the image contents expand, new bands are added to accommodate the increased capacity. This new disk image format is used in Mac OS X v10.5 and newer for FileVault encrypted home folders and network Time Machine backups.

   NOTE ▶ The sparse bundle image format is compatible only with Mac OS X v10.5 and newer and is not recommended for deployment use because it's saved as a package. Packages are not compatible with most third-party file storage and transport mechanisms.

▶   Read-only disk image—This disk image type is similar to the standard read/write image type except that the image's contents are not editable. This type is also indicated by the .dmg file extension. The only time you can add to this type of disk image is during its creation by using the contents of a folder or another disk image;

users cannot erase any part of a read-only image after it is created. Because read-only images are saved as a single monolithic file, they are a suitable format for deploying items or entire system drives.

▶ Read-only compressed disk image—This disk image type is similar to the read-only disk image except that the contents have been compressed. The algorithm used is similar to ZIP compression, so you can expect a 50 percent size reduction on average. Compressing a disk image not only halves the required storage space, it also provides increased performance during deployment because it effectively doubles available network bandwidth. Therefore, this image type is ideal for deploying items or entire system drives.

▶ DVD/CD master image (ISO/UDF)—This disk image type is primarily used for storing master copies of optical disc volumes and is indicated by the .cdr file extension. This disk image type is identical to the more common .iso image file, as it contains both ISO and UDF volume information. These images are also read-only and must be created using the contents of another volume or disk image. This type is unique because it contains a copy of all sectors of a disk regardless of whether they are used. This allows you to save and later burn a bit-for-bit copy of the original media. While this is ideal for duplicating media, it's not ideal for most Mac OS X deployment purposes. On the other hand, this is the only disk image type that is generally compatible with third-party systems.

▶ Hybrid image (HFS+/ISO/UDF)—The hybrid image type is unique in that it includes volume information about the disk image contents in three formats: Mac OS Extended, ISO9660, and Universal Disk Format. Hybrid disk images are created using the contents of another folder or volume and are therefore read-only. Disk images of this type use the .dmg file extension but have the advantage of being readable on most modern third-party systems because of the inclusion of ISO and UDF volume information.

This compatibility feature makes hybrid disk images an attractive option for deploying items to third-party systems. However, applying any of the compression or encryption algorithms used by Mac OS X will likely break compatibility with third-party systems. As a result, you cannot create compressed hybrid disk images with Disk Utility. Thus, if you're deploying only to Mac OS X systems, you're better served by compressed disk images.

Encrypted Disk Images

Disk image encryption is not tied to a specific type; you can choose encryption for any disk image type. Disk Utility in Mac OS X v10.6 offers strong 128-bit AES encryption and very strong 256-bit AES encryption. Although the 256-bit AES security algorithm is approved by the NSA for protecting top-secret information, this encryption is only as strong as the password you choose, so don't choose an easy-to-guess password for your encrypted disk images.

Mac OS X uses encrypted disk images to protect FileVault home folders. Even if you don't use FileVault, you can still take advantage of this feature by using a smaller encrypted disk image for individual items you want to secure. The encryption algorithm is highly optimized and calculated on the fly as you move items to and from the secure disk image. In most cases, you probably won't even notice a performance penalty for the added security.

Further, because the encryption occurs at the file-system level, an encrypted disk image can provide secure network storage on any network. For example, if you have an encrypted disk image stored on a network file server that you access through potentially nonsecure networks, you connect to the server as usual and leave the encrypted disk image where it is, but you mount the secure image volume on your local Mac. The data between your Mac and the server will automatically remain encrypted because the encryption/decryption calculations occur only at the file-system level on your local Mac.

NOTE ▶ Encrypted disk images are not recommended for entire system deployment use because most restore tools do not support the encrypted format.

Comparing Archive Files to Disk Images

With two viable item container technologies built into Mac OS X, you may have a hard time choosing which method is best for your deployment needs. In many cases, either method will suffice, but there are a few specific situations where one specific format has a distinct advantage.

Reasons for Choosing Disk Images over Archive Files

Disk images are ideal if you need to deploy:

▶   Any number of items from simple to complex

▶   Entire operating systems

▶   The contents of an entire file system or even multiple file systems

Disk images are also preferred if your environment requires:

▸   A storage mechanism that is easily editable

▸   A storage mechanism where compression is optional but not required

▸   Data checksums to verify the integrity of deployed items

▸   Increased security through the use of password-protected and encrypted storage

Reasons for Choosing Archive Files over Disk Images

Archive files are ideal if you need to deploy:

▸   A smaller number of items

▸   On both Mac OS X and third-party operating systems

Archive files are also preferred if your environment requires:

▸   A file format that is easily accessible for novice users to store items

▸   Quick lossless compression

▸   A file format that is compatible with nearly any operating system

General Disk Image Use

As covered previously, you can create a blank read/write disk image, and then add the deployment items to the image, or you can create a disk image from the contents of a deployment folder, volume, or entire drive. Although starting with a blank disk image can be very useful for general storage, it's not ideal for deployment. When creating a deployment disk image, it takes less time to create a read-only disk image using just the items you're going to deploy. This can also save storage space because you can compress read-only disk images.

The tasks here show you how to create a new disk image containing only the items you need to deploy. You will learn how to do this from both the graphical interface using Disk Utility and from the command line using the hdiutil tool.

> **MORE INFO** ▸ The Disk Utility application has file-system management capabilities well beyond disk image creation. To learn more about Disk Utility, please refer to *Apple Training Series: Mac OS X Support Essentials v10.6* (Peachpit Press, 2010).

Creating a Disk Image Using Disk Utility

To create a disk image containing your deployment items:

1   Open the /Applications/Utilities/Disk Utility application.

Disk Utility.app

2   Choose File > New > Disk Image from Folder.

Notice that you can also create a blank disk image or a disk image from the contents of an entire disk drive.

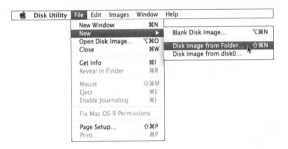

3   From the browse dialog that appears, select the folder or volume you want to use as the basis for your disk image. Then click Image to continue.

4   In the Save dialog that appears, select the name and location for the disk image file you are creating. It's safe to use the target folder's name for your disk image because the .dmg file extension will be automatically added to the name.

5   In the bottom half of the Save dialog, select the Image Format type and encryption options from the appropriate pop-up menus. Then click Save to create the disk image.

You can choose any image type you want, but the ideal image type for deploying items is compressed. You can also choose an encryption for your disk image, but that will require password authentication to access the image's contents. Although this level of security may be required in your environment, it adds a step that may interfere with automated deployment tools.

If the disk image creation process is going to take more than a few seconds, a progress dialog appears showing the estimated time required to complete the compression task. You can also choose to stop the disk image creation process by clicking Cancel.

Once the creation process is complete, the disk image file will be saved to your selected location, but it will not be mounted. If you want to view the contents of the disk image, you need to mount it as described in "Mounting Disk Images" later in this chapter.

When creating a compressed disk image, it's always interesting to compare the original items' size with the disk image's size using the Get Info or Inspector window in the Finder. As with archive files, in many cases you can expect around a 50 percent decrease in file size when using compressed disk images.

Creating a Disk Image Using the Command Line

The primary tool for handling disk images in the command line is hdiutil. The hdiutil command can perform any disk image–related task from creation to conversion to mounting. The general syntax for creating a disk image from the contents of a folder or volume starts with hdiutil create followed by any disk image options, then -srcfolder followed by the path of the items to copy, and then finally the path to the new disk image file.

MORE INFO ▶ If you are not familiar with the command line, please refer to *Apple Training Series: Mac OS X Support Essentials v10.6* (Peachpit Press, 2010).

In the following example, Michelle wants to create a compressed disk image of the DeployApps folder. Michelle first uses `ls -l` and `du -h` to view the contents and sizes of the items in the DeployApps folder.

```
MyMac:Desktop michelle$ ls -l DeployApps/
total 0
drwxr-xr-x 3 michelle staff 102 Dec 11 13:49 Bento.app
drwxr-xr-x@ 3 michelle staff 102 Mar 3 21:52 Firefox.app
MyMac:Desktop michelle$ du -h DeployApps/
...
98M DeployApps/
```

Michelle then issues the `hdiutil` command with the `-format UDZO` option, which instructs the command to create a compressed disk image identical to that created by Disk Utility. It's important to make sure to add the .dmg file extension to the name of your archive file.

```
MyMac:Desktop michelle$ hdiutil create -format UDZO -srcfolder DeployApps DeployApps.dmg
.........................................................
created: /Users/michelle/Desktop/DeployApps.dmg
```

Finally, Michelle lists the contents of her Desktop folder. At 45 MB, the disk image file is less than half the size of the original folder.

```
MyMac:Desktop michelle$ ls -lh
total 91672
drwxr-xr-x 4 michelle staff 136B Mar 16 20:12 DeployApps
-rw-r--r--@ 1 michelle staff 45M Mar 16 20:18 DeployApps.dmg
```

MORE INFO ▶ For quick access to all the disk image creation options available through `hdiutil`, enter `hdiutil create -help` at the command line. In fact, for generally any `hdiutil` command variant you can use this shortcut. To list available command variations, enter `hdiutil` with no additional arguments in the command line.

Mounting Disk Images

To access the contents of a disk image, you must mount its file system on your local Mac. You can mount disk images from the Finder or with the command `hdiutil`.

Mounting Disk Images Using the Finder

To access the contents of a disk image, simply double-click the disk image file in the Finder.

Disk Image File.dmg   Disk Image Volume

This starts the process to mount the volume contained in the disk image file as if you had just connected a normal storage device. If the disk image is encrypted, you will first be presented with an authentication dialog; otherwise, the system will continue with the mounting process unattended. By default, the system will verify the disk image integrity using a checksum contained in the disk image file. If verification succeeds, the disk image system will mount the enclosed volume(s).

TIP You can adjust how the system mounts disk images by selecting Disk Utility > Preferences from the menu bar while in the Disk Utility application.

Once mounted, the disk image volume appears on the desktop or sidebar of the Finder, depending on your preferences. Even if the disk image file is located on a remote file server, you can mount it as if it were a local drive. You can treat the mounted disk image volume as you would any other storage device by navigating through its hierarchy and selecting files and folders as you need them, and if the disk image is read/write, you can add to its contents by simply dragging items to the volume.

NOTE ▶ When you are done with a disk image volume, be sure to properly unmount and eject it as you would any other removable volume.

Mounting Disk Images Using the Command Line

You can also use hdiutil from the command line to mount and unmount disk images. The syntax for mounting a disk image is hdiutil attach followed by any disk image mounting options, and then the path to the disk image file. The syntax for unmounting and ejecting a disk image volume is simply hdiutil eject followed by the path to the mounted volume. Note that terms normally associated with physical storage, *attach* and *eject*, are applied here to virtual disk volumes.

In the following example, Michelle wants to mount, verify, and then unmount the DeployApps disk image volume she created earlier. Michelle first mounts the DeployApps. dmg volume using the hdiutil command. By default, the hdiutil command shows all checksum verification information as it processes the disk image. When the disk image volume is successfully mounted, the mount path is displayed. As with any nonsystem volume mounted on Mac OS X, the disk image volume is mounted in the /Volumes folder.

```
MyMac:Desktop michelle$ hdiutil attach DeployApps.dmg
Checksumming Driver Descriptor Map (DDM : 0)...
 Driver Descriptor Map (DDM : 0): verified CRC32 $26255419
Checksumming Apple (Apple_partition_map : 1)...
 Apple (Apple_partition_map : 1): verified CRC32 $F25B9CDD
Checksumming disk image (Apple_HFS : 2)...
.............................................................
 disk image (Apple_HFS : 2): verified CRC32 $033A14A0
Checksumming (Apple_Free : 3)...
 (Apple_Free : 3): verified CRC32 $00000000
verified CRC32 $B968F76B
/dev/disk2 Apple_partition_scheme
/dev/disk2s1 Apple_partition_map
/dev/disk2s2 Apple_HFS /Volumes/DeployApps
```

Next, Michelle lists the volume contents to verify that the volume has indeed mounted to the file system.

```
MyMac:Desktop michelle$ ls -lh /Volumes/DeployApps/
total 0
drwxr-xr-x 3 michelle staff 102B Mar 16 20:12 Bento.app
drwxr-xr-x@ 3 michelle staff 102B Mar 16 20:12 Firefox.app
```

Finally, Michelle uses the `hdiutil` command to unmount and eject the DeployApps volume.

```
MyMac:Desktop michelle$ hdiutil eject /Volumes/DeployApps/
"disk1" unmounted.
"disk1" ejected.
```

Modifying Disk Images

Only sparse and sparse bundle disk images automatically size to fit their content, but even when using this type of disk image, once you reach the maximum volume size that was defined when the image was created, you cannot add any more data to the image. Other image types are limited based on their set volume size or their read-only status.

For these reasons you may find it necessary to resize an existing disk image to fit your new storage needs. However, you can resize only a read/write disk image. Thus, you may need to convert a disk image from one type to another to meet your deployment needs. You can convert or resize existing disk images using either the Disk Utility application or the `hdiutil` command. The `hdiutil` command provides superior functionality in regard to modifying existing disk images.

> **NOTE** ▸ Disk images must not be mounted when performing any modifications using the Disk Utility application or the `hdiutil` command.

Converting an Existing Disk Image

From Disk Utility, converting an image is similar to saving another copy of any normal document. To start the process simply choose Images > Convert from the menu bar or click the Convert button in the toolbar. An open dialog will appear, letting you select the original image, then a save dialog will appear, allowing you to save the new image. At the bottom of the save dialog you can choose the new image type from a limited list of options, including encryption.

Because Disk Utility only allows for a few convert choices, you will need to use the hidutil command for converting to other disk image types. The syntax for converting a disk image is hdiutil convert -format followed by the desired disk image format type, then -o and the path to the new output disk image file, and then finally the path to the original disk image file.

Again, the hdiutil command offers a larger selection of format types than does the Disk Utility application. The hdiutil manual page lists them all, but the following are the most common disk image format types:

▶ UDRO—Read-only disk image

▶ UDZO—Compressed (zlib) disk image, default in Disk Utility

▶ UDBZ—Compressed (bzip2) disk image, yields even smaller files

▶ UDRW—Read/write disk image

▶ UDTO—DVD/CD master disk image

▶ UDSP—Sparse disk image

▶ UDSB—Sparse bundle disk image

In this example, Michelle needs to add to the previously created DeployApps.dmg. However, it was originally created as a compressed read-only disk image, so she needs to convert it to a read/write disk image. Once she has a read/write version of her disk image, she can then easily expand and add to the image using the resize techniques covered in the following section.

Michelle first reveals the image information using hdiutil imageinfo. For the sake of brevity, much of the information was removed in this example, but the important section showing the image format type is shown.

```
MyMac:Desktop michelle$ hdiutil imageinfo DeployApps.dmg
...
Format Description: UDIF read-only compressed (zlib)
...
```

Next, she uses the hdiutil command to convert her existing image to a new read/write image, which she names DeployAppsExpand.dmg.

NOTE ▶ You must always pick a new name for the output image so the system doesn't try to overwrite your original image during the convert process.

```
MyMac:Desktop michelle$ hdiutil convert -format UDRW -o DeployAppsExpand.dmg
DeployApps.dmg
Reading Driver Descriptor Map (DDM : 0)...
Reading Apple (Apple_partition_map : 1)...
Reading disk image (Apple_HFS : 2)...
.............................................................
Reading (Apple_Free : 3)...
Elapsed Time: 6.253s
Speed: 20.3Mbytes/sec
Savings: 0.0%
created: /Users/michelle/Desktop/DeployAppsExpand.dmg
MyMac:Desktop michelle$ hdiutil imageinfo DeployAppsExpand.dmg
...
Format Description: raw read/write
...
```

After the new disk image is created, she verifies its image format type and file size.

```
MyMac:Desktop michelle$ ls -lh
total 351592
-rw-r--r--@ 1 michelle staff 45M Mar 16 23:51 DeployApps.dmg
-rw-r--r-- 1 michelle staff 127M Mar 16 23:01 DeployAppsExpand.dmg
```

NOTE ▶ Even though you have to create a new image file, with a new filename, the original disk image volume name will remain the same through the convert process.

Resizing an Existing Disk Image

Resizing an image will not save another image file; instead it will modify the selected image. Again, note that you can only resize an image that isn't currently mounted. To resize an image in Disk Utility, choose Images > Resize from the menu bar, or from the volumes list select your image, then click the Resize Image button in the toolbar. From the dialog that appears, simply enter a new size for the image and click the Resize button.

As always, the hdiutil command gives you more options than Disk Utility. The syntax for resizing a disk image is hdiutil resize -size followed by the desired volume size, and then finally the path to the disk image file.

For the desired volume size, you can use any abbreviation for bytes (?), blocks (?b), kilobytes (?k), megabytes (?m), gigabytes (?g), terabytes (?t), petabytes (?p), or exabytes (?e), or you can use min and max.

Continuing from the previous example, Michelle is expanding her disk image to add another application for deployment. She starts by increasing the read/write disk image to 1 gigabyte using hdiutil resize.

```
MyMac:Desktop michelle$ hdiutil resize -size 1g DeployAppsExpand.dmg
```

Next, she verifies the resize, mounts the disk image, copies another application to the disk image volume, verifies the application copy, and ejects the image volume.

```
MyMac:Desktop michelle$ ls -lh
total 2188968
-rw-r--r--@ 1 michelle staff 45M Mar 16 23:51 DeployApps.dmg
-rw-r--r-- 1 michelle staff 1.0G Mar 16 23:56 DeployAppsExpand.dmg
MyMac:Desktop michelle$ hdiutil attach DeployAppsExpand.dmg
...
MyMac:Desktop michelle$ cp -R /Applications/SketchUp.app /Volumes/DeployApps/
MyMac:Desktop michelle$ ls -lh /Volumes/DeployApps/
total 0
drwxr-xr-x 3 michelle staff 102B Dec 11 13:49 Bento.app
drwxr-xr-x@ 3 michelle staff 102B Mar 3 21:52 Firefox.app
drwxr-xr-x 3 michelle staff 102B Mar 17 00:00 SketchUp.app
MyMac:Desktop michelle$ hdiutil eject /Volumes/DeployApps/
...
```

She next issues another `hdiutil resize` command, but this time she uses the `-size min` option to make the read/write disk image as small as possible given the volume contents.

```
MyMac:Desktop michelle$ hdiutil resize -size min DeployAppsExpand.dmg
MyMac:Desktop michelle$ ls -lh
total 595504
-rw-r--r--@ 1 michelle staff 45M Mar 16 23:51 DeployApps.dmg
-rw-r--r--@ 1 michelle staff 246M Mar 17 00:07 DeployAppsExpand.dmg
```

Now the disk image is down to 246 MB, but she decides to do even better by converting the read/write image to a compressed image, thereby creating a new image that is one-third the original size.

```
MyMac:Desktop michelle$ hdiutil convert -format UDBZ -o DeployAppsNew.dmg
DeployAppsExpand.dmg
...
created: /Users/michelle/Desktop/TEST/DeployAppsNew.dmg
MyMac:Desktop michelle$ ls -lh
total 742600
-rw-r--r--@ 1 michelle staff 45M Mar 16 23:51 DeployApps.dmg
-rw-r--r--@ 1 michelle staff 72M Mar 17 00:09 DeployAppsNew.dmg
-rw-r--r--@ 1 michelle staff 246M Mar 17 00:07 DeployAppsExpand.dmg
```

Using Disk Image Deployment Features

As you have seen, Mac OS X disk image technology provides a flexible item container system. In this section, you will explore a few more techniques that you can use to make deploying items with disk images even more flexible and easier to use.

Adding a Graphic to Help Users Deploy a Disk Image

A generic disk image is not the easiest deployment mechanism for your users. The process to install an application deployed using a disk image is simply not self-explanatory. The user has to locate the disk image file, then double-click to mount the image volume, then locate the mounted disk image volume, and then drag and drop the enclosed items into the correct location on his or her local Mac. Even experienced users can make a mistake here, and inexperienced users will probably not have any idea what to do. You can make this process much easier for your users by adding a background graphic that explains the copy process and a file-system shortcut link to the appropriate destination folder.

Implementing a background graphic for your deployment disk image requires a bit of creativity. The goal is to create a graphic that will be displayed in the image volume's Finder window that clearly shows users what they need to do to properly install the items. You can use any graphic creation tool that you like as long as the final graphic is saved as a .tiff, .jpeg, or .png file. The following graphic is an example of an appropriate background graphic for deployment purposes.

To add a background graphic and a destination link to a disk image:

1   Create an appropriate background graphic and save it as a .tiff, .jpeg, or .png file.

2   Create a read/write disk image.

   You must start with a read/write disk image because you are going to be making changes to its content. Creating a read/write disk image was covered earlier in this chapter in the "Creating a Disk Image Using Disk Utility" section.

3   Mount the disk image volume and place a copy of the background graphic and the item to be deployed at the root level of the volume.

   The root level of the volume is the first location that appears when you double-click the disk image volume in the Finder.

4   Simplify the Finder window for the root of the image volume by choosing View > Hide Toolbar, and then choose View > as Icons. Once the Finder window has been simplified, immediately close the window to save the view change.

5   Reopen the root Finder window for the image volume, and then choose View > Show View Options.

   The Finder View Options panel appears, allowing you to fine-tune the view of the Finder window.

6 From the View Options panel, select "Always open in icon view," and select Picture in the Background area.

7 Drag the background graphic stored on your disk image to the image well. Alternately you can double-click on the image well to select the background graphic from a browser window.

8 In the command line, use the mv command to rename the background graphic file by placing a period at the front of the file's name. This will make the Finder hide the graphic file from the user.

For example, if your background graphic is named diskpic.jpg, rename it *.diskpic.jpg*. In this case, you would enter mv diskpic.jpg .diskpic.jpg in the command line, assuming you had already navigated to the root of your disk image volume.

9 Return to your disk image's Finder window and verify that the background graphic file has indeed disappeared from view.

10 Open another Finder window showing the destination folder for your deployment item. The most common folder is the /Applications folder, but it can be any common folder that you would normally find on any Mac OS X system.

11 While holding down the Option and Command keys, drag the destination folder onto the disk image volume.

This creates an alias file in your disk image that links to the destination folder on any local Mac. Aliases are smarter than other file-system links, in that they will automatically adjust when moved to another system. Thus, when your disk image is mounted on another computer, the alias you just created will point to the equivalent folder on the local Mac.

12 Return to the Finder and tweak the View Options, icon placement, and window placement until the window looks good to you.

Make sure the size and placement of the volume's Finder window when opened is in an ideal location.

13 After tweaking the size and placement of the Finder window, save any changes by closing the window without opening any of its contents.

As you can see in this example, it's now pretty clear what the user is supposed to do to complete the deployment.

14 When you are done modifying your deployment disk image, protect it from changes and minimize its size by converting it to a compressed disk image, as covered in the "Modifying Disk Images" section earlier in this chapter.

Creating Internet-Enabled Disk Images

Another solution to make deploying disk images easier for your users is to create an Internet-enabled disk image. When a user downloads an Internet-enabled disk image, Mac OS X will automate much of the deployment workflow: mounting the image volume, copying all visible contents to the local Mac, ejecting the image volume, and placing the image file in the Trash.

The image contents are placed in the same folder as the image file. Thus, if the image is downloaded using a web browser, the image contents will be placed in the user's download folder. The default download folder on Mac OS X v10.5 is /Users/username/Downloads, and on any older version of Mac OS X it is /Users/username/Desktop. However, users can specify any download destination folder they want in the web browser preferences.

Creating an Internet-enabled disk image is easily handled by the hdiutil command. In the command line, enter hdiutil internet-enable and then the path to the disk image file. You can enable this feature only on read-only or compressed disk images. In the following example, Michelle uses the hdiutil command to make the Updates.dmg image Internet-enabled.

```
MyMac:Desktop michelle$ hdiutil internet-enable Updates.dmg
hdiutil: internet-enable: enable succeeded
```

NOTE ▶ Disk images must not be mounted when performing any modifications using the Disk Utility application or the hdiutil command.

Testing an Internet-Enabled Disk Image

You can test your Internet-enabled image by downloading it using the Safari browser.

To test your Internet-enabled disk image, follow these steps:

1   Before you download the Internet-enabled image in Safari, be sure the "Open 'safe' files after downloading" feature is enabled in the General preferences of Safari. If this feature is not enabled, the disk image will download, but it will not automatically deploy.

2 Download the image from a web server using Safari. You can host the file from any web server, or you can enable Web Sharing service on your local Mac to temporarily host the image for your testing.

MORE INFO ▶ To learn more about the Web Sharing service, please refer to *Apple Training Series: Mac OS X Support Essentials v10.6* (Peachpit Press, 2010).

Once the Internet-enabled disk image is fully downloaded by Safari, the image will be mounted and its contents copied to the user's Downloads folder, and the image file will be placed in the Trash.

3 To watch the progress from the Safari Downloads window, choose Window > Downloads.

4 Once the automatic deployment is complete, find the items by navigating to the Downloads folder in the Finder or by clicking the Spotlight button next to the item in the Safari Downloads window.

Creating Segmented Disk Images

When deploying exceptionally large disk images, you may need to *segment* the disk image to make it more manageable. This would certainly be the case if you needed to deploy large disk images using limited storage like that found on optical discs. Smaller segments can also help when deploying across slow or unreliable Internet connections. You can perform segmenting only on read-only or compressed disk images.

Segmenting an existing disk image is easily handled by the `hdiutil` command. The syntax for segmenting a disk image is `hdiutil segment -o` followed by the path to the new output disk image files, then `-segmentSize` followed by the desired segment size, and then finally the path to the disk image file.

For the desired segment size you can use any abbreviation of bytes (?), blocks (?b), kilobytes (?k), megabytes (?m), gigabytes (?g), or terabytes (?t). The command will automatically calculate the appropriate number of segments and number the segment filenames in order. Or, you can instead define the number of segments by using -segmentCount followed by the desired number of segments. The hdiutil command will automatically calculate the correct size for each segment based on the segment count you specify.

In the following example, Michelle needs to fit a 7.3 GB disk image onto a set of CD-Rs, which have a capacity of 660 MB. She uses hdiutil segment with the -segmentSize variable to break the DeployMedia.dmg disk image into 660 MB segments, naming the new disk image file DeployMediaSeg.dmg.

> **NOTE ▶** You must always pick a new name for the image segments so the system doesn't try to overwrite your original image during the segmenting process.

Once the segmenting process is complete, the hdiutil command shows the path to all the new segments. In this example the output has been truncated to save space.

```
MyMac:Desktop michelle$ ls -lh
total 15332064
-rw-r--r--@ 1 michelle staff 7.3G Oct 20 12:28 DeployMedia.dmg
MyMac:Desktop michelle$ hdiutil segment -o DeployMediaSeg.dmg -segmentSize 660m
DeployMedia.dmg
.........................................................
created: /Users/michelle/Desktop/DeployMediaSeg.dmg
created: /Users/michelle/Desktop/DeployMediaSeg.002.dmgpart
created: /Users/michelle/Desktop/DeployMediaSeg.003.dmgpart
...
created: /Users/michelle/Desktop/DeployMediaSeg.012.dmgpart
```

Mounting a Segmented Disk Image

Mounting a segmented disk image is very similar to mounting a normal disk image, with the exception of two requirements:

▶ All the image segments must be in the same folder in order to mount the image volume.

▶ You must specify the first segment, the only segment without a number in its name, as the image to mount.

If a segment is missing, you will be presented with an error message, and the image volume will not mount. However, if all segments are accounted for, the image volume will mount as usual.

What You've Learned

▶ Mac OS X uses unique file elements that should be placed in container file formats for safe and efficient deployment. Mac OS X provides built-in support for ZIP archive files and disk images.

▶ You can create ZIP archive files from the Finder or by using tar in the command line.

▶ Apple Remote Desktop, which must be purchased separately, can quickly and efficiently deploy any number of items to any number of remotely managed Mac computers.

▶ You can create a variety of disk image types from Disk Utility or by using hdiutil in the command line.

▶ You can employ several advanced disk image features to make deploying items even easier and more convenient for your users.

References

You can check for new and updated Knowledge Base documents at www.apple.com/support.

Mac OS X File Management

▶ TA20578, "Mac OS X: Apple Double Format Creates File Name with the Prefix '._'"

▶ HT3134, "Common Internet file formats"

Apple Remote Desktop Item Deployment

▶ TA23926, "About Apple Remote Desktop 3.0"

▶ TA24066, "Apple Remote Desktop 3: First launch dialog causes a 'Copy and Open' or Open Items task to fail"

▶ TA21523, "Apple Remote Desktop (all versions): File Copy using 'Specify Full Path' works for startup volume only"

Disk Images

▶ TA20701, "Mac OS X: Disk Image File Cannot Be Deleted While the Image Is Available"

▶ TA21118, "Mac OS X: About Encrypted Disk Images"

▶ TA21118, "Mac OS X: How to create a password-protected (encrypted) disk image"

▶ HT2059, "How to copy previously burned DVD-R video discs"

Web Resources

▶ Apple Developer Connection bundle and package documentation, http://developer.apple.com/documentation/CoreFoundation/Conceptual/CFBundles/CFBundles.html

▶ Apple Developer Connection software distribution, http://developer.apple.com/documentation/DeveloperTools/Conceptual/SoftwareDistribution/Introduction/chapter_1_section_1.html

▶ Enable Remote Management from the command line, http://docs.info.apple.com/article.html?path=RemoteDesktop/3.0/en/ARDC882.html

▶ Apple Remote Desktop resource website, www.apple.com/remotedesktop/resources.html

▶ Wikipedia entry on AES encryption, http://en.wikipedia.org/wiki/AES_encryption

Review Quiz

1. What is file-system metadata? What is AppleDouble?
2. What is a bundle? How does it differ from a package?

3. What is a container?

4. What issues arise when trying to deploy items with file-system metadata or bundles and packages?

5. What two methods can be used to safely distribute files with file-system metadata or bundles and packages?

6. What types of disk images can be created with Mac OS X v10.6? What are the key differences between these disk image types?

7. Why would you want to use disk images over archive files?

8. Why would you want to use archive files over disk images?

9. What are the names of the graphical and command-line tools for managing disk images?

10. What is an Internet-enabled disk image? How can you create one?

11. What types of disk images can be segmented? What tools can be used to segment a disk image?

Answers

1. File-system metadata is a Mac OS Extended file-system feature in which a single file is composed of a data fork and an arbitrary number of additional forks for storing additional information about the file. AppleDouble is the name of the way Mac OS X automatically saves file-system metadata to a separate data file on systems that don't support metadata. The AppleDouble file is named with a "._" followed by the name of the original file; this keeps the file invisible by default on Mac systems, but not necessarily on other systems.

2. A bundle is a common collection of software resources contained in a single folder. A package takes this concept a step further by hiding the bundle contents from users in the Finder. Thus, a package appears as a single item in the Finder. Most Mac OS X applications are packages.

3. A container is a special type of file that can contain other items. Container files allow you to combine items by making them appear as a single data file, which is easier to deploy.

4. Items with file-system metadata or bundles and packages may not be compatible with some storage and transport mechanisms.

5. Mac OS X includes the capability to save items inside ZIP archive files and disk image files.

6. Mac OS X v10.6 can create read/write disk images, which can be easily modified and expanded; read/write sparse images, which automatically expand to fit the volume contents; read/write sparse bundle images, which also automatically expand but are saved as a package of many separate file bands; read-only disk images, which cannot be modified; read-only compressed disk images, which cannot be modified either but are more efficient due to compression, making them ideal for deployment; DVD/CD master images, which are used for copying entire disks and especially optical media; and hybrid images (HFS+/ISO/UDF), which are read-only and compatible with many third-party systems. Any disk image type can be encrypted and secured with a password to prevent unauthorized access.

7. You would choose a disk image over an archive file if you need to deploy any number of items from simple to complex, entire operating systems, or the contents of an entire file system or even multiple file systems. Disk images are also preferred over archive files if your environment requires a storage mechanism that is easily editable, a storage mechanism where compression is optional but not required, data checksums to verify the integrity of deployed items, and increased security through the use of password-protected and encrypted storage.

8. You would choose an archive file over a disk image if you need to deploy only a small number of items or deploy on both Mac OS X and third-party operating systems. Archive files are also preferred over disk images if your environment requires a file format that is easily accessible for novice users to store items, quick lossless compression, and a file format that is compatible with nearly any operating system.

9. The graphical tool for managing disk images is Disk Utility and the command-line tool is `hdiutil`.

10. An Internet-enabled disk image contains a setting that tells Safari to automatically extract the disk image volume's contents and then move the original disk image into the Trash. This can be enabled from the command line with `hdiutil internet-enable`.

11. You can only segment read-only or compressed disk images. This can be done from the command line with an `hdiutil segment`.

3

Chapter 3

Deploying with Installation Packages

The techniques for deploying individual items are inadequate for deploying some of the more complex software available today. When your deployment needs require distribution of complex collections of items or greater installation control and automation options, then you should consider taking advantage of the built-in Mac OS X installation technology. The same technology that's used to install Mac OS X and other Mac software can be used to distribute any items needed for your deployment. Further, as you'll see in the next chapter, the Mac OS X installation technology plays an integral part in deployment of entire systems.

First, this chapter introduces the Mac OS X installation technology. The following sections teach you how to create custom installation packages that can be used to distribute any software or configuration to your Macs. The installation packages that you create can range from individual items or configurations to entire systems, and everything in between. Next, you will learn how to deploy and troubleshoot installation packages. Whether you're installing prebuilt or custom installation packages, the techniques you learn here can be quickly and efficiently executed on all your deployed Macs. The final section in this chapter presents third-party tools that you can also use to install items on your deployed Macs.

Although installation packages can certainly be used to install entire systems, they are not the optimal tool for deploying entire systems. The preferred method for deploying entire systems is to use the system imaging and restore tools, covered in Chapter 4, "Creating System Images," and Chapter 5, "Deploying System Images."

Understanding Mac OS X Installation Technology

The installation package technology built into Mac OS X is the preferred method for delivering software components. This technology is used not only by Apple and other software developers but by customers who need a customizable deployment solution. You can take advantage of installation package technology to further automate your software distributions.

There are several benefits to using installation packages for software distribution, including the ability to:

▶ Verify that a certain version of the operating system is already installed

▶ Verify that certain components are already installed on the system

▶ Start or stop processes and daemons

▶ Install software in multiple locations throughout the system

▶ Run custom scripts to automate administrative functions

▶ Present the user with documentation, policies, or license information

▶ Allow the user to customize the installation

In addition to these standard installation package features, Mac OS X version 10.5 introduced several new features, including:

▶ Better post-install management via the Installer package database

▶ "Flat" installation packages that are built as a single contiguous file

▶ Installation packages that automatically download the latest version

▶ Certificate-based installation package signing to verify authenticity

Understanding Installation Packages

An *installation package* is a collection of compressed files and other information used to install software on Mac OS X. The entire contents of an installation package are contained within a single package bundle or package file, which has the filename extension .pkg. As with all package bundles, the Finder displays the installation package as a single opaque item.

Custom Deployment.pkg

Installation packages are created by using the PackageMaker application, which can be found in /Developer/Applications/Utilities or by using the packagemaker command. Both tools are available when you install the Xcode Tools software development suite on your Mac.

> **MORE INFO** ▶ The Xcode Tools installer can be found on both the Mac OS X and Mac OS X Server installation discs, or it can be downloaded from the Apple Developer Connection website: http://developer.apple.com/.

Installation packages can be installed using the Installer application, the Apple Remote Desktop (ARD) administrator application, or the installer command-line tool. All of these tools will install the software in its designated locations, run any scripts designated for the installation, and create a receipt for future maintenance. The Installer application, located in the /System/Library/Core Services/ folder, is primarily used by the user and will display the custom welcome, Read Me, and license information screens and allow the user to customize the installation, if customization is allowed. For deployment purposes, however, the ARD administrator application and the installer command-line tool are more appropriate.

Understanding Installation Metapackages

Installation metapackages allow you to present multiple packages as a single installation package. An installation metapackage doesn't install files itself; instead, it references other installation packages, which perform the actual installations. These reference installation packages are often stored inside the installation metapackage, which can be identified by a slightly different icon than the standard installation packages and the .mpkg filename extension. You can designate each package within the metapackage as optional or required, allowing your users the flexibility to choose what they want to install.

Just as with standard installation packages, the user need only click a single installer package icon in the Finder. The same Installer interface appears, but there is one difference.

With installation metapackages the user is offered a Customize interface, which displays a list of all of the packages being installed, as well as checkboxes to enable or disable each package. However, when you create the installation metapackage, you can prevent users from making customized installation selections if you deem customization unnecessary.

Installation metapackages are useful if you have files that are common to all users but also need to allow separate groups to have their own collections of additional files. For example, you could create a single installation package that contains both group-specific files and the files for all users. However, as soon as one of the files used by everyone changes, you need to re-create every group installation package. The solution, as shown in the following figure, is to create separate installation metapackages for each group, each also containing a common package for all users. This way, each group will have a single installation metapackage, but if a common file changes, you will have to update only the common installation package.

Installation metapackages are also useful for large software deployments, when you have a large set of files you want to distribute that requires frequent updates. As in the previous example, you could create an installation metapackage that refers to three separate packages:

▶ The main application—This package might come directly from the vendor, or if you were repackaging it, it would be updated with every revision of the application.

▶ Configuration presets—This package might include default preferences for all of your users, as well as license information that you want to distribute directly in a file rather than having to type a license code at every workstation. This package would rarely need to be updated.

▶ Plug-ins and support files—This package might contain third-party plug-ins and other support files. It would rarely need to be updated. If additional plug-ins were needed later, you would simply add another installation package to your installation metapackage.

Understanding Flat Installation Packages

As you learned in the previous chapter, deploying bundled items introduces third-party compatibility issues that require the use of file containers. Thus, when you deploy standard bundle-based installation packages or metapackages, you may need to place them inside a container file. This is why every installer package you download from a website is contained inside an archive file or, more commonly, a disk image.

To alleviate this deployment hindrance, Mac OS X v10.5 introduced a new package format in which the package is flattened to a single contiguous data file. Though this new flat installation package format is compatible only with Mac OS X v10.5 or newer, it offers several advantages over the traditional bundle-based installation packages.

Flat installation packages and metapackages are:

▶ Compatible with third-party file storage and transmission technologies

▶ Completely opaque in the Finder, so users cannot easily see the installation package contents

▶ Signable with a certificate to ensure authenticity

These advantages have made the flat format the default for all Mac OS X v10.5–targeted installation packages and metapackages. The flat package format uses the same .pkg or .mpkg filename extensions and Finder icons that standard installation packages and meta-packages do, so the formats are indistinguishable to most users. The easiest way to tell whether an installation package is a flat package is by right-clicking or Control-clicking it in the Finder. If the Show Package Contents command is not available from the shortcut menu, then it's a flat package. However, if you have the Xcode Tools installed, you should be able to open the flat installation package with the Flat Package Editor application.

Understanding Installation Package Contents

An installation package or metapackage is made up of a collection of files that tell the installation tool what to install, how to install it, and how to verify what was installed. For bundle-based installation packages, these items reside in the Contents folder inside the package. As with any package on Mac OS X, to view its contents, right-click or Control-click the package and choose Show Package Contents from the shortcut menu. This opens a new Finder window, in which the package contents are displayed. For flat installation packages, you can view the contents using the Flat Package Editor application, which is installed as part of the Xcode Tools.

> **NOTE ▶** The specific content of bundle-based and flat installation packages varies slightly. Differences are noted in the following list.

The main content of an installation package includes:

- ▶ Archive.bom (bundle-based)/Bom (flat package)—The binary bill of materials (BOM) file describes the contents of the installation package. This file contains a list of every file and folder that is to be installed by the installation package, along with ownership and permissions information for each item.

- ▶ Archive.pax.gz (bundle-based)/Payload (flat package)—This file contains the actual content to be installed, saved inside a single archive file that is compressed.

- ▶ Distribution—This script file was introduced with Mac OS X v10.4 to allow greater control over the installation process. Flat installation packages always include this file, and some bundle-based installation metapackages are also included in this file. Some examples of information found in this file are Installer interface customizations and installation requirement specifications.

- ▶ Info.plist (bundle-based) / PackageInfo (flat package)—This property list file contains general installation information, such as whether authorization is required for installation and whether the package requires the computer to be rebooted after installation.

- ▶ Resources folder—This folder contains any additional resources that are used by the installation process, including items used to customize the installation. Some examples of items in this file are background images, Read Me files, license-agreement files, and scripts. You don't actually need to create all of the resources. If any resources are missing, they will be skipped or a default will be presented. For example, if the welcome message is missing, a default pane asks the user to proceed to the installation. If the license file is missing, no license pane will appear. To use localized (language-specific) versions of the resources, create folders with the name *languagename*.lproj, and put the resources for that language in that folder. Note that the scripts cannot be localized, but any of the information presented to the user can be localized.

▶ Packages folder—This folder is found only in bundle-based installation metapackages. (Flat installation metapackages store each installation package at the root of the package.) It contains the installation packages that make up the complete installation metapackage.

Creating Installation Packages

In this section you will learn how to create custom installation packages and metapackages from items already installed on your source Mac. The items you intend to deploy using an installation package are generally referred to as the installation *payload*. The first step in creating a custom installation is to properly organize the payload items. Then you will use the PackageMaker application to create and customize your installation. Along with creating your installation package or metapackage, PackageMaker saves an editable copy of your installation settings. This file is known as the PackageMaker project file and uses the filename extension .pmdoc.

PackageMaker.app   PackageMaker
                       Project.pmdoc

This discussion assumes that you have the PackageMaker application installed. If you don't already have PackageMaker installed, you can install it from the Utilities folder of the Mac OS X Server Administration Tools disc. It's also installed as part of the Xcode Tools, which provides many additional tools and considerable additional documentation, so you are encouraged to install it on your administration Mac. With Xcode Tools installed, you can open the PackageMaker application from the /Developer/Applications/ Utilities/ folder.

MORE INFO ▶ Though PackageMaker use is covered in this book, you can find more detailed documentation at the Apple Developer Connection, http://developer.apple. com/documentation/DeveloperTools/Conceptual/PackageMakerUserGuide/.

Preparing the Payload Items

The first step in creating a custom installation package is to locate and prepare the items to be installed. The PackageMaker application can create an installation package from items stored in nearly any location on your Mac. If you need to install only a single item, such as a single configuration file or a simple application that appears as a single item in the Finder, you don't really need to prepare it for packaging. When creating the installation package, you can simply drag the single item into PackageMaker.

However, if you want to install multiple items as part of a single installation, you may want to prepare a separate deployment root folder: a folder dedicated to storing just the collection of items that you want to install. For example, if you want to install multiple items from the Applications folder, the best practice is to create copies of only the items you want to install and save them in a deployment folder separate from the main Applications folder. Then create the installation package based on the contents of the deployment folder instead of the main Applications folder.

The main advantage of using a separate deployment folder is that it prevents you from unintentionally installing other, unwanted items from the original source folder. Folders currently in use by your Mac, such as the main Application and Library folders, have contents that change often during normal use. When building installation packages, you want to be sure of the content, so a folder that changes often is a bad choice as an installation source.

NOTE ▶ Take note of items that are symbolic links or aliases to other items. Your payload items should reflect the actual locations of the files, and they should not use paths that include symbolic links or aliases. For example, files that are found at the /etc/ symbolic link actually exist at /private/etc/.

Creating Basic Installation Packages

Mac OS X v10.5 introduced a new PackageMaker application that is much easier to use than previous versions. It takes only a few minutes to set up a basic installation project with your custom deployment content, and then with one click ProjectMaker will build your installation package.

> **NOTE** ▶ The following instructions assume that you have already created your payload structure in a deployment root folder as described in the preceding section of this chapter.

To create a basic installation package:

1 Open the PackageMaker application.

When you open the PackageMaker application directly, as opposed to opening a PackageMaker project file, it starts by creating a new installation project for you.

2 Set the following basic installation properties, and then click OK:

▶ Enter the Organization information in a reverse URL format. This information will be used to identify installation projects that belong to your organization and will be part of the installation package identifier. For example, if your organization is com.pretendco, and you title the installation package *Base Items*, the identifier will be com.pretendco.baseitems.

▶ Choose a Minimum Target from the pop-up menu. The selection you make here will determine the type of installation package that will be created by PackageMaker. If you choose Mac OS X v10.5 as your target, a flat installation package will be created, whereas selecting earlier Mac OS X versions will create bundle-based installation packages.

> **TIP** ▶ The Minimum Target setting is not the ideal way to define minimum installation requirements. The PackageMaker interface has a dedicated section for defining installation requirements, covered in the "Setting Installation Requirements" section later in this chapter.

After you click OK, PackageMaker creates a new installation product. In PackageMaker the installation product is a reference to the contents of an entire installation package. PackageMaker then displays the Configuration pane for the installation product.

TIP You can access the installation properties settings again by double-clicking the name of the installation in the column to the left above the word "Contents."

3 Specify the general settings for your installation as a whole.

▶ Enter a Title for your installation. This will be the title as it appears in the Installer application. This does not set the filename of the final installation package, project file, or installation identifier.

▶ From the User Sees pop-up menu, choose whether the user can use the Easy Install or Custom Install interface, or both. The Custom Install interface is useful only when creating installation metapackages.

▶ Select the Install Destinations by enabling the appropriate checkboxes. Users will not be able to install to destinations that are disabled. If you choose the "System volume" destination, the installation will require administrator authentication.

▶ If you are targeting Mac OS X v10.5 systems, you can select a certificate file to sign your flat installation package. This will help others verify the authenticity of your installation.

▶ In the Description field, you can add a brief description of your installation. This is not intended as a substitute for other, more detailed, information you need the user to view during installation. For instance, you would not want to put your license or policy information here.

MORE INFO ▶ Installation product settings in the Requirements pane will be covered in the "Setting Installation Requirements" section; the Actions pane will be covered in "Using Installation Action Workflows," both later in this chapter.

4 Define the installation payload by dragging your deployment items to the Contents list or click the Add (+) button at the bottom of the list to use a file browser to locate your deployment items. In most cases, you will select the deployment root folder that you created earlier.

The PackageMaker application will scan the deployment items you've selected, and then create a new installation package component in the Contents list. In PackageMaker an installation package component is a reference to the settings for a single payload inside your full installation. The deployment items themselves will remain in the same location on your Mac but will be copied into the payload archive when you later build the installation package. This allows you to easily add to the deployment root folder when you need to build new installation packages in the future.

Once PackageMaker has scanned the deployment items, the interface changes to reveal the installation package component's Configuration settings.

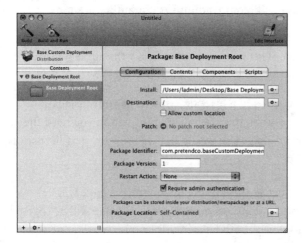

TIP Clicking once on the installation product name above the Contents list will return you to the installation product settings. Double-clicking the installation name will bring back the Installation Properties dialog.

5 Define the location where items will be installed by entering a path in the Destination field. You can also browse to the location by clicking the Action button (labeled with a gear) to the right of the Destination field.

In this example, the items that will be installed are applications, so the appropriate destination folder is /Applications. If you define a destination that does not exist on the target Mac, the proper folders will be created during installation.

NOTE ► Use caution when entering Install or Destination paths. A typo here can install the wrong items or create a new folder with an incorrect name on the target system. This results in an installation package that may not behave correctly, and misnamed folders are often very difficult to diagnose later.

6   In the Configuration pane, you can set other general options for the selected installation payload:

►   Selecting the "Allow custom location" checkbox will allow the user to specify the install location. This option should be avoided for any installation that places items in the system or local domains.

►   The Package Identifier name is automatically created based on your organization name and installation package name. This identifier is used by the system to track each specific installation, so the identifier should be unique for each of your packages.

►   The Package Version is used by the installer to identify whether the installation package is an update of an older package. If an older version of this installation is found on the target Mac, the items will be upgraded.

►   The Restart Action pop-up menu allows you to require a logout, restart, or shutdown after installation takes place.

►   Selecting the "Require admin authentication" checkbox is necessary any time your installation destination is the system or local domains. You could obviously also select this option to prevent standard users from being allowed to install the installation package.

►   The Package Location setting allows you to set a custom location for the installation payload, including external locations to the installation package. The default setting here is ideal in most situations.

7   Click the Contents tab to adjust the installation payload content and permissions. Expand the folder contents by clicking the disclosure triangles to navigate through your installation payload structure.

►   Deselect checkboxes next to items that you do not want to include in the installation package. For example, you should not include the invisible .DS_Store files. These files are used by the Finder to store window settings and are rarely required for deployment.

▶ In most cases you should also deselect the "Include root in package" checkbox. This will prevent the installation of the deployment root folder itself, which is ideal in most cases. In the following example, only the two applications should be installed on the target Mac, but not the Base Deployment Root folder.

▶ Optionally, you can select any item in the listing, and then at the bottom you can adjust ownership and permissions settings. These settings will be applied to the item during installation on the target Mac. In general, most items installed in the system or local domain should be owned by the root user and the admin group. If you're not sure what to select here, you can click the Apply Recommendations button and PackageMaker will apply some logical defaults.

TIP At this point you can choose to accept the default settings for your installation and move on to step 9 to build your installation package. However, the next step provides detailed information about installation settings that you may find useful.

8 Click the Components tab to specify a few more settings specific to bundles and packages in your installation payload. PackageMaker will automatically identify these items and display them in the components list.

▶ Allowing relocation will attempt to track down a component that you may be updating but that has moved from its original target destination. For instance, if a user moves an earlier version of an installed application, the installation process will attempt to locate that moved application and apply the update in the relocated destination. Clicking the Relocation button at the bottom will allow you to specify relocation search settings.

▶ Allowing downgrade will tell the Installer to replace a newer version of the component with the version in the installation package. For instance, if a user installs a newer version of an application on his own, the installation process will delete the newer application and replace it with the version in the installation package.

MORE INFO ▶ Installation package component settings in the Scripts pane will be covered in the "Using Scripts in Installation Packages" section later in this chapter.

9 When you are satisfied with your installation settings, click the Build icon in the toolbar to create the installation package.

10 In the Save dialog that appears, select a name and location for the installation package file, and then click Save to start the build process.

The PackageMaker window shows you the build process for your installation package. Any build errors or warnings that occur appear below the built process. If any problems appear, click the Spotlight icon to view more information about the error or warning.

After the build successfully completes, you can click the appropriate button to open the installation package, view the package in the Finder, or return to editing the installation settings.

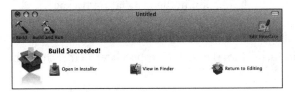

11 If you are done using PackageMaker, click the Close button. Choose Yes to save a project file.

You should always save a project file if you intend to improve and update the installation package.

NOTE ▶ Always test a custom installation package before you deploy it. Exploring the results of an installation is covered in the "Inspecting Installation Packages" section later in this chapter.

Creating Installation Metapackages

With PackageMaker, it's easy to add items to an existing installation product. If you want to keep your installation as a single package, you can simply add more items to your deployment root folder, and then rebuild the installation project. PackageMaker will reevaluate the deployment items and build a new installation package with an updated payload.

TIP To quickly find a deployment root folder while using PackageMaker, right-click or Control-click the installation package component in the Contents list, and then choose "Reveal in Finder" from the shortcut menu.

You can also choose to add new items by upgrading your existing installation package project to an installation metapackage project. This will give both you and your users more control over the installation process. Upgrading to an installation metapackage project is as easy as adding deployment items to your Contents list. When you rebuild the modified installation product, PackageMaker will automatically format the internal structure of your installation as a metapackage.

NOTE ▶ Again, the following instruction assumes that you have already created your payload structure in a deployment root folder, as described previously in the "Creating Installation Packages" section in this chapter.

To add to an existing installation and create a metapackage:

1 Open an existing PackageMaker project or create a new one as outlined in the preceding section.

2 If you're working from a previous PackageMaker project, choose File > Save As and save a new project file.

TIP ▶ It's always best to keep archives of your PackageMaker project files so that you can easily go back and check previous configurations. These project files are very small, so there is no harm in saving multiple files and versions for a deployment project.

PackageMaker always opens to the installation product Configuration settings.

3 Review these settings and at the very least change the Title and Description to match the new installation metapackage that you are creating.

4 Define additional installation package components by dragging your deployment items to the Contents list.

You can add as many items as you need for your deployment. However, pay special attention to exactly where in the list you drop the new items because the location of the items will directly affect your *installation choices*. PackageMaker defines an installation choice as a group of one or more installation package components. When a user opens an installation metapackage and chooses Custom Install, each installation choice will be represented as a separate item in the Custom Install list.

If you drop the new items on top of the previous installation choice or installation package component, it will be added to that installation choice. In this case, from the user's point of view, you will not have a true installation metapackage because the two payloads will be installed as one.

However, if you drop the new items below the previous installation package component, an additional installation choice is created. In this case, you will have a true installation metapackage where each payload can be individually configured and installed.

If you have decided to create a true installation metapackage, the Contents list will show that you now have two separate installation choices, which are indicated by a blue dot next to the installation choice name. As you can see, each installation choice contains separate installation package components.

To review, the PackageMaker interface is now showing three levels of installation organization. The top item is the *installation product package* and is used to define settings for the entire installation. The first item in the Contents list is an *installation choice*, which defines the individual choices users will see if they perform a custom install. Each installation choice can have one or more *installation component packages*, which define the actual items to be installed.

Installation Product Package

Installation Choice

Installation Component Package

NOTE ▶ You cannot easily rearrange items in the Contents list. To fix a mistake in the Contents list placement, you must remove the item by selecting it and pressing the Delete key, and then add the item back in the correct location.

5 From the Contents list, select each installation choice in turn. In the Configuration settings tab that appears at the right, configure appropriate settings. You can also choose to accept the default settings.

▶ The Choice Name field specifies the name that users see listed if they attempt to perform a custom installation. Remember, you can choose to allow or disallow the Custom Install feature by selecting the installation project, shown above the Contents list, and changing the User Sees setting.

▶ The Identifier field sets the order for the Custom Install listing. Obviously choice0 will appear before, or above, choice1 in the Custom Install list.

▶ The Initial State checkboxes specify how the installation choice appears in the Custom Install listing. Select the Selected checkbox if you want the installation choice installed by default. Select Enabled to allow the user to decide whether the installation choice is installed. If the Enabled option is not selected, during installation users cannot select, or more importantly, deselect the installation choice. Select Hidden if you don't want the user to even see the installation choice.

▶ In the Destination field you can specify an alternate installation target.

▶ The Tooltip and Description fields will be displayed at the Custom Install screen. Use them to describe the installation choice to the user.

6   Select any new installation package components that you have added and adjust the
    Configuration, Contents, and Components settings accordingly, or accept the default set-
    tings. Remember that each installation package component has its own unique settings.

7   Once you are satisfied with your installation settings, click the Build icon in the tool-
    bar to create the installation metapackage. When the Save dialog appears, make sure
    to save the installation metapackage with a different and appropriate name.

    NOTE ▶ If your minimum target is Mac OS X v10.5, PackageMaker will create a flat
    installation metapackage that may still use the .pkg filename extension. Though not
    necessary, if it makes you feel better or you just prefer the installation metapackage icon,
    you can change the filename extension to .mpkg and it won't affect the performance of
    the installation.

    The build process will be identical, except for the longer build time, to the process for
    building a standard installation package.

    After the build has succeeded, you can click the appropriate button to open the installa-
    tion package, view the package in the Finder, or return to editing the installation settings.

8   If you are done using PackageMaker, click the Close button and make sure to save the
    changes to your project file. You should always save the project file if you intend to
    improve and update the installation package.

NOTE ▶ Always test a custom installation package before you deploy it. Exploring the results of an installation is covered in the "Inspecting Installation Packages" section later in this chapter.

Customizing the Installation Interface

To create a truly professional-looking installation, or to fulfill policy and licensing requirements, you can customize the interface that the user sees during installation. This customization can be viewed only if you use the graphical Installer application— in other words, not if you're deploying using the installer command or ARD.

To customize the interface of an installation:

1   Open an existing PackageMaker project or create a new one as outlined previously. If you're working from a previous PackageMaker project, choose File > Save As and save a new project file.

2   In the toolbar, click the Edit Interface button.

The PackageMaker Interface Editor window opens. This is a simulated Installer application window that allows you to customize the interface for your installation.

TIP ▶ At the bottom of the Interface Editor, a pop-up menu allows you to define custom localized interfaces for multiple languages. Each language you enable can have its own separate custom interface settings for your installation. This feature allows you to create a single installation that supports many languages.

The first customization choice in the list at the left is background image. The default choice is the generic Mac OS X application icon, but you can specify any GIF, JPEG, TIFF, or PNG image file.

3   To specify a custom background, drag an image file into the content area of the Interface Editor window. You can also enter the image file's path in the File field or browse to the image file by clicking the Action button (labeled with a gear) in the right side drawer. If the background does not fit correctly, you can adjust the Alignment and Scaling from the pop-up menus in the right side drawer as well. When you are done, click Continue.

TIP ▶ It's best to use a simple background with lots of white space so as not to interfere with the information text. If you're using just a logo image, you can use alpha channels so the background will show through.

TIP ▶ The default Installer window size in Mac OS X is 620 by 420 pixels.

When the installation package is built, PackageMaker will copy the specified image file into the Resources folder of the installation package.

4   Select Introduction if you want to set custom introduction text. The Introduction screen is the only required information screen, and it is the first screen that appears when a user opens an installation with the Installer application, so your users will see the default introduction text if you don't make a change here. To specify custom introduction information, do one of the following, and then click Continue:

▶ Select the Embedded button in the drawer to the right, and then create your introduction text inside the content area of the Interface Editor window. When the installation package is built, the embedded text will be saved in the distribution file inside your installation package.

TIP ▶ Embedded Installer text can use full rich text formatting. You can access a full range of text formatting options from the Formatting menu in the menu bar.

▶ Select the File button and drag a TXT or RTF text file into the content area of the Interface Editor window, or enter the text file's path, or browse to the text file by clicking the Action button below the File button. In this case, when the installation package is built, PackageMaker will copy the specified text file into the Resources folder of the installation package.

5 You can add Read Me, License, or Finish Up information to your installation using the methods described in Step 4.

These information screens are not required, so if you leave the default setting of None, these screens will not appear.

The Read Me and License screens will appear before the installation starts, and the Finish Up screen will appear when the installation is complete. Therefore, if you have to distribute policy information to your users along with the payload, you can put it on a screen that appears prior to the actual installation.

6 When you are satisfied with your customization settings, close the Interface Editor window and return to the main PackageMaker window.

At this point, you can build your installation package to test your customized interface. Be sure to save your changes to the installation project file.

Advanced Installation Customization

If you need to make modifications beyond what the normal PackageMaker interface allows, you can use PackageMaker's Raw Editing Mode. To enter this mode, choose Project > Raw Editing Mode. The PackageMaker interface will switch to show you the raw files that make up the installation, allowing you to directly manipulate these items. Using the Raw Editing Mode is beyond the scope of this book, but you can find out more at the Apple Developer Connection website (http://developer.apple.com.)

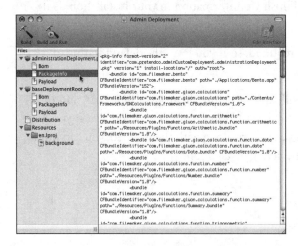

NOTE ► It's very easy to make a mistake when using Raw Editing Mode that results in an inoperable installation. Because of this, you should always work from a second copy of the project file.

Setting Installation Requirements

Setting software and hardware requirements for the systems on which your installation will be deployed will improve the reliability of your deployed items by preventing installation on substandard or incompatible systems. PackageMaker includes a thorough selection of requirement criteria that you can set for your installation packages.

To specify installation requirements:

1   Open an existing PackageMaker project or create a new one as outlined previously. If you're working from a previous PackageMaker project, choose File > Save As and save a new project file.

2   From the Contents list, select either the installation product package or another installation choice.

 If the target computer does not meet the requirements set for the installation product package, the entire installation will not be allowed.

 Similarly, if the target computer does not meet the requirements set for another installation choice, the contents for that choice will not be allowed. However, in this case, all other installation choices that do meet the installation requirements will still be allowed.

3 Click the Requirements tab to reveal the installation requirements list for the selected item.

PackageMaker allows you to create multiple installation requirements, and if any requirement in this list is not met, then the installation for the selected item will not be allowed.

4 To add a new installation requirement, click the Add (+) button below the list.

A dialog appears, allowing you to create a new installation requirement.

In the top half of the installation requirements dialog you can define the requirement criteria; in the bottom half you can define specific failure actions when the requirement is not met.

5 From the If pop-up menu, choose the requirement criteria. You can return to this menu repeatedly to select as many requirements you need.

NOTE ▸ A System requirement will query whether the criteria is met for the Mac running the installation, whereas a Target requirement will query whether the criteria is met for the selected installation target volume.

You can set your installation package to check requirements such as these:

▸ Amount of free space available on the target volume—This is the most important installation requirement, especially if you have unusually large payloads. Also remember every Mac should have at least 1 GB of free space on the system volume for virtual memory operations, so you should always assume 1 GB plus your payload size.

▶ Hardware specifications—These requirements are very important if you're redistributing high-end software packages or require special hardware attachments.

▶ Version of the installed operating system—Setting the operating system version is a good way to ensure consistent performance for your custom installation.

▶ Selection state of other installation choices—You can set dependencies within the choices of an installation metapackage.

▶ Whether a specific file, bundle, or property list exists—Use this option to determine whether previous required installations have taken place.

▶ Any criteria based on a custom script—You can use scripts to set any other requirement criteria you want.

The requirement criteria settings will change depending on the specific requirement criteria you choose from the If pop-up menu. In some cases you will need to specify only the path to an item, but usually you will need to specify an operand and a variable.

6 From the "is" pop-up menu, choose an operand. Choices include equal to (==), not equal to (!=), less than (<), less than or equal to (<=), greater than (>), and greater than or equal to (>=). Enter your variable in the field next to this menu.

For example, you might specify the If and "is" fields like this: "If the megabytes on available target is greater than 1100," or "If system OS version is greater than or equal to 10.6.2."

7 After you have established the requirement criteria, enter the failure settings:

► For the failure of installation package product requirements, enter a short message. This message should give the user enough information to quickly figure out the problem.

► For the failure of installation choice requirements, set whether the installation choice status will be changed to Selected, Enabled, or Hidden. These installation choices were covered in the "Creating Installation Metapackages" section previously in this chapter.

8 When you are satisfied with your new installation requirement, click OK to return to the requirements list and set more requirements.

From this list you can also double-click a requirement to modify it, or you can select a requirement and click the Minus (–) button to delete it.

9 If you are setting installation package product requirements, you can set a few more options from the requirements list:

► In the Required column, click an entry, and from the pop-up menu choose whether you want the item to be optional. An optional requirement will allow the installation to continue even if the requirement isn't met, but an error message will be displayed.

► In the "Pass if" column, click an entry to specify whether the criteria is met if the statement in the Description column is true or false.

Now you can build your installation package to test your new installation requirements. Be sure to save your changes to the installation project file.

Using Installation Action Workflows

Installation packages can be used for more than just installing items; they can also be used to execute a command or perform a specific task on the target computer by setting up actions or scripts. Actions and scripts allow an installation package to serve as a deployment mechanism for both files and administrative tasks.

With PackageMaker you can easily create an automated workflow to accompany your installation without having to create a complicated script. These workflows are based on *installation actions* that are very similar to the Automator actions used to automate other Mac OS X tasks.

You can set actions only for the installation product package, meaning that you can define actions only for the installation as a whole, not per installation choice or per installation package component. However, you can define a preinstall action that occurs right before the installation process, and you can create a postinstall action that occurs immediately after the installation process.

To create an installation action workflow:

1   Open an existing PackageMaker project or create a new one as outlined previously. If you're working from a previous PackageMaker project, choose File > Save As and save a new project file.

2   Select the installation product package from above the Contents list, and then click the Actions tab.

3   To add a new installation action workflow, click the Edit button below either the Preinstall Actions list or Postinstall Actions list, depending on which type of action you want to create.

A new dialog appears, allowing you to create an installation action workflow, with the available actions listed at the right.

Significant installation actions include the ability to do the following:

▶   Create a file-system alias of an installed item for the user in a convenient location—For instance, placing a shortcut to an application on the user's desktop (as a postinstall action).

▶   Locate an open application and quit or kill that application—For instance, if you're going to replace that application during installation (as a preinstall action).

TIP ▶   To use the Get Application action, you will have to specify the application's identifier. This identifier can be found in the Info.plist file inside the application package contents. When you open the Info.plist file, look for the Bundle Identifier value, which should be in reverse URL notation. For example, the Firefox application's bundle identifier is org.mozilla.firefox.

▶   Load or unload a kernel extension—For instance, if a kernel extension or kernel extension dependency is being replaced during installation (as a preinstall action).

▶   Open a specified file or reveal it in the Finder—For instance, to reveal an important document or item that was installed as part of the installation (as a postinstall action).

▶   Open a specified URL in the default web browser—For instance, to direct the user to important web-based information (as a postinstall action).

4   Drag the desired actions from the Actions list to the workflow area at the right. You can add as many actions as you want. Use care when placing actions in the workflow area because the order of the workflow list will determine the order in which the actions are performed. To reorder the workflow, simply drag any action above, below, or between the other actions in the workflow listing.

5   Each action requires some form of input, whether from a previous action or from static information you have entered:

▶   For static actions, enter the appropriate input information in the action window.

▶   For actions that require additional input, place the action directly below the other action that will provide the input information. For example, set the Get Application action static input to locate a specific application. Then place either the Quit Application or Kill Application action below the Get Application action.

6   After you are satisfied with your workflow, click Save.

The interface returns to the installation product package Actions pane. From here you can view your complete action workflows or continue to edit them by clicking the Edit button.

Now you can build your installation package to test your new installation actions. Be sure to save your changes to the installation project file.

Using Scripts in Installation Packages

Though easy to use, the variety of available installation actions is limited. To perform additional actions, you can create your own scripts. The capabilities of custom installation scripts are unlimited. You can use installation scripts to perform tasks you deem necessary to prepare for installation and to clean up after an installation is completed. You can use them to create needed resources, add configuration options to existing files, start and stop dependent services, and verify that setup is performed correctly.

Understanding Installation Scripts

The creation of installation scripts requires knowledge of scripting. General scripting instruction is beyond the scope of this book, but there are plenty of resources online. You can refer to *Apple Training Series: Mac OS X Support Essentials v10.6* (Peachpit Press, 2010). You can also learn by example by examining other installation packages, as covered in the "Inspecting Installation Packages" section later in this chapter.

If you are prepared to create scripts for your installation packages, you should be aware of a few key arguments. When an installation script is run, the installer process passes four main arguments to the script that contain useful information about the installation process:

▶ $1—The full path to the installation package being installed; for example, /Volumes/
Projects/Testing/PackageName.pkg

▶ $2—The full path to the installation target destination; for example, /Applications

▶ $3—The mount point of the destination volume; for example, / or /Volumes/
External_Disk

▶ $4—The root folder for the current system, that is, /

You should preface most of the paths in your script with the third argument ($3 in a shell script or $ARGV[2] in a Perl script). In most cases, this is all that is necessary to allow your package to be installed on volumes other than your system volume. Also, remember that volume names commonly have spaces in them, so you should place quotation marks around every path.

Within PackageMaker you can define installation scripts separately for each installation package component. For installations with a minimum target of Mac OS X v10.5 (flat package), you can also define installation scripts separately for each bundle inside the payload.

Additionally, you can set the point at which a script is executed during the installation process. The following list shows the available script types and the order in which the scripts are executed during the installation process:

▶ Preflight (bundle-based packages only)—These scripts run before all other scripts and before the installation or upgrade takes place. It's important to note that when you use a custom preflight script, the Installer application will warn the user that a program must run first before installing.

▶ Preinstall—For bundle-based packages, these scripts run after the preflight script, but only when the Installer determines that this is a new installation. For flat packages, these scripts run before the associated installation package component or payload bundle item is installed.

▶ Preupgrade (bundle-based packages only)—These scripts run after the preflight script but only when the Installer determines that the installation is an upgrade.

▶ Postinstall—For bundle-based packages, these scripts run after the initial installation. For flat packages, these scripts run after the associated installation package component or payload bundle item is installed.

▶ Postupgrade (bundle-based packages only)—These scripts run after an upgrade installation.

▶ Postflight (bundle-based packages only)—These scripts run after all other scripts.

MORE INFO ▶ The "upgrade" status of an installation is based on the existence of a receipt from a previous similar installation. Receipts are covered in the "Installation Package Maintenance" section later in this chapter.

Adding Installation Scripts to Your Installation Project

PackageMaker makes it easy to incorporate scripts into your installation packages. When you build an installation with scripts, PackageMaker automatically makes a copy of those scripts inside the installation package. Installation scripts can refer to other scripts and resources, but those items must be included as part of the installation package. In PackageMaker you can define a scripts resources folder that will also be copied into the installation package during the build process.

To add scripts to an installation:

1 Open an existing PackageMaker project or create a new one as outlined previously. If you're working from a previous PackageMaker project, choose File > Save As and save a new project file.

2 Select an installation package component from the Contents list, and then click the Scripts tab.

If your minimum target is Mac OS X v10.5 (flat package), you will be able to add preinstall and postinstall scripts.

If your minimum target is Mac OS X v10.4 or v10.3 (bundle-based package), you will be able to add preinstall, postinstall, preflight, postflight, preupgrade, and postupgrade scripts.

NOTE ▶ When creating bundle-based packages, if you want to be sure that the installation scripts always run, set them as preflight and postflight scripts.

3   Add the scripts to your installation by dragging them to the appropriate fields or by clicking the Action button to the right of the field and using a browser window to navigate to the script file.

4   If you want, set a Scripts directory, or folder, that contains additional scripts and script resources.

The entire contents of this folder will be copied into your installation package when built.

5   If your minimum target is Mac OS X v10.5, you can also set installation scripts per bundle inside your installation payload:

▶   With your installation package component selected, click the Components tab. This will list all the bundles inside your installation payload. Select the specific item you want to set a script for, and then click the Scripts button at the bottom.

▶   In the new dialog that appears, choose whether to add a preinstall or postinstall script for this payload item. Then add the scripts by dragging them to the appropriate fields or by clicking the Action button to the right of the field and using a browser window to navigate to the script file.

▶   When you have set your scripts, click Save to close the dialog.

Now build your installation package to test your new installation scripts, and be sure to save your changes to the installation project file.

Creating Payload-Free Installation Packages

A *payload-free installation package* is an installer that contains no items to install but instead contains actions and scripts for automating tasks. Payload-free installation packages are created using the same methods as for regular installation packages but with no items in the installation payload.

For instance, you can use a payload-free installation package to enable users to run UNIX commands on their computers without having to work with UNIX; simply include the commands in a postinstall script in a payload-free installation package, which the user can install by double-clicking.

You can also use payload-free installations that contain scripts to fix a known problem, alter a system configuration, or create additional user accounts.

To create a payload-free installation package:

1   In the Finder create a new folder called *Empty*; do not put anything inside the folder.

2   Open PackageMaker and create a new installation. Configure the installation properties and installation product package settings as covered previously in this chapter.

3   Drag the Empty folder to the Contents list.

This creates a new empty installation package component.

TIP Notice that by default the new installation package component's Configuration settings require administrator authentication. You should leave this setting enabled if the scripts you intend to add to this installer require administrative access.

4 To prevent anything from installing, disable the Empty folder from installing. Select the Empty installation package component, and then click the Contents tab. Deselect the checkbox next to the Empty item in the contents list.

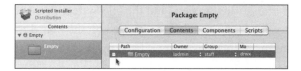

Now your payload-free installation is ready to accept your actions and scripts.

5 Using the techniques covered previously in this chapter, add as many actions and scripts as you need to accomplish the task requirements.

It's best to set postinstall actions and scripts for payload-free installations so the scripts run only if the user chooses to complete the installation process.

Once you have added all the necessary actions and scripts, you can build your payload-free installation package to test it. Be sure to save any changes you made to an installation project file.

Creating Snapshot Installation Packages

When you're deploying complex systems, using a uniform set of tools reduces the risks of software incompatibilities and mistakes. This is one of the primary reasons for creating your own custom installation packages using the built-in Mac OS X installation technology. However, creating installation packages from third-party software can be a difficult task because some products use nonstandard installation techniques, making it difficult to track where the software resources are placed on your Mac.

This is where the new *snapshot package* feature of the Mac OS X v10.5 or newer version of PackageMaker comes in handy. The snapshot feature can monitor any system changes, and then automatically generate a new set of installation package components based on changes to the file system. PackageMaker accomplished this feat by taking advantage of a system service introduced with Mac OS X v10.5 called File System Events. This service allows applications to quickly track changes in the file system as they happen.

Within PackageMaker you start the snapshot monitoring process, and this tells the File System Events service to track any system changes. Now you can run any installation process you need to capture, including third-party and Apple installations. Returning to PackageMaker, you stop the snapshot monitoring process, and the File System Events service returns a list of all the items that were either installed or changed on the Mac during the monitoring period, which makes it incredibly easy to repackage any software installation as a custom installation package.

NOTE ▶ The snapshot feature will scan all file systems currently mounted to your Mac. However, it is limited by the permissions of the user who is running the snapshot scan.

To create a snapshot installation package component:

1   Open an existing PackageMaker project or create a new one as outlined previously. If you're working from a previous PackageMaker project, choose File > Save As and save a new project file.

2   Choose Project > Add Snapshot Package. In the snapshot dialog that appears, click Start.

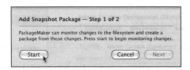

PackageMaker starts monitoring file-system changes, as indicated by the spinning gear next to the word "Watching" that appears in the snapshot dialog.

3   Use any method to install the new items that you want to make part of your snapshot installation package.

4   Return to PackageMaker. Click Stop to cease the monitoring process, and then click
Next to continue.

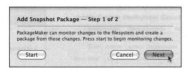

NOTE ▶ Clicking Start again at this point will restart the monitoring process, and any
changes that were recorded during the previous monitoring period will be lost.

A second snapshot dialog appears that allows you to filter out unwanted items that
have been installed or changed during the monitoring period.

5   Use the disclosure triangles to reveal items inside folders, and deselect any items that
you do not want to include in your new snapshot contents.

Mac OS X has many background processes that continually update items, which you
do not want to include in your installation package. For example, you should filter
out log files, cache files, and unrelated preference files that have changed during the
snapshot monitoring period.

6   After you have filtered out any unwanted items from your snapshot contents, enter a
Snapshot Title, and then click Save to create the new installation package component.

In the Contents list, you will see a new installation choice with a new installation
package component referencing the snapshot contents you just captured.

With the exception of not being able to change the installation snapshot contents, you can configure any other settings that you would normally associate with a custom installation package component.

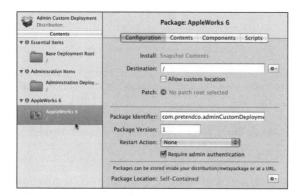

At this point you can build your installation package to test your new installation snapshot package. Be sure to save your changes to the installation project file.

Inspecting Installation Packages

When you authenticate as an administrator and then launch an installation, you essentially are giving the installation process free reign over your Mac. It can install any item in any location or perform any task as dictated by the creator of the installation package. A poorly made installation package could destroy the software on your Mac, and a malicious installation package could perform an action that puts your personal information at risk or even violates the law. Because of the potential for mayhem from a bad installation package, you should always inspect installation packages that you are unfamiliar with before you deploy them.

Basic exploration of installation packages was covered in the "Understanding Installation Package Contents" section previously in this chapter, where you saw how the contents of bundle-based installation packages can be easily viewed in the Finder and how the contents of flat installation packages can be viewed with the Flat Package Editor application. In this section you will dig deeper into the installation package to see and even extract the installation payload items.

Verifying Installation Packages

When installing packages downloaded from third-party sources, you should always question the validity of the installer. One method to verify the authenticity of the downloaded files is to use a checksum comparison. Many sites provide a programmatically generated checksum number that you can use to verify an installer package. Specifically, Apple provides SHA-1 cryptographic checksums for its downloads. In fact, Apple's Software Update mechanism uses this checksum technology to automatically verify downloaded updates.

In cases where you manually download an installation package, you also have to manually verify the checksum. For example, the Mac OS X v10.6.1 update downloads page (www.apple.com/downloads/macosx/apple/macosx_updates/macosxv1061update.html) includes the following text: "SHA1= 2e20c303e0078a488702172d782cb1b882eef543". This is the SHA-1 cryptographic hash associated with the disk image file containing the update installation. Thus, when you download the disk image containing the update, if valid, you should be able to calculate the exact same string of text using the SHA-1 algorithm.

In the command line you can generate the SHA-1 hash with the openssl command. The syntax is simply openssl sha1 and then the path to the downloaded item. In the following example, Michelle generates the SHA-1 hash for the previously mentioned system update (inside a disk image) downloaded from Apple's website.

```
MyMac:Downloads michelle$ openssl sha1 MacOSXUpd10.6.1.dmg
SHA1(MacOSXUpd10.6.1.dmg)= 2e20c303e0078a488702172d782cb1b882eef543
```

As you can see in this example, the hash numbers match, indicating the downloaded content is identical to that of the original. If you perform a check like this and they don't match, it means that at some point the installer has been compromised. This could be accidental due to connection failure or an intentional act of sabotage. Either way, you shouldn't install the update, but instead try to acquire the update again and compare the SHA-1 hash results a second time.

If you plan on hosting your own installation packages for download via a website, consider generating an SHA-1 hash and posting it as well. This simple step will allow others to perform the same action to verify that the downloaded update hasn't been compromised.

Expanding Flat Installation Packages

As covered previously in the "Understanding Flat Installation Packages" section, you can use the Flat Package Editor application to view the contents of a flat installation package.

However, Flat Package Editor only provides a basic interface for exploring installation contents. For example, you can't see the ownership or permissions of the items to be installed from Flat Package Editor. Thus, before you can really dig into a flat installation package, you must expand it from its flattened form.

The pkgutil command allows you to expand a flat installation package. The syntax is pkgutil --expand followed by the path to the flat installation package, followed by the path to a destination folder for the expanded installation content. In the following example, Michelle uses the pkgutil command to expand the FlatInstallation.pkg into a folder called UnFlatInstallation.

```
MyMac:Desktop michelle$ ls -lh
total 86296
-rw-r--r-- 1 michelle staff 42M Mar 31 00:01 FlatInstallation.pkg
MyMac:Desktop michelle$ pkgutil --expand FlatInstallation.pkg UnFlatInstallation
MyMac:Desktop michelle$ ls -lh
total 86296
-rw-r--r-- 1 michelle staff 42M Mar 31 00:01 FlatInstallation.pkg
drwxr-xr-x 6 michelle staff 204B Mar 31 00:02 UnFlatInstallation
```

She then verifies the installation contents by listing the items inside the UnFlatInstallation folder. She obviously expanded a flat installation metapackage because multiple installation packages were expanded. Further, both installation packages appear as folders at the command line so their contents have been expanded as well.

```
MyMac:Desktop michelle$ ls -lh UnFlatInstallation/
total 16
-rw-r--r-- 1 michelle staff 5.1K Mar 30 17:13 Distribution
drwxr-xr-x 3 michelle staff 102B Mar 31 00:02 Resources
drwxr-xr-x 5 michelle staff 170B Mar 31 00:02 administrationDeployment.pkg
drwxr-xr-x 6 michelle staff 204B Mar 31 00:02 baseDeploymentRoot.pkg
```

Listing the Installation Bill of Materials

As covered previously, installation packages contain a bill of materials (BOM) file, which lists every item that is part of the installation payload and the items' ownership and permissions. This file is a binary encoded document, so you cannot read it with a text reader; instead, you use the lsbom command-line tool to read BOM files.

To use this command, enter `lsbom -p MUGsf` and then the path to the BOM file inside the installation package. The `-p MUGsf` parameter will list the payload contents, similar to the way that entering `ls -l` at the command line does. The BOM file for bundle-based installation packages is named Archive.bom, and the BOM file for flat installation packages is named Bom. It's important to remember that each installation package inside an installation meta-package contains its own BOM file. Further, to view any BOM file inside of a flat installation package, you should first expand the package as described in the preceding section.

> **TIP** ▶ You can view the BOM of a flat installation package without expanding the installation package by using `pkgutil -payload-files` and entering the path to the flat installation package. However, this will not show you any ownership or permissions information about the payload.

The following example builds on the previous example where Michelle expanded a flat installation package to a folder named UnFlatInstallation. Michelle now uses the `lsbom -p MUGsf` command to list the BOM for baseDeploymentRoot.pkg inside the UnFlatInstallation folder. The contents are listed, but they have been truncated here to save space. As you can see, the payload items are listed with their permissions, ownership, size in bytes, and full path. You can also see that the `lsbom` command does not hide any detail but instead shows you every single item, including invisible items and the full contents of packaged items.

```
MyMac:Desktop michelle$ lsbom -p MUGsf UnFlatInstallation/baseDeploymentRoot.pkg/Bom
drwxr-xr-x   root admin          .
drwxrwxr-x   root admin          ./Applications
-rwxr-xr-x   root admin    82    ./Applications/._Firefox.app
drwxr-xr-x   root admin          ./Applications/Firefox.app
-rwxr-xr-x   root admin    82    ./Applications/Firefox.app/._Contents
drwxr-xr-x   root admin          ./Applications/Firefox.app/Contents
-rwxr-xr-x   root admin    82    ./Applications/Firefox.app/Contents/._MacOS
-rwxr-xr-x   root admin    82    ./Applications/Firefox.app/Contents/._Plug-Ins
-rwxr-xr-x   root admin    82    ./Applications/Firefox.app/Contents/._Resources
-rw-r--r--   root admin    3396  ./Applications/Firefox.app/Contents/Info.plist
...
```

> **TIP** ▶ Use the greater than operator (>) at the command line to save the BOM listing to a more manageable text file: `lsbom -p MUGsf pathtoBOMfile > pathtotextfile.txt`.

Extracting Items from Installation Payloads

The installation payloads are saved inside the installation package as ZIP compressed PAX archives. This format can easily be expanded using the Mac OS X Finder. The payload file for bundle-based installation packages is named Archive.pax.gz, and the payload file for flat installation packages is named Payload. Again, remember that each installation package inside an installation metapackage contains its own payload file. Further, to view any BOM file inside a flat installation package, first expand the installation as outlined previously.

To extract items from an installation package payload:

1 Locate the payload file inside the installation package. Then use the Finder to copy it to a temporary working folder or your desktop.

You should do this because the Finder extracts archive content into the same folder as the original archive. Therefore, if you were to use the Finder to extract the payload in its original location, the payload's contents would be duplicated in the installation package.

2 After you copy the payload file to a temporary working folder or your desktop, simply double-click the payload file from the Finder.

The Archive Utility opens and extracts the items.

The Archive Utility must perform two extraction tasks. First it decompresses the PAX archive, and then it extracts the items from the archive. Thus, bundle-based payloads will be extracted to a folder named Archive, but flat payloads will be extracted to a folder named Payload 2 2. The root of this folder will match the deployment root of the installation package, which in many cases was targeted to be installed at the root of your system volume.

3 Now that the payload items are extracted, drag them to any location or manually install the items by dragging them to their intended location. You should also refer to the installation package BOM as outlined in the preceding section to ensure that the appropriate ownership and permissions are applied. If any item's ownership or permissions are not properly set, you may experience unexpected results. To fix these items, you will have to manually adjust the ownership and permissions to match what is listed in the installation BOM.

TIP If you need to create new flat installation packages from previous bundle-based installation packages, you can simply drag any extracted archive folders to a new PackageMaker project that has a minimum target of Mac OS X v10.5.

Inspecting Installation Scripts

Installation packages can contain scripts of questionable intent or quality. In general, for bundle-based installations, scripts are located in the Resources folder of each installation package; for expanded flat installations, the scripts are located in the Scripts folder of each installation package. If the installation has a Distribution file, this can also be a location that contains scripts. If you are unable to decipher what an installation script is doing, but you are concerned about the script content, you can always extract the payload items as outlined previously and manually copy them to their appropriate target destinations.

Deploying Installation Packages

All the hard work that goes into making an installation package truly pays off when it comes time to deploy. Because nearly all of the installation parameters are included with the installation package, little or possibly no additional input is needed to run the installation process, which not only makes the installation process easy for users to complete by themselves, but also allows you to quickly deploy installation packages with little additional configuration.

There are four primary methods for deploying software via installation packages:

▶ Hosted on a server for manual installation—This is the most common method used by software developers for distributing their products. Installation packages can be hosted on a file server using nearly any file protocol, but they are most commonly hosted on web servers so they can be easily accessed using a web browser. This method assumes you trust your users with the task of properly downloading and installing the installation package. This also assumes that the users have administrator access on their own computers. For these reasons this is not a viable deployment solution for most managed systems and is not covered further here.

NOTE ▶ If you're hosting bundle-based installation packages from a file server, you should place the installation packages inside disk images to prevent the bundles from being corrupted when using third-party storage and transport mechanisms. Using disk images for deployment is covered in Chapter 2, "Deploying Individual Items and Containers."

▶ Deploying installation packages using Secure Shell (SSH)—This method uses command-line tools via a remote SSH connection to transfer the installation package to the target computer, and then run the installation. This method has the advantage of being transparent to the currently logged-in user on the target Mac, which makes it ideal for deploying new items to active computers. Further, this method can be scripted to automate the process. However, unless you already have a working script, this method isn't ideal for large-scale managed deployments.

▶ Deploying installation packages using ARD—This method uses the ARD administrator application to copy and install the installation package to one or more targeted Macs. This method is completely transparent to the currently logged-in user. Using this method, it's much easier to deploy an installation package to multiple computers simultaneously, making it the ideal solution for managed deployments.

▶ Deploying installation packages through a variety of other third-party commercial and open-source solutions—Most client management solutions on Mac OS X support package deployments in a similar fashion to ARD. If you already have a management solution for your Windows systems, it's possible you can use it on your Mac OS X systems as well.

Deploying Installation Packages with SSH

Deployment using SSH assumes that you have SSH remote login access and an administrator account on the target Macs where you will be deploying the installation package. This method involves three basic steps: copying the installation package to the target Mac using the scp command, logging in to the target Mac using the ssh command, and performing the installation using the installer command.

This is just one example of how to leverage ssh for package deployment. The beauty of this solution is that you can customize it for your specific environment. For example, you can pull the packages down from a web server instead of using scp to copy them.

MORE INFO ▶ To learn more about using SSH, please refer to *Apple Training Series: Mac OS X Support Essentials v10.6* (Peachpit Press, 2010).

The syntax to copy the installation file from the source administration Mac to the target Mac is scp installation_package_path target_user_name@target_host_name:target_path. In the following example, Michelle copies the Deploy.pkg to the /tmp folder on a Mac named SnowMac.local using the ladmin account. She has never connected to this computer before using SSH, so she must agree to the authenticity warning by entering "yes." Then she must authenticate with the password for the ladmin account to continue. The copy process is complete when the command shows "100%".

```
MyMac:Desktop michelle$ scp Deploy.pkg ladmin@SnowMac.local:/tmp/
The authenticity of host 'SnowMac.local (fe80::20a:95ff:feb7:6eb0%en1)' can't be
established.
RSA key fingerprint is 7b:1c:33:9f:f3:73:6e:65:8d:04:b2:83:fe:e5:bf:1e.
Are you sure you want to continue connecting (yes/no)? yes
Warning: Permanently added 'SnowMac.local,fe80::20a:95ff:feb7:6eb0%en1' (RSA) to the
list of known hosts.
Password: (password not shown)
Deploy.pkg 100% 42MB 3.0MB/s 00:14
```

NOTE ▶ Ideally, when using remote login you will have configured a preshared key pair for authentication so you do not have to enter any passwords at the command line and you can verify the authenticity of the target computer. To learn more about shared keys, please refer to *Apple Training Series: Mac OS X Security and Mobility v10.6* (Peachpit Press, 2010).

The syntax to log in to the target Mac is ssh target_user_name@target_host_name. In the following example, Michelle logs in to the SnowMac.local Mac using the ladmin account. She must again authenticate with the password for the ladmin account to continue. Once she is logged in, she navigates to the /tmp folder. Then she lists the items there to verify that the installation package was copied properly.

```
MyMac:Desktop michelle$ ssh ladmin@SnowMac.local
Password: (password not shown)
Last login: Sun Mar 30 23:16:37 2008
SnowMac:~ ladmin$ cd /tmp
SnowMac:tmp ladmin$ ls -lh
total 86296
srwxrwxrwx 1 root  wheel  0B  Mar 26 18:02 ARD_ABJMMRT
-rw-r--r-- 1 ladmin wheel 42M Mar 31 14:36 Deploy.pkg
drwx------ 3 ladmin wheel 102B Mar 26 18:02 launch-M1IOF5
...
```

TIP ▶ The /tmp folder is a good temporary location for deployment items because it's assumed the items in this folder are temporary.

Finally, the syntax to run the installation is sudo installer -pkg installation_package_path -target destination_path. In the following example, Michelle installs the Deploy.pkg installation package to the system volume "/". She must preface the installer command with sudo to allow the installation process to place items in the system or local domains. Once again, she must authenticate to continue with the installation. When the process is nearly complete, the installer command informs Michelle of any installation warnings; in this case, the currently logged-in user must log out for the installation to fully complete. Once the installation process completes, Michelle logs out of the remote Mac using the exit command.

```
SnowMac:tmp ladmin$ sudo installer -pkg /tmp/Deploy.pkg -target /
Password: (password not shown)
installer: Package name is Admin Custom Deployment
installer: Installing at base path /
installer: The install was successful.
installer: The install requires logging out now.
SnowMac:tmp ladmin$ exit
logout
Connection to SnowMac.local closed.
```

NOTE ▶ This example shows basic ssh and installer command use, which both require user interaction. If you were to script this process, you would have to use both commands in modes that don't require user interaction. The manual pages for these commands describe how to enable unattended features.

Deploying Installation Packages with ARD

By far the quickest, easiest way to deploy installation packages is to use the ARD Install Packages feature. With this feature you can copy and install multiple installation packages to multiple target Macs. Further, ARD uses its built-in multicast copy system to reduce the amount of time it takes to copy installation packages to multiple Macs, and it can encrypt the network traffic to secure the transfer.

NOTE ▶ This task assumes that you have already set up your ARD administrator application to access remote computers. Setting up the ARD client management system is covered in Chapter 2, "Deploying Individual Items and Containers."

To deploy installation packages with ARD:

1   Open the /Applications/Remote Desktop administrator application and authenticate if necessary.

2   From a computer list in the sidebar, select the target Macs to which you will be deploying the items. Then click the Install button on the toolbar, or choose Manage > Install Packages.

An untitled ARD Install Packages window will open, allowing you to set installation deployment options.

3   Drag installation packages from the Finder to the Packages list, or click the Add (+) button to open a browser dialog and locate the items.

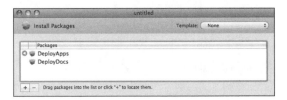

NOTE ▶ A small icon with a white triangle inside a gray circle indicates that the selected installation package requires a system restart.

4 Select your installation settings from the options in the middle of the Install Packages window.

You can set installation package options to do the following:

▶ Restart the computer after installation, either first allowing users to save or forcibly restarting the computer immediately.

▶ Specify the ARD system that will execute the installation using either the Remote Desktop application or the ARD Task Server.

MORE INFO ▶ Using the ARD Task Server is covered in Chapter 7, "System Maintenance."

▶ Stop the installation package task on all selected Macs if a copy error occurs. For small deployments this is acceptable, but for larger deployments it is generally a bad idea, especially when using a Task Server. Remember, you can always go back to the History list and rerun the Install Package task for computers that have failed.

▶ Encrypt the network transfer for increased security, or limit the network bandwidth if needed.

5 At the bottom of the install window, check the status of any selected Macs.

Your installation will not complete on any Macs that are sleeping or otherwise unresponsive unless you are using a Task Server, in which case the installation will complete the next time those Macs are available. To resolve unreachable connections, don't close the copy window. Simply return to the main Remote Desktop window and attempt to wake or reconnect to the unreachable Macs.

NOTE ▶ Your install will not complete on any Macs that are sleeping or otherwise unresponsive unless you are using a Task Server, in which case the installation will complete the next time those Macs are available.

6 When you are satisfied with the installation settings, click Install.

You will automatically return to the Active Tasks list, where you can view the progress of the install task. If the installation progress appears to stall, you may have experienced a network interruption. Click the Cancel button to the right of the progress bar to stop the installation. You can easily reattempt the installation by accessing it from the History list.

TIP ▶ Don't forget about the Schedule and Save buttons at the bottom of the ARD copy window, which offer two important time-saving features. The Save button allows you to place a shortcut for this task in the Remote Desktop sidebar, and the Schedule button allows you to set a specific time for the installation process to take place.

Verifying the Installation

If you are performing the installation yourself, you can easily tell whether the installation process has completed. The Installer application will present you with an "Install Succeeded" screen; the `installer` command will return "installer: The install was successful"; and in the History list, ARD will report "Succeeded."

However, if you did not personally witness the installation process, you can verify that an installation package was installed by inspecting the installer log. Any time the installation process is run, it writes information to the installer log located at /var/log/install.log. You can read this file using the command-line tool `less` or in the graphical interface using the /Applications/Utilities/Console application.

TIP ▶ You will likely find multiple install log files because the system automatically archives older logs whenever they surpass 100 KB. You can use the Console application and zcat to decompress and view these log files in one step.

The install log is incredibly detailed, showing every item installed, deleted, upgraded, or even just touched. It also shows nearly every installation setting along with any script activity. To find the beginning of an installation session in the log, look for the "Opened from:" string, which lists the path to the installation package. To locate the end of an installation session, look for the "Summary Information" string.

Installation Package Maintenance

One of the primary tasks of the Mac OS X installation architecture is to keep track of what has been previously installed. If you are having problems with previously installed items, or you're simply curious about what has been previously installed, you need to know how to access the historical information maintained by the installer architecture. In this section you will learn how to leverage this installation information for both assessment and maintenance purposes.

Understanding Installation Receipts

Immediately after an installation completes, a *receipt* entry is created for the installation package. Mac OS X uses receipts to keep track of installed items. For example, the install process checks for the existence of a receipt to determine whether to install or upgrade the payload items. If a receipt exists and version information exists for the software being installed, the installation process can skip some files that don't need to be upgraded.

For bundle-based installation packages, the install process executes the preupgrade and postupgrade scripts instead of the preinstall and postinstall scripts that are run during a first-time installation.

Snow Leopard Installation Receipts

The quickest method to list the receipt items is to run pkgutil --pkgs at the command line on the target computer. This command returns a list of receipts for all installed packages, bundle-based or flat, in the receipts database. The list uses the installation identifier for each receipt name—for example, com.apple.pkg.BaseSystem. This list is also presented in chronological order with the oldest installed items appearing at the top of the list.

Mac OS X v10.6 stores installation receipts in the /var/db/receipts/ folder. In this folder you will find two receipts files for every installation package that has been installed while running Mac OS X v10.6. The first receipts file, named with the installation identifier followed by ".bom", is the bill of materials (BOM) file from the installation package. As covered previously, the BOM file contains a full listing of the installation payload items. The second receipts file, named with the installation identifier followed by ".plist", is a file containing general installation information including when the item was installed.

TIP ▶ You can use the Finder's Quick Look feature to view the contents of any .plist file by simply selecting the file and hitting the Space bar. Further, if you have the Xcode developer tools installed, double-clicking on a .plist file will open Property List Editor.

Legacy Installation Receipts

Versions of Mac OS X prior to v10.6 stored installation receipts in the /Library/Receipts/ folder. If you have performed an upgrade install to Mac OS X v10.6 or used Migration Assistant to move items from an older Mac, then you will likely have legacy installation receipts in this folder. These items are still useful as you can access the BOM file from these previous installations to uncover what they installed to the Mac.

MORE INFO ▶ Interestingly, even though Mac OS X v10.6 has moved its primary receipts folder to /var/db/receipts/, you will find an InstallHistory.plist file in the /Library/Receipts/ folder. This file contains a basic history of all of the items installed while running Mac OS X v10.6.

The legacy method for handling receipts of bundle-based installations consists of a near-complete copy of the original installation package, including the contents of any Resources folder. Most importantly, the BOM file will be inside the installation receipt package. The only piece missing from a bundle-based receipt was the payload archive, so these receipts don't take up much space. Receipts for bundle-based installations were saved as packages inside the /Library/Receipts folder and have the same name as the original installation package. Thus, you can use the contents of this folder as a reference list for previously installed bundle-based installation packages.

The legacy method for handling receipts of flat installation packages includes only the BOM and a few other pieces of installation information. The BOM files were written to /Library/Receipts/boms/, while the remainder of the install information was saved inside a database located in the /Library/Receipts/db/ folder.

Viewing Receipt Content

Once you have located the receipt entries left by any previously installed installation packages, you can easily determine which items were installed by viewing the contents of the BOM file associated with the receipt. You can use the same techniques outlined in the "Listing the Installation Bill of Materials" section previously in this chapter to examine the receipt BOM files, with the only difference being the location of the BOM files. Receipt BOM files are located in the /Library/Receipts/ folder rather than in the original installation package.

For example, to view the BOM from a package installed by Mac OS X v10.6, enter the following in the command line:

```
lsbom -p MUGsf /var/db/receipts/installation_id.bom
```

For another example, to view the BOM for a legacy bundle-based installation package receipt, enter the following at the command line:

```
lsbom -p MUGsf /Library/Receipts/installation_package.pkg/Contents/Archive.bom
```

> **TIP** You can also view the BOM of a flat installation package receipt by entering `pkgutil --files` and the installation identifier. However, this will not show you any ownership or permissions information about the installed items.

Repairing and Replacing Installed Items

Mac OS X also uses certain system installation receipts to repair ownership and permissions for previously installed items. For example, many installation payloads include common folders such as /Applications and /Library to guide the install process to the target location of the payload items. Improperly built installation packages may contain incorrect ownership and permission settings for these common items. If authorized by an administrator, the installation process will dutifully change the ownership and permissions settings to reflect the improperly built installation package.

The repair permissions process uses the BOM information stored in the receipt database to determine the correct permissions for a specific list of system items. This list, known as the standard packages list, is set by Apple and repairs only items that are part of the standard Mac OS X operating system. You can view the list by entering /usr/libexec/ repair_packages --list-standard-pkgs at the command line.

Repairing Permissions for Standard Packages

There are two common methods to initiate the repair permissions process on Mac OS X. In the graphical interface, you can use the Disk Utility application, and at the command line you can use the `diskutil` command.

To use Disk Utility to repair permissions for previously installed items:

1 Open Disk Utility and select the target system volume from the items listed at the left.

2   Click the First Aid tab, and then click the Repair Disk Permissions button.

You may not see any progress for a few moments as the receipt database is rebuilt, but once that process is complete the system will start repairing any incorrect ownership and permissions. Any corrections will appear in the history window.

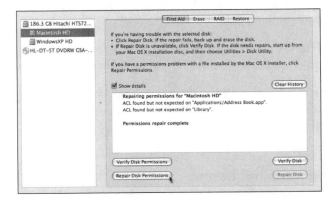

To use the command line to repair permissions for previously installed items, enter `diskutil repairpermissions` and then the path to the target volume. In most cases this will be the system volume, so you would enter `diskutil repairpermissions /` at the command line. Again, initially you may not see any progress as the receipt database is built, but if any repairs do occur they will be listed as the process executes.

Replacing Installed Items

If you have determined that a previously installed file has become corrupted or is missing, you should replace that item to resolve the problem. To do this, you can trick the install process into performing a full installation by removing the associated receipts. When you do this, the install process no longer knows that you previously installed the package and will treat the next installation like a first-time installation.

To remove a receipt for a flat installation package, you must use the `pkgutil` command to delete the item from the receipts database. The syntax for this is `sudo pkgutil --forget` followed by the installation identifier, and then `--volume` followed by the target volume. If no target volume is given, the `pkgutil` command assumes the current system volume.

In the following example, Michelle removes the receipt for com.pretendco. adminCustomDeployment.administrationDeployment.pkg on her current system volume. The installation identifier in this example is so long because this installation package is part of an installation metapackage. The `pkgutil` command returns a message saying the receipt item for that installation package was successfully forgotten.

```
MyMac:~ michelle$ sudo pkgutil --forget
com.pretendco.adminCustomDeployment.administrationDeployment.pkg --volume /
Forgot package 'com.pretendco.adminCustomDeployment.administrationDeployment.pkg' on '/'.
```

To remove a receipt for a bundle-based installation package that was installed before installation of Mac OS X v10.6, remove the receipt package file from the /Library/Receipts folder.

Third-Party Installation Tools

The installation tools built into Mac OS X, the Xcode Tools suite, and ARD fulfill the installation deployment needs for many administrators. However, you may find some third-party installation tools more convenient or appropriate for your deployment needs. Popular third-party installation tools for Mac OS X include Pacifist by CharlesSoft, Composer by JAMF Software, Iceberg by WhiteBox, InstallEase by LANrev, and VISE X 3 by MindVision Software.

MORE INFO ► Website links to all of the third-party tools discussed here are available at the end of this chapter in the "Web Resources" section.

Pacifist by CharlesSoft

Pacifist is a commercial tool that allows you to graphically browse and extract items from installation packages and metapackages. If you often have to locate and pull out items inside installers and containers created by others, Pacifist is a valuable tool. The following figure shows the use of Pacifist to search for a specific application within the Mac OS X installer.

Composer

Composer is part of the Casper Suite by JAMF Software. Composer allows you to create packages using a snapshot feature similar to the one in PackageMaker. The primary advantages of Composer are that it integrates with the Casper Suite, which provides an advanced, full-deployment solution for Mac OS X, and that it can create snapshot packages from installations that require reboots.

Iceberg

Iceberg by WhiteBox is a free third-party installation package creation tool. In many ways it's similar to the PackageMaker application. Prior to the release of the Mac OS X v10.5 version of PackageMaker, Iceberg enjoyed a popular following because it was generally more advanced than previous versions of PackageMaker. Iceberg can still be used to create bundle-based installation packages, but it is not compatible with flat installation packages.

InstallEase

InstallEase is part of the LANrev management suite, but it's also available for free as a standalone product. InstallEase allows you to manually create installation packages or create installations using a snapshot feature similar to the one in PackageMaker. The primary advantage of InstallEase is that it integrates with the LANrev suite, which provides an advanced, full-deployment solution for both Mac OS X and Windows.

VISE X 3

VISE X 3 by MindVision Software uses a proprietary installation architecture. Because of this, the VISE installation software creates a fully self-contained installation environment in a single installation file. This file is a Mac OS X application that, when opened, executes the proprietary VISE installation process. This proprietary system gives you much greater control over the installation process and interface than does the Installer application. The VISE system also allows you to create uninstall files that can remove the items installed by a previous VISE installation.

What You've Learned

► Mac OS X uses an advanced installation system that makes it easy to deploy complex collections of items or automate management tasks.

▶ You can create custom installation packages using the PackageMaker application
   included with the Xcode Tools suite.

▶ The PackageMaker snapshot feature can monitor file-system changes on your Mac to
   automatically create installation package payloads.

▶ Apple Remote Desktop is an Apple-created deployment tool for installation packages.

▶ Mac OS X tracks installed items via an installation database that can be used for
   future maintenance, including for repairing incorrect permissions.

References

You can check for new and updated Knowledge Base documents at www.apple.com/support.

Troubleshooting Installation

▶ TS1394, "Mac OS X: Troubleshooting installation and software updates"

▶ HT2956, "Troubleshooting Mac OS X installation from CD or DVD"

▶ HT2632, "Mac OS X: Troubleshooting the Mac OS X Installer"

▶ TA24974, "Some installer package files work with Mac OS X 10.5 only"

▶ TS2200, "Mac OS X 10.5: Installer destination window does not show drives"

Web Resources

▶ Apple Developer Connection, http://developer.apple.com

▶ PackageMaker User Guide, http://developer.apple.com/documentation/
   DeveloperTools/Conceptual/PackageMakerUserGuide

▶ Composer by JAMF Software—Installation package creation tool,
   www.jamfsoftware.com/products/composer

▶ Iceberg by WhiteBox—Installation package creation tool,
   http://s.sudre.free.fr/Software/Iceberg.html

▶ InstallEase by LANrev—Installation package creation tool,
   www.lanrev.com/solutions/package-building.html

▶ Pacifist by CharlesSoft—Installation archive examination tool, www.charlessoft.com

▶ VISE X 3 by MindVision Software—Proprietary installation tool,
   www.mindvision.com/vise_x.asp

Review Quiz

1. What are the main benefits of using installation packages for deployment?

2. What are installation packages, installation metapackages, PackageMaker projects, payloads, and receipts?

3. What are the main differences between a flat installation package and a bundle-based installation package? What versions of Mac OS X support flat installation packages?

4. When creating an installation package, what format is recommended for the installation package identifier?

5. What types of scripts can be added to an installation package? When is each type of script executed?

6. Why is installation package inspection an important step prior to installation?

7. How does file checksumming help to provide greater security for downloaded installation packages?

8. What are three methods for deploying installation packages?

9. How does Mac OS X track previously installed installation packages?

10. How do you display a list of files that were installed by an installation package?

11. How does the repair permissions process determine which permissions to check and repair?

Answers

1. The main benefits of installation packages include these abilities: verifying that a certain version of the operating system is installed and that certain components are installed on the system; starting or stopping processes and daemons; installing software in multiple locations throughout the system; running custom scripts to automate administrative functions; presenting the user with documentation, policies, or license information; and allowing the user to customize the installation.

2. An installation package is a collection of configuration files, scripts, resources, and archives that is used to install collections of items on a Mac OS X system. An installation metapackage contains multiple installation packages inside a single item. A PackageMaker project is a file saved by PackageMaker, which contains all the settings required to build an installation package product. A payload is the archive of items stored inside an installation package that will be installed on the target computer. A receipt is created during the installation of each package. At the very least,

a receipt includes a BOM file containing a list of the items installed for the associated installation package. Mac OS X uses receipts to keep track of installed items.

3. A flat installation package is built as a single contiguous file that can be installed only on Mac OS X v10.5 or v10.6. A bundle-based installation package is built as a folder containing a collection of items that is hidden from the user in the Finder. Bundle-based installation packages can be installed on versions of Mac OS X earlier than Mac OS X v10.5.

4. It's recommended that the installation package identifier is formatted in a reverse URL style that includes your organization followed by a descriptive name; for example, com.pretendco.admintools.

5. Installation packages that have a minimum target of Mac OS X v10.5 can include preinstall and postinstall scripts, installed in that order. Installation packages that have a minimum target of Mac OS X v10.4 and v10.3 can include preflight, preinstall, pre-upgrade, postinstall, postupgrade, and postflight scripts, installed in that order.

6. Installation package inspection is important prior to deployment because poorly made or malicious installations can cause serious damage to your system's software or compromise the security of the system.

7. File checksumming helps you verify the integrity of a downloaded installation package by comparing a known key to a key generated by scanning the downloaded contents. For Apple installation packages (inside a disk image) the known keys can be found on Apple's support website. You can determine the generated key from the command line using `openssl sha1` and then the path to the downloaded item.

8. Installation packages can be deployed manually from a server share, manually or scripted using SSH remote login, or automatically to multiple systems using ARD.

9. Mac OS X tracks previously installed items using a receipts database maintained in the /var/db/receipts/ folder. The /var/db/receipts/ folder contains bill of materials (.bom) files for every previously installed package. These .bom files list every item installed and that item's owner and permissions.

10. You can view a list of files installed by an installation package by accessing the receipt .bom for that installation. View the .bom from any package receipt by entering the following at the command line: `lsbom -p MUGsf /var/db/receipts/package_id.bom`.

11. The repair permissions process determines the appropriate permissions by referencing the .bom files stored in the receipts database. By default the repair permissions process only checks Apple installation packages. You can verify this from the command line with `/usr/libexec/repair_packages --list-standard-pkgs`.

4

Chapter Files	Deployment Planning Template.pdf, available at www.peachpit.com/acsa.deployment
	Mac OS X v10.6 installation media
Time	This chapter usually takes approximately 4 hours to complete, but it could take much longer depending on the complexity of your deployment.
Goals	Select a system imaging technique that meets your deployment needs
	Integrate advanced Mac OS X managed preferences with your system image
	Create a cloned system image using Disk Utility
	Create basic network disk images using System Image Utility
	Build a modular NetRestore image using System Image Utility

Chapter **4**

Creating System Images

For many deployments, the best solution is a unified system disk image, which involves creating an ideal system, saving it to a disk image, and then deploying that system to all your computers. A unified system image requires a significant time investment up front, but it saves a great deal of time in the long run. Computers with identical configurations are much easier to manage; the fewer the differences between your deployed systems, the more uniform their performance and the less time spent diagnosing problems, updating software, and reconfiguring hardware.

A unified system image also greatly accelerates the deployment process for any deployment larger than a dozen computers. Once you have fully configured, tested, and created a custom system image on one computer, it can take as little as five minutes to copy it to another machine. Compare this with the time needed to deploy the system individually on every computer, and it's easy to see the benefit of a deployable system disk image. In this chapter you will learn two general methods for creating deployable system disk images: cloning from a model system and building a modular system.

Understanding System Image Creation

Before starting the process of creating a system image, you must consider your deployment requirements: what software and configuration settings will be part of your system image? Consider your users, your systems, and the limitations of identical-system deployment on multiple computers. You also need to consider which of the two image creation methodologies will best suit your needs and abilities. The choices you make while planning your system image will affect every computer on which this system is deployed.

> **MORE INFO** ▶ A great deal of system deployment information is presented here, but you can also download the Apple System Imaging and Software Update Administration guide at http://images.apple.com/server/macosx/docs/System_Imaging_and_SW_Update_Admin_v10.6.pdf.

Defining System Image Requirements

When identifying all the specific items and configuration settings that you want to include in your system image, you must take into consideration the requirements of your users, the technical requirements of your systems, and the limitations of deploying an identical system on multiple computers.

User Requirements

Your primary focus when developing system image requirements should be on maximizing system usability, for both users and administrators. In some cases your target audience or usage policies may require tighter system control. This is often the case when users are inexperienced or cannot be trusted to manage any part of their systems. In this scenario you would limit application access and lock down as many system configuration settings as possible. You would also want to make things easy for the user by preconfiguring any system setting you can. In scenarios where you will be performing a significant amount of client management, you should incorporate directory services–based managed preferences.

> **MORE INFO** ▶ Implementing managed preferences is detailed later in the "Integrating with Managed Preferences" section of this chapter.

In professional or creative environments, you may not need to be as restrictive in the application or settings, but you should still make sure to prepare the system based on the users' needs; for instance, install third-party applications and peripheral drivers for inclusion with your system image.

No matter the level of your users, your system image should be as fully configured as possible, with both Apple and third-party software installed and updated, any necessary support files such as third-party drivers and fonts installed, and any systemwide configuration settings implemented. Note, though, that many settings are not well suited to deployment via a unified system image—more on this topic later in this section.

> **MORE INFO** ▶ Common system customizations often included with system images are covered in the "Customizing System Configuration" section later in this chapter.

Computer-Specific System Requirements

Before you create your system image, you must determine which version of Mac OS X you intend to use. A major administrative advantage of using Mac OS X v10.6 and Mac OS X Server v10.6 is that they include all the hardware drivers necessary to work with any Mac that meets the minimum system requirements, allowing you to build a single system image that can work on any Mac.

Although creating a unified system image for computers that support Mac OS X v10.6 is simple, creating a system image for brand-new Macs can present a significant problem. In many cases, because the release of new Mac computers is not in sync with the release of the retail version of Mac OS X, a custom intermediate version of Mac OS X is created just to support the new hardware. However, new Macs cannot run versions of Mac OS X released prior to their introduction—that is, the oldest version of Mac OS X supported by a new Mac computer is the version that it ships with from the factory.

Thus, a previously created system image will not work on new Mac computers, and you will have to create a new system image based on the version of Mac OS X that shipped with the new Macs. Further, these custom intermediate versions of Mac OS X may technically work with older Mac computers, but they are not officially supported by Apple to do so, presenting a problem when you are trying to build a single unified system image.

> **MORE INFO** ▶ You can find out which version of the Mac OS shipped with your Mac in Knowledge Base article HT1159, "Mac OS X versions (builds) included with Intel-based Macs."

Fortunately, every general Mac OS X version update includes support for all Mac computers introduced prior to the update. For example, if you were to acquire new Macs that were introduced this week, the next general update of Mac OS X will include support for those new Macs and will support older hardware as well. Therefore, if you can wait to build your system image until you can base it on the next general update for Mac OS X, you can create a single system image for all your Macs. If you can't wait that long, you will need to create a separate system image just for your new Macs.

It's important to note that custom intermediate versions of Mac OS X for new computers do not use different version numbers from the general releases. They do, however, have different build numbers, which can be identified by clicking once on the version number from the About This Mac window.

Software Update Requirements

You should strive to build your system image using the latest versions of your selected software. To do this, you'll need to collect and keep track of all the necessary software update installers that you'll apply when building your system image.

> **NOTE** ▶ Although in most cases it's best to deploy the latest versions of software, only with thorough testing can you verify this.

First you need to determine and acquire the latest version updates for Apple software. Apple's downloads website, www.apple.com/downloads/, lists all the latest updates and can be searched and browsed so you can locate and then download specific Apple software updates. However, it may not seem obvious which Apple updates are needed; for this reason you can open Software Update from the Apple menu.

Apple Software Update will compare your Mac's current installed software with the latest versions available from Apple. Obviously, you should run this on one of your test deployment systems to verify exactly which updates are necessary. The Mac OS X v10.6 version of Software Update no longer allows you to download updates without installing them. Thus, if you want to acquire the updates for later installation or deployment, you will have to do so from Apple's downloads website.

> **NOTE** ▶ Avoid using "delta" or single-point Mac OS X updates for your system images. You'll get better results and spend less time installing by using the Mac OS X "combo" updates. These updates not only contain all previous delta updates, they also contain all previous system security updates.

You should also verify that you are using the latest versions of third-party applications and drivers. Many third-party products feature a built-in automatic update system that will check online for updates. However, few of these third-party update systems will allow you to download the individual update installer so that you can later use it to build your system image. Again, in this case, visit the software developer's website to download the individual update installers.

Limitations of a Unified System Image

You should include as many configured settings as possible with your system image so you don't have to spend time setting these items on each individual computer. However, there are many settings that you should not, or cannot, deploy with the same configuration to every computer.

For example, in most cases, user-specific settings should not be included with your system image. Computer-specific settings also should not be configured on the system image. For instance, a unique IP address and network name needs to be set for every Mac. Both user- and computer-specific settings are best handled using dedicated client management tools and techniques.

In deploying a Mac OS X Server system image, your primary goal will be to strike a balance between what you can safely configure as part of the generic server system image and what settings you must leave for after deployment.

> **MORE INFO** ▶ Chapter 6, "Postimaging Deployment Considerations," deals specifically with managing settings that are best handled after deploying your system image.

Choosing a System Image Methodology

When using the tools built into Mac OS X to create a deployable system disk image, you have a choice between two different methodologies: cloned system images and modular system images.

With a *cloned system image*, you first set up a model computer that is configured with all the software and settings you intend to deploy. Then you create a duplicate copy of the system volume saved to a disk image that has been specially prepared for deployment.

The *modular system image* methodology, a newer method, requires a bit more work up front, but it has several advantages over the older method and is the Apple-recommended best practice. With this method you build a fresh system by installing a series of installation packages to a sparse disk image. The installations include the full Mac OS X system, any software updates, any additional Apple software, any third-party software, and any custom installation packages that you have created to set up your system image. This sparse image is then converted to a disk image that has been prepared for deployment.

Cloned System Image Pros and Cons

► Pro—Easier workflow for novice administrators

► Pro —Less time spent creating initial system images

► Con—Requires that the model computer be purged of any unnecessary or troublesome files

► Con—Prone to issues if model not properly "cleaned"

► Con—Prone to more issues when deploying to different models

► Con—Increased workload when creating multiple system images

► Con—Increased workload when it's time to update system images

► Con—New system images are never consistent with prior images

► Con—Difficult to document and audit system image configurations

► Con—Increased workload to test system image modifications

Modular System Image Pros and Cons

► Pro—System images are clean because they have never been booted.

► Pro—System images have no model-specific settings.

► Pro—Apple updates won't interfere with your customizations because they are always applied before your customizations.

► Pro—Your workload is lighter when creating multiple system images that require unique software and configurations.

► Pro—Your workload is decreased when it's time to update system images.

► Pro—Multiple and updated system images are perfectly consistent for similar items every single time.

▶ Pro—All configurations are easily documented and easily audited.

▶ Pro—Testing of updates and image modifications are simpler.

▶ Pro—System image creation process is automated.

▶ Pro—It's easy to integrate modular system images with system maintenance work-flows and third-party deployment tools.

▶ Con—Workflow is more difficult for novice administrators.

▶ Con—You must create custom installation packages for some third-party items and any configuration settings.

▶ Con—You will spend more time creating an initial system image.

The cloned system image methodology requires less effort up front, and you can get your first image set up quickly. However, in the long run you'll have to spend much more time fixing bugs, updating software, and adding modifications than with a modular system image. The modular system image methodology requires more initial effort to properly configure your first system image, but maintaining your systems will be much easier because you'll be able to build new modular images with additional items and updated software.

Integrating with Managed Preferences

If you have used the Parental Controls preferences to manage a local Mac or the Preferences pane of Workgroup Manager on a Mac OS X Server to manage networked Macs, then you have used preference management. Both of these features are facilitated by the underlying managed preferences architecture. The Mac OS X managed preferences architecture, sometimes called MCX, is a method to control both system and user settings from a centralized source. In other words, you can use managed preferences to define policy for all your clients from a single administrative resource.

In this section, you will learn how you can leverage Mac OS X's managed preferences as an alternative to deploying static settings as part of a system image. Planning and implementing this type of client management system is the best way to enforce usage policies and maintain a consistent configuration across your deployed systems. Nevertheless, managed preferences are not required to deploy system images. In fact, the flexibility of this system means that you could choose to deploy managed preferences well after you have deployed your system images.

For many deployments the managed preferences source is a network directory service that the client computers are bound to, like a Mac OS X Server with the Open Directory service enabled. By relying on a network directory service for acquiring configuration, you have much greater flexibility for deploying user and system settings. Storing configuration information on a directory server means you don't have to include this configuration as part of your system image. Further, when managing preferences from a network directory service you can easily change configuration settings after your initial deployment.

Understanding the Managed Preferences Architecture

Mac OS X's managed preferences architecture allows you to define policy at four different account levels; user, group, computer, and computer group. The background process MCXCompositor, found inside the /System/Library/CoreServices/ManagedClient.app bundle, is responsible for assessing any available managed preferences. At system startup the compositor process queries directory services for computer and computer group managed preferences, and during login queries for user and group managed preferences. These preferences are then cached to the local computer so the management remains active even if the Mac is disconnected from the directory service.

As you can see, managed preferences rely on directory services as the source for policy information. This allows you to store managed preferences in any location that Mac OS X's directory service can access. This includes the local account database, a properly configured Lightweight Directory Access Protocol (LDAP) server like the one hosted from a Mac OS X Server, or a properly configured Active Directory (AD) server.

If you choose to host managed preferences in the local account database, then you will want to include this configuration in your system image. The downside is that your managed preferences are no longer centrally managed, and you will have to deploy changes to each client using a manual method.

A more common configuration is to have a network directory service like LDAP or AD host the managed preferences information. In this case, to take advantage of managed preferences, your system image must include steps for binding to the network directory service, as covered in Chapter 6, "Postimaging Deployment Considerations."

> **MORE INFO** ▶ Full coverage of directory service concepts is beyond the scope of this reference guide. To find out more please refer to *Apple Training Series: Mac OS X Directory Services v10.6* (Peachpit Press, 2010).

Using Managed Preferences

The most comprehensive tool for configuring managed preferences is Workgroup Manager (WGM), located in the /Applications/Server folder on your Mac OS X Server computer. This application can also be installed as part of the Server Admin Tools v10.6 on any Mac OS X v10.6 computer. In fact there are several managed preferences settings that can be properly set only when you open WGM from a Mac client. For example, when building an allowed applications list, WGM can add applications to this list only from the Mac it's currently open on. Many Mac servers don't have all the additional applications that Mac clients use; thus you need to open WGM from a Mac client.

> **MORE INFO ▶** The Server Admin Tools v10.6 installer can be found on the Mac OS X Server installation discs, or it can be downloaded from the Apple website, http://support.apple.com/kb/DL914.

> **MORE INFO ▶** While a brief introduction to using WGM is presented here, the primary goal of this section is to cover advanced managed preferences techniques. In-depth coverage of the account management options in WGM is available in *Apple Training Series: Mac OS X Server Essentials v10.6* (Peachpit Press, 2010).

To apply basic managed preferences settings using WGM:

1   Open /Applications/Server/Workgroup Manager.app and a server connection dialog will appear.

2   Perform one of the following tasks to connect and manage a directory service:

   ▶   If you're going to manage a network directory service, enter the address and directory administrator authentication information for the server hosting the directory.

   ▶   If you are going to manage the local directory service on the local Mac client, click the Cancel button to dismiss the server connection dialog and then choose Server > View Directories from the menu bar.

3 Verify that you have connected to the correct directory and are allowed to make changes by inspecting the selected Directory Node, which appears directly under the WGM toolbar.

If the lock icon to the right still appears "locked," click it and authenticate as an administrator so you can edit accounts.

4 Select or create the account type you wish to manage—a user, group, computer, or computer group—and then click the Preferences button in the toolbar.

This will display a pane showing the categories of preferences that can be easily managed with WGM. In this example a computer group has been selected. Note that computer and computer group accounts have more preference management options in WGM.

TIP Remember that in WGM you can select multiple accounts by holding down the Shift or Command keys and then clicking your selections.

TIP If your plan is to apply preference management at the local level, then a quick and easy method to apply settings to all computers is to create and manage a guest computer account. Any computer that is not part of a specific computer or computer group account will by default fall into the management set on the guest computer record. To create a guest account select Server > Create Guest Computer from the menu bar.

5   Select a preference icon to display an interface that allows you to manage the associ-
    ated preferences. The following example shows the Dock Display preferences.

6   To manage a preference only the first time a user logs into the system, select the Once
    button. To permanently mange a preference, thus disallowing a user to make changes,
    select the Always button.

    Selecting the Never button will "turn off" managed preferences for the selected items.

7   Once you have made your selections, click the Apply Now button to save the managed
    preferences.

8   Click the Preferences button in the toolbar to return to the main Preferences view.

    Note the small arrow icon next to any preference that is being managed.

Finally, when configuring managed preferences, it's important to thoroughly test these settings from a client Mac to verify the correct behavior. Any new preference changes will be
applied the next time a user logs into any system that is currently connected to the directory
service. If you're having problematic results, try some of the troubleshooting tips covered in
the "Troubleshooting Managed Preferences" section later in this chapter.

Understanding Custom Managed Preferences

Workgroup Manager (WGM) also provides a managed preferences Detailed view that allows you to import and manage preferences that don't have a graphical interface in WGM's default Preferences view. This includes the ability to centrally manage the preferences for both built-in and third-party applications that support Apple's standard preference format, the property list or ".plist" file. In fact, the underlying format for managed preferences is the same XML (eXtensible Markup Language) encoded key/value pairs that you'll find in local preference .plist files.

> **MORE INFO** ▶ Details regarding manual modification and deployment of .plist-formatted files is covered in Chapter 6, "Postimaging Deployment Considerations."

There are three methods for importing, and thus managing, a preference with WGM:

▶ The primary method is via a mechanism known as a *preference manifest*. A preference manifest is a file embedded inside an application bundle that describes the application's customizable preferences. When you select an application's icon to import into WGM, it will scan the application for a preference manifest to import. Not only will the preference manifest include all the manageable key/value attributes, it often also includes examples and plain-text description of the items. In short, the existence of a preference manifest makes it much easier to define custom managed preferences settings for an application or service.

▶ Another method is to import the application's preference file directly into WGM. This can be done by locating the specific .plist file, or by selecting the application's icon. If the application lacks a preference manifest, then WGM can import the application's preference file instead. The primary drawback here is that the application may not react well to preference management. Further, you will likely have to experiment to figure out which key/value pairs represent the preferences that you wish to manage.

▶ The last method is really just a shortcut to many of the included Apple preference manifests. The /System/Library/CoreServices/ManagedClient.app application bundle contains roughly two dozen preference manifests for various Apple system and application preferences. WGM can import all of these preferences at once for optional management. Preference manifests in the ManagedClient.app include several significant manageable preferences including Bluetooth, Desktop Picture, Folder Redirection, iTunes, Safari, Screen Saver, Sidebar, and VPN settings.

The primary caveat to custom managed preferences is that some items are difficult if not impossible to manage because they don't fully support Mac OS X's preference architecture. In fact, most third-party preferences do not respect the Always managed preferences option, thus making permanent management difficult. Because of this limitation, when you import custom preferences for management you are allowed a fourth management option, Often. Setting a preference to be managed Often instructs the MCXcompositor to rewrite the .plist file, wherever its default storage location is, every time the user logs in. The result is that the user may still be able to change the setting, but every time she logs into the Mac, the preference will be set to the managed state.

Using Custom Managed Preferences

To import and manage custom preferences:

1   Open /Applications/Server/Workgroup Manager.app and authenticate to the directory that will be hosting the custom managed preferences.

2   Select the account(s) that you wish to manage, then click the Preferences button in the toolbar, and then the Details tab. This will reveal WGM's preference editor interface.

If you have previously configured managed preferences settings using WGM's normal graphical interface you will see those items in the preference editor list with a pointer icon adjacent to the items' names.

3   To import a new preference manifest or preference file, click the small plus button at the bottom of the preference editor list and an import dialog will appear.

4   From this dialog you can import manageable preferences by selecting any one of the following items:

   ▶   An application's icon, which will import the preference manifest, if found, or the application's related preference files as long as they are in .plist format

► A specific .plist preference file that you wish to manage

► The /System/Library/CoreServices/ManagedClient.app, which will import many of the included Apple preference manifests all at once

5 Optionally, if you selected an application or preference file to import, you will note that the options at the bottom of the import dialog may have activated. These options can be used to automatically import the management settings along with the preference items:

► Selecting the "Import my preferences for this application" checkbox will import the current preference state of the selected item and use that as the set management options.

► The "Manage imported preferences" pop-up menu allows you to choose how you want the preference to be managed. The default selection of Often is the safest choice as it's compatible with most custom preferences. The other two options are Once and Always. Again, selecting the Once option only sets the preference the first time the user logs in to a Mac, while the Always option attempts to prevent the user from changing the preference. It's important to note that many third-party preferences do not respect the Always option, making the Often option your only recourse.

▶ Selecting the "Import as ByHost preferences" checkbox is necessary if the preference is designed to be user and computer specific. This option instructs the managed preferences system to change the ByHost preference file's name so that it can apply to any managed user or computer. An example ByHost preference is ~/Library/Preferences/ByHost/com. apple.scheduler, which is used to set the automatic Software Update schedule.

MORE INFO ▶ You can learn more about ByHost preferences in Chapter 6, "Postimaging Deployment Considerations."

6 Once you have selected the item you wish to import and any additional options, click the Add button to import the item into WGM.

The following screen shot shows the results of importing the preferences of the Safari application and the preference manifests inside the ManagedClient.app bundle. Note that any managed preferences will be displayed with an adjacent arrow icon, thus only those preferences that you have manually configured or imported with settings will be managed.

7 To manage a preference simply double-click on its name in the preference editor list.

This will open the preference editor, which allows you to edit the individual key (shown in the Name column) value pair of the preference file. Use the disclosure triangles to expose the managed key/value pairs under each management option— Once, Often, Always. You can modify existing key/value pairs by clicking on them. Use the New Key button to add new key/value pairs and the Delete button to delete any unnecessary items.

Any key/value item listed will be part of the managed preference entry. In many cases you will have to experiment to get the best set of managed key/value pairs. For instance, the previous screen shot shows an imported Safari preference, which contains many extraneous key/value pairs that should be deleted from management.

8   When you have completed the necessary managed preferences modifications, click the Apply Now button to save the changes.

Again, note the small arrow icon next to any preference that is being managed.

Finally, when configuring managed preferences, it's important to thoroughly test these settings from several client Macs to verify the correct behavior. This is especially true when dealing with custom managed preferences. It will probably take several attempts to nail down the exact combination of managed preferences options and settings to achieve your policy goals.

Again, any new preference changes will be applied the next time a user logs into any system that is currently connected to the directory service. If you're having problematic results, try some of the troubleshooting tips covered in the following section.

Troubleshooting Managed Preferences

With so many different technologies responsible for implementing managed preferences, troubleshooting managed preferences issues can be complicated. As with any complicated issue, breaking it down into specific trouble spots is always the best plan.

Managed Preferences: Verify Directory Services

Start by troubleshooting any potential directory service issues, since this is the system through which the Mac acquires the managed preferences settings. Basically, you need to verify connectivity to the directory service hosting the managed preferences. You can do this by viewing the Network Account Server status in the Login Options pane of the Accounts preferences.

Network Account Server: ⊜ server.nivek.net   (Edit...)

You can further verify connectivity by logging into the Mac with a network user account or use id username, where "username" is the account name of a network user account, in the command line to verify that your Mac can see a network account. If any of these tests fail, then you need to resolve the directory service issue before you hunt down the managed preferences issue.

If you are able to verify that directory services is working properly, then you can verify that the directory service is providing managed preferences information. The dscl command allows you to read the directory information, including any managed preferences settings. In the following example Michelle uses the dscl command with the -mcxread option to verify that the "lab1" computer group contains managed preferences settings.

```
MyMac:~ michelle$ dscl localhost -mcxread /Search/ComputerGroups/lab1
App domain: com.apple.dock
Key: autohide
State: always
Value: 0
...
```

Note that dscl indeed returns management settings. Also note that the output has been truncated to save space. It's not uncommon for dscl to return several pages of text when asked to query managed preferences information. When using dscl in this manner, if you want to search for a different account type, simply enter that in the search path: for example, /Search/Users/user_name, /Search/Groups/group_name, or /Search/Computers/computer_name.

If you are unable to retrieve user information using the id command, or are unable to retrieve management settings using dscl, you will need to troubleshoot the directory services setup. Common issues include a loss of network connectivity, DNS problems, and not having the directory service node in the search path on the client.

Managed Preferences: Verify Compositor Output

Once you have verified that the Mac can view managed preferences settings from directory services, it's time to verify the results of the MCXcompositor. As covered previously, the MCXcompositor collects all the managed preferences settings and then applies those to the user's session during login. Managed preferences issues at this level stem from having unexpected MCXcompositor results. The symptoms are easily identified by simply logging in as a user and then opening various applications and system items to verify your managed preferences settings.

While logged in as a user with managed preferences, you can view the managed preferences results by opening /Applications/Utilities/System Profiler.app and selecting Managed Client from the Contents list. This will show the managed preferences results of this specific user logged in to this specific Mac.

You can test other managed preferences combinations using the mcxquery command. This command allows you to test the managed preferences results by specifying a user, group, and/or computer account combination. The following example shows Michelle querying for the managed preferences results of user "logan" in the group "dev" on the computer "lab1_12."

```
MyMac:~ michelle$ mcxquery -user logan -group dev -computer lab1_12
com.apple.dock
    autohide              wgmuser (User)   always  0
    autohide-immutable    wgmuser (User)   always  1
    largesize             wgmuser (User)   always  128
...
```

In this example, again the results have been truncated to save space. If the compositor is returning what you think are improper results, then you have one of two main paths to follow. First, you can return to WGM on the server and try to verify the managed preferences settings. In this case, don't forget to look in the WGM Details view, where you can manually inspect every key/value pair. The second path is to reset the Mac client's managed preferences related service and settings, as covered next.

Managed Preferences: Reset Services and Caches

To enhance performance and provide for offline access, managed preferences are cached locally on each Mac. Sometimes the cache can become out of sync with the primary settings hosted from the directory servers. Mac clients will try to refresh on every directory service transition, such as a user login or network state change. You can also simulate this by restarting the directory service process, which may clear up any directory service issues as well. From the command line simply enter:

```
MyMac:~ michelle$ sudo killall DirectoryService
```

Another option, new in Mac OS X v10.6, is to use the mcxrefresh command. This command will attempt to re-query the managed preferences results and rebuild any local caches. In the following example Michelle refreshes the managed preferences results for the user "logan".

```
MyMac:~ michelle$ sudo mcxrefresh -n logan
```

Finally, as a last resort you can manually clear out the local managed preferences cache and restart the Mac. Simply delete the /Library/Managed Preferences/ folder and restart. If you are having problems with a particular user's preferences, you can delete just that individual user's folder from within the Managed Preferences folder.

Customizing System Configuration

In this section, you will learn to perform advanced customizations to further optimize your system image for deployment. All the custom configurations demonstrated in this section are optional and can be used individually. However, including them in your system image allows you to present the user with a Mac system that is tightly integrated with your organization and its policies.

Rerunning the Setup Assistant

The Setup Assistant is the first interface most Mac OS X users see when they start a new Mac for the first time. The Setup Assistant guides the user through the process of configuring initial settings, including the creation of an administrative user account. However, after this initial setup is complete, the Setup Assistant no longer appears at startup. You can force the Startup Assistant to run at the next system startup to give users some control over their own computers, including the ability to create their own user accounts.

If you want to make the Startup Assistant run at the next system startup, simply remove the /var/db/.AppleSetupDone file. If you also want Setup Assistant to present the user with a choice to bind to a directory server, remove /var/db/.AutoBindDone. These files are protected by root access, so the quickest method to remove them is to enter `sudo rm /var/db/.AppleSetupDone` and `sudo rm /var/db/.AutoBindDone` at the command line. When a user restarts the computer, the Setup Assistant will launch, allowing the user to make several configuration changes. This potentially includes changes that are not ideal for your deployment, including the following:

▶ The user will be allowed to set the default keyboard and language, enter registration information, his Apple ID, and MobileMe information, and reset the time zone.

▶ If networking is already set up, the user will not be allowed to configure any network settings at this point.

▶ If you remove the .AutoBindDone file, the user will be able to bind to a network directory service.

▶ The user will be able to create an additional administrative user account.

▶ The Setup Assistant will enable automatic login for the newly created user.

▶ The Setup Assistant will change the computer's name using the following convention: new user's name followed by the computer model.

Unfortunately, you cannot limit what the Setup Assistant allows the user to configure. If you still want to use the Setup Assistant but you need to limit the changes, you can implement a script to automatically reset some of these items after the Setup Assistant finishes. Techniques for implementing such a script at first startup is covered in Chapter 6, "Postimaging Deployment Considerations." If you change your mind about restarting the Setup Assistant, you can easily replace the appropriate files by entering `sudo touch /var/db/.AppleSetupDone` or `sudo touch /var/db/.AutoBindDone` at the command line.

> **TIP** The best time to remove the .AppleSetupDone and .AutoBindDone files is when you are purging the model system of files that shouldn't be part of the system image. This is covered in the "Cloned Image: Clean Up System" section later in this chapter.

Customizing the Setup Assistant

To customize your users' new Mac experience, you can change the QuickTime video and MP3 audio files played at the introduction of the Setup Assistant. You can use any content-creation tool you like to create custom organization-specific replacements for these files. For instance, you could create a movie that reminds the user of your organization's usage policies, or you could create replacements that essentially play nothing. When creating your custom introduction media, keep in mind that the video and audio files start playing simultaneously, but the video ends before the audio file to allow the user to continue the setup process accompanied by background music.

> **NOTE** ▶ The Startup Assistant must have a QuickTime file and an MP3 file to play to continue the setup process. Thus, you cannot completely remove these files or replace them with empty documents.

The files you must replace are located inside the Setup Assistant package, in the /System/ Library/CoreServices/Setup Assistant.app/Contents/Resources/TransitionSection.bundle/ Contents/Resources folder. In this folder you will need to replace the intro.mov and intro-sound.mp3 files. These files are protected by root access, and you should back them up just in case you need to return the Setup Assistant to its original state.

In the following example, Michelle uses the command line to back up the original audio and video files, and then replace them with two custom files that she has created on her desktop. Michelle first navigates to the appropriate folder inside the Setup Assistant package. Notice that she uses the sudo command to bypass the file-system permissions.

```
MyMac:~ michelle$ cd "/System/Library/CoreServices/Setup Assistant.app/Contents/
Resources/TransitionSection.bundle/Contents/Resources"
MyMac:Resources michelle$ sudo mv intro.mov intro.mov.old
MyMac:Resources michelle$ sudo mv intro-sound.mp3 intro-sound.mp3.old
MyMac:Resources michelle$ sudo cp /Users/michelle/Desktop/custommoive.mov intro.mov
MyMac:Resources michelle$ sudo cp /Users/michelle/Desktop/customsong.mp3 intro-sound.mp3
```

Customizing the Login Screen

You can also customize the login screen to meet your organization's deployment needs; for instance, display information such as usage policies. Ideally, you should configure custom login screen settings using managed preferences settings hosted on a directory server. Workgroup Manager (WGM) includes a specific Login preferences interface for easily configuring the login screen behaviors and appearance. Using managed preferences is covered in the "Integrating with Managed Preferences" section previously in this chapter.

NOTE ▶ To require the user to interact with the login screen, make sure to also disable automatic login. This can be accomplished locally from the Accounts preferences or from WGM in the Login preferences under the Options tab.

However, if you have decided against deploying managed preferences settings, you can configure login screen settings on your model system and make them part of your system image deployment. The login screen is managed by the loginwindow process, which references settings located in the /Library/Preferences/com.apple.loginwindow.plist preference file. You could edit this file using the Property List Editor application included with the Xcode Tools suite, but it's much quicker to use the defaults write command to customize this file. Because the file is protected by root permissions, you would use the sudo command to bypass those restrictions.

MORE INFO ▶ The defaults command can be used to edit any property list preference files. This is command is detailed in Chapter 6, "Postimaging Deployment Considerations."

Using the defaults command, you must add a new property key, LoginwindowText, to the loginwindow preference file. The value for this new key will be the string of text you want shown at the login window inside quotation marks. For example, to customize the login window text with a usage policy notice, you would enter the following at the command line:

```
sudo defaults write /Library/Preferences/com.apple.loginwindow LoginwindowText
"By logging in to this computer you are agreeing to the usage policies found in
Pretendco document UP-1052. Thank you, and have a nice day."
```

To test your custom configuration, log out of your current session and observe the login screen behavior.

Customizing the Desktop Background and User Template

Some deployments require a static desktop background as part of their deployment policy. It's common in open or lab environments to maintain a consistent desktop background between sessions. Perhaps the desktop background includes instructive text or administrator support information that you have decided should always be easily available.

In Mac OS X the desktop background is a per-user preference, so every user is allowed to set her own background. This makes permanently setting the background for all users a bit more complex. There are two methods for accomplishing it; use managed preferences, or modify the user template on your model system. Again, as you'll see, the best solution is to set the desktop background using managed preferences.

> **NOTE** ► This technique takes advantage of file-system permissions to lock the desktop background image file, thus preventing users from being able to change the desktop background. These file-permission settings can be reversed if your users are allowed administrative access and have knowledge of the command line.

Set the Desktop Background

Either method you choose requires that the desktop picture be located on the local Mac and locked from editing. So the first step is to prepare and secure the desktop background image file on your model system.

To install, set, and protect a custom desktop background picture:

1 Log in to your model computer with an administrative account.

2 Place the image file you want to set as the desktop background in a location that all users will be able to access, such as the /Library/Desktop Pictures folder.

3 Open the Desktop & Screen Saver preferences and set the desktop background for the administrative account to the desired image file. You will have to drag the image file from the desktop into the image well area at the upper-left corner of the preference pane.

> **TIP** ▶ You can set a cycling "slideshow" of desktop background images by dragging a folder full of sequentially numbered images to the image well area. You can then adjust the duration of each image from the "Change picture" pop-up menu.

4 Set any additional desktop background features, and then close the Desktop & Screen Saver preferences.

This creates a properly formatted desktop property list preference file in the administrator's home folder.

5 Protect the desktop image file from modification. This requires changing the files' ownership to be writable only by root but still readable by everyone else.

Again, because this image file will have root permissions, the quickest method is to use the command line. In the following example, Michelle changes the ownership for the pretendco.jpg image file.

```
MyMac:~ michelle$ sudo chown root:wheel "/Library/Desktop Pictures/pretendco.jpg"
```

6 Now that you have set the desktop background and protected the selected image from changes, use one of the methods in the next two sections to permanently set the background for all users.

Use Managed Preferences to Force a Desktop Background

Once you have set the desktop background on a model system, it takes only a few steps to apply that setting as a custom managed preference. Again, this instruction assumes you are familiar with the topics outlined in the "Integrating with Managed Preferences" section earlier in this chapter.

To configure managed preferences to force a desktop background:

1   Make sure you are logged in to your model Mac with the administrative account that you used previously to set the custom desktop background.

2   Open /Applications/Server/Workgroup Manager.app and authenticate to the directory that will be hosting the custom managed preference.

3   Select the account(s) that you wish to manage, click the Preferences button in the toolbar, and click the Details tab. This will reveal WGM's preference editor interface.

If you have previously configured managed preference settings using WGM's normal graphical interface you will see those items in the preference editor list with a pointer icon adjacent to the items' names.

4   To import the desktop background preferences, click the small plus button at the bottom of the preference editor list and an import dialog will appear.

5   Browse to and select the ~/Library/Preferences/com.apple.desktop.plist file.

6   Make sure Always is selected as the management option and then click the Add button to import your desktop settings into WGM.

7   You will return to the Details view, then double-click on the Desktop Picture preference. This will open the preference editor, allowing you to verify the desktop background setting.

8   Click the disclosure triangle next to Always to reveal the imported key/value pairs. The import will have included many extraneous key/value pairs that you will need to delete.

9   Select and delete all items except for Background > Default Image > Image Path. The results should look like the following screen shot.

10 When you have completed the necessary managed preference modifications, click the Apply Now button to save the changes.

Again, note the small arrow icon next to any preference that is being managed.

11 To test the settings, log in to another user account and verify that your desktop background has been set and that you cannot change it from the Desktop & Screen Saver preferences.

Modify the User Template to Force a Desktop Background

Whenever a local or mobile user account is created, the system also creates a local home folder for that user. The contents of these created home folders are based on the system's user template. You can customize this user template to prepopulate new users' home folders with any items, including preference settings.

As always, the ideal solution to set specific user settings is to use managed preferences, as covered previously in this chapter. However, as an alternative solution, you can place user-specific preference files containing the settings in the user template on your model system and make them part of your system image deployment.

NOTE ▶ Modifying the user template will only apply to new user home folders that are created on the local clients. If you already have established home folders, or network home folders, then you will need to manage the desktop background using custom managed preferences.

Thus, you can customize the user template to set a default background for every user. However, the desktop background is saved as a per-user setting, and the user can normally change it at any time from the Desktop & Screen Saver preferences. To prevent the user from making this change, you will have to set special permissions that lock the preference file from changes.

TIP ▶ Although this example is specific to setting the desktop background preference, you can use a similar technique to deploy custom user home folders as part of your system image.

To modify the user template to force a desktop background:

1   Make sure you are logged in to your model Mac with the administrative account that you used previously to set the custom desktop background.

2   Copy the com.apple.desktop.plist file from the administrative account's ~/Library/ Preferences folder to the appropriate folder in the user template: /System/Library/User Template/English.lproj/Library/Preferences/.

    This folder is protected by root access, so you will have to use the command line to copy this file into the appropriate location. In the following example, Michelle uses her administrative account to copy the desktop preference file into the user template.

    ```
    MyMac:~ michelle$ sudo cp "/Users/michelle/Library/Preferences/com.apple.desktop.
    plist" "/System/Library/User Template/English.lproj/Library/Preferences/"
    ```

3   Protect the desktop preference file from modification. This requires changing the files' ownership and permissions to be writable only by root but still readable by everyone else, and then setting the lock flag.

    Again, because these items will have root permissions, the quickest method is to use the command line. In the following example, Michelle changes the ownership, permissions, and lock flag for the desktop preference file inside the user template.

```
MyMac:~ michelle$ sudo chown root:wheel "/Library/Desktop Pictures/pretendco.jpg"
"/System/Library/User Template/English.lproj /Library/Preferences/com.apple.
desktop.plist"
MyMac:~ michelle$ sudo chmod 644 "/Library/Desktop Pictures/pretendco.jpg" "/System/
Library/User Template/English.lproj /Library/Preferences/com.apple.desktop.plist"
MyMac:~ michelle$ sudo chflags uchg "/Library/Desktop Pictures/pretendco.jpg"
"/System/Library/User Template/English.lproj /Library/Preferences/com.apple.
desktop.plist"
```

Normally when the user template items are copied to create the new user's home folder, the ownership and permissions are set so the items belong to the user. However, because you set the lock flag, the copied desktop preference file will retain the original ownership and permissions you have set here. Thus, users will not be allowed to change the desktop background setting even if they have access to the Desktop & Screen Saver preferences. The system preference will remain active and allow the user to interact with the settings, but the desktop background will never change.

Creating a Hidden Administrator

Perhaps the cleverest advanced customization you can make to your model image is hiding the local administrative user's account from the primary users of the computer. If the administrator's account isn't hidden, users can view the local user list at the login window, the fast user switching menu, and the Accounts preference; they can also see other users' home folders in the /Users folder from the Finder and command line and when connecting remotely to a Mac that has file-sharing services enabled.

The technique covered here will hide all these clues from every user and will even hide the account from other administrative users. Although an administrative user who knows exactly what to look for can easily uncover and delete your hidden administrator, the vast majority of users will have no idea that the account is even there.

> **TIP** Another way to implement a hidden administrator account is to use a network directory–based administrative account. To learn more about network accounts, please refer to *Apple Training Series: Mac OS X Directory Services v10.6* (Peachpit Press, 2010).

To create a local hidden administrative account:

1 Log in to your model computer with an administrative account.

2   Open the Accounts system preference, click the Login Options button, and set "Display login window as" to "Name and password." Disable automatic login if you haven't done so already.

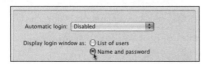

3   While still in the Accounts system preference, create a new administrative user account. Choose an appropriate short name as this user's primary login name. Also, do not activate FileVault for this user. Click Create Account when you are done.

4   In the accounts list, right-click or Control-click the entry for your new administrative account and choose Advanced Options from the shortcut menu.

5   In the Advanced Options dialog, change the user ID to *499* and the home directory location to any path that an average user would never navigate to. For instance, you could choose any folder normally hidden in the Finder. Then click OK.

A good location to store the hidden administrator's home folder is inside the /var folder. You can further "hide" the home folder by giving the home folder a name that begins with a period. For example, if your hidden administrator's short name is hadmin, a good hidden home folder path would be /var/.hadmin.

6   Move and rename the hidden administrator's home folder and set the appropriate ownership.

Step 5 changed the hidden administrator's user record, but in doing so you effectively removed access to this account's original home folder. You must move the original home folder to the new path you chose in step 5 and correct the ownership for the home folder items.

Because you're modifying another user's home folder, the fastest method to restore access is to use the command line. In the following example, Michelle will move and rename the hidden administrator's home folder, and then set the appropriate ownership.

```
MyMac:~ michelle$ sudo mv /Users/hadmin /var/.hadmin
MyMac:~ michelle$ sudo chown -R hadmin /var/.hadmin
```

7   Remove the Public and Sites folders from the hidden administrator's home folder.

Even though we have moved the hidden administrator's home folder, it may still show up when various network sharing services are enabled. This is easily remedied by removing the Public and Sites folders from this home folder.

Again, because you're modifying another user's home folder, the fastest method is to use the command line. In the following example, Michelle will remove the shared folders in the hidden administrator's home folder.

```
MyMac:~ michelle$ sudo rm -R /var/.hadmin/Public /var/.hadmin/Sites
```

8 Modify the loginwindow settings so the hidden administrator account and any account with user IDs below 500 are not shown. This will also prevent the Accounts preference and the fast user switching menu from showing accounts with user IDs below 500.

The quickest method to set these custom settings is to use the defaults command. Note that you could also set this using custom managed preferences, as covered previously in this chapter. In the following example, Michelle will modify the loginwindow preferences to hide accounts with user IDs below 500, and then hide the hadmin account.

```
MyMac:~ michelle$ sudo defaults write /Library/Preferences/com.apple.loginwindow
Hide500Users -bool TRUE
MyMac:~ michelle$ sudo defaults write /Library/Preferences/com.apple.loginwindow
HiddenUsersList -array hadmin
```

9 Test your work by logging out of your current account and then logging in as the hidden administrator.

10 If everything is working properly, delete your initial administrator account because it's not hidden.

Aside from having an interesting location for the home folder, your hidden administrator account is identical in function to any other administrative account.

NOTE ▶ Don't forget to reconfigure the Remote Management settings in the Sharing preference to allow the hidden administrator to use Apple Remote Desktop to manage the client.

Cloned Image: Overview and Preparation

Creation of a cloned system image suitable for deployment involves just a few main steps:

1. On a model system, install and update all necessary software, configure system settings, and perform any additional customizations.

2. Purge the model system of files not suited for deployment.

3. Use the Disk Utility application or the hdiutil command to copy the model system to a read-only (optionally compressed) disk image.

4. Use the Disk Utility application or the asr command to prepare the system image for deployment.

The first step, configuring the model system, will require the most time and expertise. Assuming you meet the prerequisite level of knowledge suggested by this guide, equivalent to the requirements for Apple Certified Technical Coordinator certification, you should already have a good idea of how to configure your model system. Further, the previous two sections in this chapter, "Integrating with Managed Preferences" and "Customizing System Configuration," provide additional techniques for system management and customization that you should consider including with your system image.

Required Equipment

To create a cloned system image, you need either two Mac computers or one Mac with two bootable volumes that have Mac OS X v10.6 installed.

If you have two Mac computers, one will be used to build the model system, and the second will be used to create the cloned system image. In this case both Macs will need to be equipped with built-in FireWire ports. You will also need a FireWire cable to connect the two so you can clone the model system to the creation system. If you are working with a Mac that does not have a FireWire port, you should use the suggested techniques for working with a single Mac.

If you are working with a single Mac, you will need two separate bootable volumes, one volume will be used to build the model system, and the other volume will be used to create the cloned system image. You could accomplish this with a single internal drive with two partitions, but a more flexible solution is to use the internal drive as the model system and the external drive as the creation system.

> **TIP** When working on a single Mac to build a cloned system image, using separate physical drives, such as FireWire drives, for each volume will significantly reduce the amount of time it takes to clone and prepare the system image. Having the drives on separate data buses (for instance, one on the internal SATA bus and one on the FireWire bus) will speed the process even further. FireWire is preferable to USB, as real-world performance of FireWire 400 can be up to three times faster than USB 2.0.

> **TIP** In Mac OS X v10.6, Disk Utility can be used to split a single partition into multiple partitions without having to reformat the original volume. You should always use the new volume to build your model system image.

> **TIP** Every Intel-based Mac can boot from an external USB drive as long as it's partitioned using the GPT format, contains a Mac OS X Extended volume, and has an installed copy of Mac OS X.

Finally, make sure that both the model and creation volumes have enough room to build your cloned system image. The model volume needs enough room to install the system and any additional items you intend to deploy, and the creation volume needs at least twice the available space used on the model volume. Thus, if your model volume uses 10 GB of storage space, your creation volume needs 20 GB of available space.

Cloned Image: Clean Up System

After you have completed all your model system customizations, you need to purge the model system volume of any items that should not be deployed to multiple computers, such as computer- and user-specific preferences and cache files that are not appropriate for other systems.

Once you have cleaned up the model system, be sure not to reboot it, otherwise many of the files you have purged will be re-created. If you must reboot the model system to make a correction, you will have to clean the system again. In fact, any time in the future when you need to update the cloned system image, you will have to reclean the model system volume before you can create a new cloned system image.

> **NOTE ▶** Remember that you will need to reset some computer-specific configuration settings after this image has been deployed to your systems. See Chapter 6, "Postimaging Deployment Considerations."

Working from the Creation System

It's easiest to properly clean your model system volume from your creation system.

1   Whether you're using two separate Macs or two bootable volumes, shut down the model system.

2   Now start using the creation system. You will need administrative access on the creation system.

3   Mount the model system volume on the creation system.

▶   If you're using two separate Macs, restart the Mac with the model system volume in target mode by clicking the Target Disk Mode button in the Startup Disk system preference. Using a FireWire cable, plug the Mac with the model system into the booted Mac that will act as the creation system.

▶   If you're using a single Mac, use the Startup Disk system preference to set the creation system volume as the startup volume and restart the Mac.

4   With the model system volume mounted on your creation system, rename the model system volume in the Finder. When you create a deployable system image, the name of the system volume will persist through the entire deployment to each system, so choose a name wisely.

You could stick with the default Macintosh HD name, but to prevent accidentally targeting the wrong volume, and to further designate this as a custom system, you should change the model system volume name to something organization specific.

Removing User-Specific Files

Remove from your model system volume any user-specific files that are not necessary or are tied to computer-specific settings. In most cases the only local account left on your model system volume at this point is an administrator account. If you do have multiple local user accounts still on your model system volume, you will need to clean out each individual user's home folder.

The following example presents a list of the user-specific files that should be removed from the model system volume. This example assumes the model system volume is mounted to a creation system and is named PretendcoHD, and that the only local user account on the model system is Michelle. The only command needed is `sudo rm -rf`, so you could enter all these items in a single command, but they are on separate lines here for easier reading.

```
sudo rm /Volumes/PretendcoHD/Users/michelle/Send Registration
sudo rm -rf /Volumes/PretendcoHD/Users/michelle/Desktop/*
sudo rm -rf /Volumes/PretendcoHD/Users/michelle/Downloads/*
sudo rm -rf /Volumes/PretendcoHD/Users/michelle/Library/Caches/*
```

Removing Computer-Specific Files

You should also remove from your model system volume any computer-specific files that are not necessary. The following example presents a list of the computer-specific files that should be removed from the model system. This example assumes the model system volume is mounted to a creation system and is named PretendcoHD. Again, the only command needed is sudo rm -rf, so you could put all these items in a single command, but they are on separate lines here for easier reading.

```
sudo rm -rf /Volumes/PretendcoHD/Documentation/old_*
sudo rm -rf /Volumes/PretendcoHD/Library/Caches/*
sudo rm -rf /Volumes/PretendcoHD/System/Library/Caches/*
sudo rm -rf /Volumes/PretendcoHD/Library/Managed\ Preferences/*
sudo rm -rf /Volumes/PretendcoHD/Users/Shared/*
sudo rm -rf /Volumes/PretendcoHD/private/etc/ssh_host*
sudo rm -rf /Volumes/PretendcoHD/private/var/db/volinfo.database
sudo rm -rf /Volumes/PretendcoHD/private/var/vm/swap*
sudo rm -rf /Volumes/PretendcoHD/private/var/vm/sleepimage
```

TIP ▶ This would also be a good point to remove the /var/db/.AppleSetupDone and /var/db/.AutoBindDone files on the model system volume if you want the Setup Assistant to run at startup on your deployed systems.

If you plan to use computer-based managed preferences, perform authenticated binding to an Open Directory server, or take advantage of other local Kerberos authentication features, then you will also need to reset the Local Kerberos Distribution Center (LKDC). The following commands present the easiest method to remove the current model's LKDC and force it to rebuild on the next startup:

```
sudo rm -rf /Volumes/PretendcoHD/private/var/db/.configureLocalKDC
sudo rm -rf /Volumes/PretendcoHD/private/var/db/krb5kdc
sudo rm -rf /Volumes/PretendcoHD/private/etc/krb5.keytab
sudo rm -rf /Volumes/PretendcoHD/Keychains/System.keychain
```

NOTE ▶ This LKDC reset method requires the removal of the System.keychain file, which may contain items that you need to deploy in your system image. For further details regarding the LKDC please refer to Chapter 6, "Postimaging Deployment Considerations."

There are several folders of computer-specific preferences that may also cause you problems when deploying to different types of hardware or computers destined for users with different levels of managed preference settings. Whether you have to remove files from these folders depends on your specific deployment scenario. In some cases you may have to modify these items after system deployment, as covered in Chapter 6, "Postimaging Deployment Considerations."

However, if you experience configuration problems when testing your deployment, these folders will contain your primary suspects:

▶   ~/Library/ByHost/—This folder is in every user's home folder and holds preference files that are both user specific and computer specific. By design, none of these preferences will work on other systems.

▶   /Library/Preferences/SystemConfiguration—This folder contains fundamental system configuration information, such as power management and network settings. Many of these settings don't translate to systems with different hardware configurations.

▶   /Library/Preferences/DirectoryService—This folder contains all the Directory Service settings. In general, if you do any sort of authenticated binding, including Active Directory binding, these items do not work when deployed to multiple systems.

Cloned Image: Create Restore Image

Once you have prepared and cleaned your model system volume, it's finally time to create a restorable image from the model. The method covered in this section is essentially the "manual" method for creating a restorable image of a cloned system.

NOTE ▶ This guide also covers an alternative method for creating a cloned system image by using System Image Utility. If you plan on deploying your system image using the NetBoot Service, then you will be better served by using System Image Utility to create your restore image. For details on this alternate method, start with the next section in this chapter, "Understanding System Image Utility (SIU)."

Create the Cloned Disk Image

Before you create the image, it's a good idea to use Disk Utility's Repair Disk feature on the model system volume. This will clean up potential volume structure issues that could have cropped up while you were building your system volume. If Disk Utility reports issues, you should run the Repair Disk process again until no issues are reported.

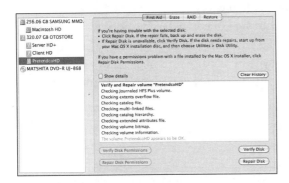

TIP If Disk Utility is unable to completely repair the volume structure of your model system volume, then consider purchasing DiskWarrior by Alsoft, available at www.alsoft.com/DiskWarrior/index.html. This third-party utility provides a much more robust Mac OS X Extended volume repair algorithm that can fix many issues Disk Utility is incapable of resolving.

As you learned in Chapter 2, "Deploying Individual Items and Containers," it's fairly easy to create a disk image using the contents of a folder or volume. You can create disk images in the graphical interface using the Disk Image application and at the command line using the hdiutil command.

Here are a few tips to keep in mind when creating a cloned system disk image:

▶ It's usually best to choose a new Disk Image from Folder and then select the model system volume as the source. This will always build an image with zero additional free space, so you can restore it to any drive that's larger than the system image contents.

▶ Make sure to specify just the model system image volume, not the physical drive, as the source for the cloned system image.

▶ The cloned system image format must be read-only (optionally compressed) and not encrypted.

▶ If you choose to create a compressed image, make sure to have roughly twice the amount of free space available on the creation volume as the amount of used space on the model system volume.

▶ Using separate physical drives for the model system volume and the destination for the cloned system image will greatly speed up the disk image creation process.

▶ If you are unable to create the cloned system image because the system is reporting Resource Busy errors, unmount, but do not eject, the model system volume and then remount it again to create the cloned system image.

TIP ▶ As an alternative to manually creating a system disk image, you can use System Image Utility (SIU) to create a deployable system image. This is covered later in the "Creating Basic Images with SIU" section of this chapter.

Preparing the Cloned System Image for Deployment

There is one last step to prepare your cloned system image for deployment. The cloned system image must be scanned in preparation for the Apple Software Restore (ASR) process. As you will learn in greater detail in Chapter 5, "Deploying System Images," the ASR process is used to restore the system image contents to a storage volume for deployment. The image scanning process can be performed by the Disk Utility application or the asr command.

The image scan process calculates additional data checksums for the cloned system image and stores this information in the disk image file. This checksum data is later used to verify the system restoration process. The image scan process will also reorder the cloned system disk image file if it is not properly ordered for the network ASR process. If the disk image file needs to be reordered, the system will have to rewrite the file to the same volume. This reordering process is why you need roughly twice the free space on the creation system to prepare the cloned system image for deployment.

To scan your cloned system image from the Disk Utility application:

1   Open Disk Utility and choose Images > Scan Image for Restore.

2   In the Open dialog that appears, select your cloned system image.

3   Authenticate as an administrative user to initiate the scan process.

Depending on the size of your system image and the speed of your hardware, it can take anywhere from a few minutes to a few hours to complete the image scan process. During this time Disk Utility will show a progress bar dialog. When the process is complete, this dialog will let you know whether the image scan process was successful.

Scanning your cloned system image from the `asr` command is nearly as easy. The syntax is `sudo asr imagescan -source` followed by the path to the cloned system image. In the following example, Michelle scans the cloned system image she previously created, ClonedSystem.dmg, on the external Storage volume. The `asr` command also displays image scan progress and success messages.

```
MyMac:~ michelle$ sudo asr imagescan -source /Volumes/Storage/ClonedSystem.dmg
Password: (password not shown)
Block checksum: ....10....20....30....40....50....60....70....80....90....100
asr: successfully scanned image "/Volumes/Storage/ClonedSystem.dmg"
```

Updating a Cloned System Image

One of the primary disadvantages of a cloned system image is that updates and changes are not easily made. Once a deployable system image is created, the image file itself can never be changed. Essentially, you have to replace your outdated cloned system image with a new cloned system image.

This process of having to build new cloned system images with every change is especially frustrating when you are testing and trying to work the kinks out of a new system deployment. Even the smallest change requires that you completely rebuild the entire system image.

There are three methods that you can use to update an existing cloned system image and still use your previous work as a starting point:

▶ Retain the original model system volume and apply your updates to the model system. Once the model system is updated, create a new cloned system image as outlined previously in this section.

▶ Restore the cloned system to a bootable volume as outlined in Chapter 5, "Deploying System Images." Treat this restored volume as the new model system and apply your updates. Once your updates are complete, create a new cloned system image.

▶ Convert the cloned system image to a read/write disk image as outlined in Chapter 2, "Deploying Individual Items and Containers." Mount the new read/write disk image that contains your cloned system and apply the changes to the mounted volume. Once your updates are complete, convert the system disk image back to a read-only format and then rescan the image for restore.

Understanding System Image Utility (SIU)

System Image Utility (SIU) is an application that you can use to create Mac OS X v10.6 network disk images. SIU is located in the /Applications/Server folder on your Mac OS X Server v10.6 computer, or it can be installed as part of the Server Admin Tools v10.6 on any Mac OS X v10.6 computer. Network disk images are modified system images that have been created for use with the NetBoot service. As you can probably tell from the name, NetBoot allows you to start multiple Mac computers via a network connection to network disk images hosted on a Mac OS X server. NetBoot is Apple's primary network-based system deployment mechanism, and as such, is one of the primary topics of Chapter 5, "Deploying System Images."

MORE INFO ▶ The Server Admin Tools v10.6 installer can be found on the Mac OS X Server installation discs, or it can be downloaded from the Apple website, http://support.apple.com/kb/DL914.

Though SIU is primarily designed to facilitate the NetBoot service, it's introduced in this chapter because it's the only Apple tool that provides an easy-to-use automated method for creating deployable system images. Specifically, SIU in Mac OS X v10.6 introduces a new network disk image type, NetRestore, which can be used to create and deploy system images. Further, even if you don't intend to use the Mac OS X NetBoot service, you can still use SIU as an automated tool for creating full system images to be deployed using another mechanism.

Selecting a Network Disk Image Source

Although Mac OS X Server v10.6 supports hosting images with previous versions of Mac OS, the 10.6 version of SIU can only create network disk images of Mac OS X v10.6.x or Mac OS X Server v10.6.x. Therefore, if you wish to create network disk images of previous versions of Mac OS X you must also use previous versions of the Mac OS X Server administration tools.

As when creating a standard system image, you must have a source from which to create your network disk images. SIU can create network disk images of Mac OS X or Mac OS X Server from two primary sources; Mac OS X installation media or any system volume that is not currently booted. Additionally, SIU treats the contents of a mounted disk image identically to that of a standard volume. Thus, if a disk image volume's contents constitute a copy of the Mac OS X installation media, SIU will recognize the mounted volume as installation media. Conversely, if a disk image volume's contents are that of an installed and configured system, SIU will recognize the mounted volume as a nonbooted system volume.

TIP ▶ Your model Mac, when set to target disk mode and plugged into your SIU creation computer, certainly qualifies as a valid nonbooted system volume from which you can create a network disk image.

TIP ▶ If your source is a system image, it's a good idea to use Disk Utility or DiskWarrior by Alsoft to verify and/or repair the volume structure before using SIU to create the network disk image.

Network Disk Image Types

System Image Utility creates three types of network disk images:

▶ A standard *NetBoot image* provides a typical computing experience, albeit one that is hosted from a NetBoot server. When started from a NetBoot image the Mac operates nearly identically to a locally booted Mac OS X client or server. Although this is an ideal configuration for systems that will remain running from the NetBoot image, it is not generally used for system deployment purposes. This is because most Mac computers come with ample local hard drive space, and more often than not, are portable computers. Thus, relying on a permanent network connection for the system volume generally isn't the best use of resources.

> **TIP** A popular use for NetBoot is to create an administration, maintenance, and recovery NetBoot system, for use when a Mac cannot start up from its internal volumes. In this case you can create a bootable Mac system, hosted on your network, that has all your favorite utilities and tools.

▶ A *NetInstall image* starts up to the Mac OS X Installer, much like when you start up from the Mac OS X installation media. In essence, you're simply taking the original Mac OS X installation media and making it available on the network. Thus, NetInstall allows you to perform an installation of the operating system to a local Mac. This is an alternative to pure system imaging techniques that restore a premade system image to the local Mac. The advantage to NetInstall is that you can pick and choose the individual packages that get installed, as opposed to performing a system restore, which always includes the entire contents of the system image.

▶ New to Mac OS X v10.6, a *NetRestore image* starts up to an interface that appears to be identical to the Mac OS X Installer. However, instead of performing an install of Mac OS X, it will restore a system image to the local Mac. The restored system image is based on either a clone of your model system or a modular system built by SIU. This is the deployment mechanism of choice for many because it provides the fastest method for deploying a fully configured system.

> **TIP** Both NetInstall and NetRestore images also include all the utilities found on normal Mac OS X Installation media, like Disk Utility and Reset Password. Thus, you could use one of these network disk image types as a network hosted maintenance system.

SIU Network Disk Image Results

SIU features a two-mode interface that allows you to create either basic network disk images with just a few clicks or more complicated images based on a customized workflow. This chapter focuses on the "basic" mode while Chapter 5, "Deploying System Images," focuses on building customized network disk images with SIU.

When using the "basic" SIU mode, there are two main choices you make; selecting the Mac OS X system source and choosing the network disk image type. The resulting image created by SIU will vary based on the selected source and type of image you are creating.

	NetBoot Image	NetInstall Image	NetRestore Image
Installation Media	Clients start to full generic system	Clients start to default Mac OS X installer interface	Clients start to an interface that will restore a generic system image
Prepared System	Clients start to full system based on selected source		Clients start to an interface that will restore a system image based on selected source

If your system source is *Mac OS X installation media*, and you choose to create a...

▶ NetBoot image—A Mac booting from this image will start up to a fully functional, though completely generic, version of Mac OS X based on the installation media. This is not a very useful build combination when using SIU in "basic" mode.

▶ NetInstall image—A Mac booting from this image will start up to an installer interface identical to that based on the installation media. This allows you to provide access to the installation media from the network.

▶ NetRestore image—A Mac booting from this image will start up to an interface allowing you to restore a generic system image based on the installation media. In other words, SIU will build a restorable system image by installing Mac OS X to a disk image based on the default installation settings. Again, when using SIU in "basic" mode this is not a very useful build combination. However, this combination provides the basis for building a modular system image, as covered later in this chapter.

If your system source is a *nonbooted system volume*, and you choose to create a...

▶ NetBoot image—A Mac booting from this image will start up to a system identical to that of the source system volume. This allows you to provide access to a fully configured system from the network. This combination is used most often for "diskless" deployments wherein the local Mac does not have a system installed; it instead relies solely on a NetBoot system. This combination is also used to create an administration, maintenance, and recovery system that can be accessed from the network.

▶ NetInstall image—SIU will not let you select this combination because the source is not valid Mac OS X installation media.

▶ NetRestore image—A Mac booting from this image will start up to an interface allowing you to restore a system image based on the source system volume. In other words, SIU will build a restorable system image by cloning the source system. While you could certainly do this yourself using the manual methods outlined previously in this chapter, SIU takes this to the next step by "wrapping" the restore system image in a NetRestore system. The image built by this combination, when hosted from a NetBoot server, is the easiest method to deploy a cloned system image via the network.

NOTE ▶ When creating a NetRestore image of a system volume, SIU will automatically "clean" the restore image of system items that are problematic for deployment. This includes removing swap files and sleep files and resetting the LKDC. However, SIU is not as thorough as the steps outlined in the "Cloned Image: Clean Up System" section previously in this chapter.

Creating Basic Images with SIU

In this section you will learn how to create and modify basic network disk images. You can create network disk images using SIU from any Mac OS X v10.6 computer. All you need is a system with access to your source media and enough storage space to save the newly created image files. Similar to when you create cloned system images, the destination volume needs roughly two times the amount of available space as there is used space on the source volume.

TIP ▶ When creating a network disk image, using separate physical drives for the source volume and save destination will significantly reduce the amount of time it takes to create the image.

Once you have created your network disk images, you can host them from a NetBoot server, as detailed in Chapter 5, "Deploying System Images." It's important to note that you don't have to create the network disk image on the server where it will eventually be hosted. You can save the image to your Mac client's system drive or an external drive, and then copy it to the appropriate location on your NetBoot server.

Create a Basic Network Disk Image

To create a basic NetBoot, NetInstall, or NetRestore image:

1   Mount your source system volume.

The source system can be either Mac OS X v10.6.x or Mac OS X Server v10.6.x. The source volume can be the original installation media, a nonbooted system volume, or a disk image containing either.

2   Open /Applications/Server/System Image Utility.

You will be presented with the basic NetBoot image-creation interface. System Image Utility automatically scans all mounted volumes for valid sources and lists them under Sources in the left column.

3   Select the system volume you wish to make an image of from the Sources list.

4   Select the appropriate button to define the type of image you want to create; NetBoot, NetInstall, or NetRestore.

NOTE ▶ You can only create a NetInstall image if your source is a Mac OS X installation volume.

5 Click the Continue button once you have made your selections.

MORE INFO ▶ Clicking the Customize button will allow you to create a workflow-generated NetBoot image, as covered in the "Understanding SIU Workflows" section later in this chapter.

6 Enter an image name and description.

The image name will be displayed by any interface that allows you to select this image, including the Server Admin application and Startup Disk preferences.

7 If you intend to host this network disk image on multiple servers, select the "Image will be served from more than one server" checkbox.

Selecting this option will set the network image ID to a range that tells the NetBoot service to automatically provide load balancing if the image is shared from more than one source. If you're not sure, simply leave the default setting, as this can be easily changed later.

8 If you are creating a NetBoot or NetRestore image from installation media, you will need to configure a local administrator account.

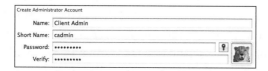

Enter a name, short name, and password (twice) to define the new local administrator account. You can also set the account picture by clicking the image at the right.

9 When you are satisfied with your network disk image settings, click the Create button.

10 Agree to the software license agreement to continue with the network disk image creation process.

11 When prompted, enter a name and select a location to save the network disk image.

The name you choose here is only used to set the name of the folder that contains the network disk image resources; it does not affect the image name you specified earlier.

The save location can be any writable destination that has enough space to hold a copy of your network disk image. However, if you're creating this image on the server that will be hosting it, you can save time by choosing the NetBoot share point. The default location for the NetBoot share point is the /Library/NetBoot/NetBootSP0/ folder.

12 Click the Save button and then authenticate as an administrative user to initiate the network disk image creation process.

Creating a network disk image can take from a few minutes to a few hours, depending on the size of the image source, the type of image you're creating, and the speed of your hardware configuration. SIU will show the progress of the creation process, and you can always click the Cancel button to stop it. For a more detailed log of the creation process, choose View > Show Log.

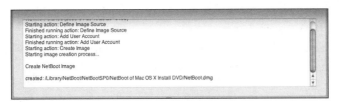

Modifying Network Disk Images

Modifying an existing network disk image is easy, as long as you don't need to apply a major Mac OS X update to the system volume. System updates that change the Mac OS X version—for instance, from version 10.6.1 to 10.6.2—usually replace core system components such as the UNIX kernel. Because of the special system image format of a network disk image, a major Mac OS X update installation will not properly replace these items. If you need to update the version of Mac OS X in a network disk system volume, you will have to create a new image.

NOTE ▶ Never modify a network disk image that is currently in use by the NetBoot service.

Network disk images are created by SIU as folders named with the .nbi extension. The system image file that Mac computers start up from when using the NetBoot service is inside the network disk .nbi folder. Inside a NetBoot image folder you will find "NetBoot. dmg," while inside NetInstall and NetRestore images you will find "NetInstall.dmg." Most modifications of network disk images are as simple as mounting this read/write system image volume, applying your changes, and then ejecting the volume. NetBoot system images usually have about a gigabyte of free space for making changes, but NetInstall and NetRestore images have very little room for making changes.

MORE INFO ▶ You can expand disk images using the techniques covered in Chapter 2, "Deploying Individual Items and Containers."

Modifying the Deployable System

Standard NetInstall images created from Mac OS X installation media can technically be modified, but making any useful change is difficult because the Mac OS X installation process is not easily editable.

TIP ▶ You can build custom NetInstall images using SIU that will install additional packages along with the Mac OS X installation. This technique is detailed in Chapter 5, "Deploying System Images."

However, you can easily access and replace the system image that is restored by a NetRestore image. Inside the NetRestore image folder you'll find the "NetInstall.dmg" system image; mount this image by simply double-clicking on it. You'll note the content of this disk image is the system used to start up Mac computers via the NetBoot service. This image content also includes the prepared system restore disk image located at /Volumes/NetInstall/System/Installation/Packages/System.dmg.

If you wish to use another deployment mechanism to restore this system image, simply copy the System.dmg out of the mounted NetInstall volume and deploy it as you wish. Conversely, you can replace this disk image with any other prepared (scanned for ASR) system image. Providing the system image file is named "System.dmg" and is in the correct folder, the NetRestore process will restore that system instead.

> **TIP** ▶ You can build custom NetRestore images using SIU that can restore from multiple system image sources. This technique is also detailed in Chapter 5, "Deploying System Images."

Modular Image Overview and Preparation

The workflow for creating a modular system image suitable for deployment is a bit more involved than what is needed to create a cloned system image. However, as you'll see, this technique yields cleaner system images and an easier upgrade path and is easy to automate.

Understanding Modular System Images

A modular system image is a disk image that uses installation packages for every item and setting in the configuration to create a fully customized Mac OS X system. That is, instead of installing the operating system and all your custom software and configurations to a booted Mac system, you install these items directly to a disk image.

The use of installation packages for every item and setting in your system configuration results in a truly modular system image creation workflow. The only requirement is a base system image with an installation of Mac OS X. After that you can add as many more installation packages as you want to your system image. This allows you to easily create multiple system images by simply adjusting the number of installation packages applied to the image during the creation process. Further, updates and configuration changes are easily handled by adding installation packages to your creation workflow.

The workflow to create a modular system image can be split into two primary stages, each with several steps. In the first stage, the preparation stage, you collect or create the installation packages that you will use to build your modular system image. There is no particular order or even an end point to this stage, as you will continue to add installation packages as your needs change and as your software needs updating. Most of your time will be spent in this stage locating or creating the appropriate installation package modules.

In the second stage, the build stage, you actually create the system image using the installation packages you prepared during the first stage. With previous versions of Mac OS X the build stage must be performed manually or using a third-party tool. The Mac OS X v10.6 version of SIU, with the introduction of NetRestore, provides an automated mechanism to easily build modular system images. This build process is covered in the "Understanding SIU Workflows" and "Building Modular NetRestore Images with SIU" sections later in this chapter.

> **MORE INFO ▶** The methodology discussed here is based on the pioneering work done by the InstaDMG project; see www.afp548.com. If you require more control over the system build process, consider InstaDMG as an alternative to SIU.

Required Equipment

To build a modular system image, all you need is one Mac OS X v10.6 system with access to enough storage space to contain all your installation packages and disk image files.

Nevertheless, the use of a separate scratch drive will speed up the modular system image creation process. In this scenario, your installation packages are stored on your primary drive, and during the SIU build process you save the image on the scratch drive. This method ensures that while the system image is being built, one drive is always reading while the other drive is writing, thus maximizing drive bandwidth and reducing build time.

> **TIP ▶** You're probably going to end up with quite a few installation packages and disk images while using the modular system image methodology, so you should create several folders to keep your work organized.

Preparing for a Modular System Image

Before you begin building a modular system image you need to prepare a collection of installation packages that includes the Mac OS X v10.6 installation, any software updates, any additional software, and any custom configuration installation packages. Once you have prepared all the installation components that will make up your modular system you can move on to the build process using SIU.

> **NOTE ▶** With the exception of the Mac OS X installer, you should copy all installation packages that have been stored inside a disk image to a convenient location on your build Mac. Installing "naked" installation packages requires less work during the build process because you don't have to mount the disk image volume.

Preparing the Mac OS X v10.6 Installation

All system images must include an installation of Mac OS v10.6. However, by default, the system installation process isn't conducive to the modular system image workflow. The primary issue is that the Mac OS X installation usually resides on inconvenient media: an optical disc. You will need more frequent access to this installer, so you should create a disk image of the Mac OS X Install DVD or the Mac OS X Server Install Disc.

As you learned in Chapter 2, "Deploying Individual Items and Containers," it's fairly easy to create a disk image using the contents of a folder or volume. In the graphical interface, you can use the Disk Image application, or at the command line you can use the hdiutil command.

Mac OS X Install DVD.dmg

> **TIP ▶** You can also make disk images from the computer-specific installation media included with all new Macs.

Preparing Additional Software and Updates

Preparing additional software and updates can be easy or difficult depending on what additional items your modular system image requires. The key is that all additional items must be added to your modular system image through an installation package. All Apple software and many third-party items are distributed this way, so preparing these items is as simple as collecting all the necessary installers in a convenient location on your build system.

> **NOTE** ▶ Some installation packages, even those created by Apple, do not react well to being installed on a nonsystem volume, as dictated by the modular system image workflow. Examples include certain iLife updates and the Cisco VPN installer. Troubleshooting these items is beyond the scope of this text, but the InstaDMG forum (www.afp548.com/forum/index.php?forum=45) provides solutions for issues you may encounter with additional installers.

However, third-party items distributed using simple file containers or non-Apple installers will need to be repackaged inside a custom-built installation package, as outlined in Chapter 3, "Deploying with Installation Packages." Specifically, the PackageMaker snapshot technology can help you easily repackage third-party items.

You can use your build system to create these installation packages, but a better option is to use a second dedicated "clean" system for building and testing your custom installation packages. During the testing process, you will undoubtedly come across installation packages that don't deploy as expected. Use the techniques covered in the "Installation Package Maintenance" section of Chapter 3 to inspect and troubleshoot problem installation packages.

Creating Configuration Installation Packages

For most administrators the process of creating configuration installation packages is the most difficult and time-consuming step of the entire modular system image workflow. Essentially, you have to research and develop a payload or script to be built into an installation package, which performs all the custom configurations, including configuring system settings, creating users, and configuring any user-specific settings, that you would normally do manually to a model system.

> **TIP** ▶ Using managed preferences settings hosted from a network directory service will greatly reduce the amount of customization you have to include with your modular system image.

It's possible to set any Mac OS X configuration by using the appropriate command or by replacing the appropriate file as illustrated previously in the "Customizing System Configuration" section of this chapter. Nearly all the customizations presented earlier can be automated and made part of an installation package. Exploring all the possible configuration options that can be automated is beyond the scope of this text, but the following references (all from Peachpit Press, 2010) should get you started:

▸ *Apple Training Series: Support Essentials v10.6*—Specifically, Chapter 3 of this guide includes a command-line and scripting primer.

▸ *Apple Training Series: Mac OS X Directory Services v10.6*—This is a comprehensive guide to both local and network directory services and user accounts in general.

▸ *Apple Training Series: Mac OS X Security and Mobility v10.6*—This is a general guide to advanced Mac OS X and Mac OS X Server configuration.

Understanding SIU Workflows

The Mac OS X v10.5 version of SIU introduced an entirely new way to create custom network disk images to suit your specific deployment needs, through an easy-to-use graphical interface that allows you to define custom images and system deployment workflows.

About Automator Actions

To implement a flexible network disk image customization system, SIU uses Mac OS X's Automator technology. The Automator application, located in the /Applications folder, allows you to automate repetitive application tasks. This technology is based on AppleScript, a much older technology. AppleScript is a very powerful application scripting language, but like any computer programming language, it has a learning curve. With Automator, even novice computer users can take advantage of the powerful automation features of AppleScript without having to know how to write code.

Automator accomplishes its work through Automator actions, each of which presents a small graphical interface that allows you to perform a very specific automated task in a specific application. You can use these actions as building blocks, combining multiple Automator actions into an ordered list to build an Automator workflow that can be used to perform a repetitive task.

MORE INFO ► To can find out more about Mac OS X automation, please refer to *Apple Training Series: Mac OS X Server Essentials v10.6* (Peachpit Press, 2010) or www.macosxautomation.com.

In many cases the order of the Automator actions in a workflow matters, not only because it defines the order in which actions take place, but also because adjacent actions can communicate to one another through inputs and outputs. For example, an Automator action for the Finder can mount a disk image volume, but first it requires input from another action that identifies the specific disk image to mount. The first action selects the disk image file and outputs that information so the action that mounts the disk image knows which image to mount. The following figure shows a simple example of an Automator workflow. Notice the input-output connection between the two actions.

Automator Action
Input-Output
Connection

TIP ► You should consider using Automator for more than just creating NetBoot images. Automator workflows can be created for all manner of automated administration and deployment tasks.

Automator has proved so successful in simplifying complex tasks in standard applications that Apple based the creation of network disk images on this technology. Included with SIU is a suite of Automator actions tailored to the creation of custom network disk images. By using the same simple technique of ordering Automator actions into an Automator workflow, you can create a custom workflow-generated network disk image, which previously would have required a significant amount of skill and time to manually configure and code.

Creating Images with SIU Workflows

System Image Utility in Mac OS X v10.6 includes 11 Automator actions for the creation of custom network disk images. Although you can access the SIU-related Automator actions from the Automator application, an easier method is to start with SIU to build your workflow-generated network disk images. Within SIU, simply click the Customize button to enter SIU workflow mode. The workflow mode will open with the two primary SIU actions already in place, Define Image Source and Create Image.

These two actions are the primary SIU actions required for creating network disk images. The Define Image Source action allows you to select the system image source, and the Create Image action allows you to configure the network disk image settings. These two primary SIU actions must always be the first and last actions for any workflow that builds a network disk image. All other SIU actions are optional and can be placed in between the two primary SIU actions. Think of the two primary actions, Define Image Source and Create Image, as bookends for the network disk image creation process.

> **NOTE ▶** Although the Create Image action is always required to create a network disk image, as an alternative you can start with the Define NetRestore Source action. This action creates a special kind of NetRestore image, which is covered in Chapter 5, "Deploying System Images."

You may have noticed that the SIU workflow mode also opens an Automator Library window showing you all the SIU-related Automator actions. Selecting an action from this list shows a brief description of the action at the bottom. To incorporate an action into a workflow, simply drag it to where you want it in the workflow.

Using Automator instead of SIU allows you to incorporate other non-SIU actions into a workflow. Just make sure not to interrupt the connection flow between the primary "bookend" SIU actions and the other optional SIU actions; otherwise your workflow may fail to complete the image build. Note that if you want your workflow to perform other tasks besides building a network disk image, you can place those actions before or after your set of SIU actions. For example, you could add actions after the Create Image action that mount a server share and then copy the newly created network disk to the appropriate folder on the NetBoot server.

Ultimately your goal shouldn't be just to build a network disk image; your goal should be to develop workflows that can automate building images for you now and in the future. This is why there is a Save button next to the Run button at the bottom of SIU. Once you build a workflow, save it. In the future, use your previous workflows as building blocks for new, possibly more sophisticated workflows.

The workflow files saved by SIU are actually formatted as Automator workflows, so they open directly in Automator when double-clicked on in the Finder. This is no accident, as you'll find that Automator provides a more complete interface for building more sophisticated workflows. Using Automator you can combine SIU actions with other non-SIU actions, use variable substitution, integrate with other applications using the Services menu, and even other scripting technologies including full AppleScript and shell scripting.

> **MORE INFO ▶** This introduction to SIU workflows provides context for the next section of this chapter, "Building Modular NetRestore Images with SIU." However, the majority of SIU-related actions are tailored to system deployment tasks, and are thus covered in Chapter 5, "Deploying System Images."

Building Modular NetRestore Images with SIU

Assuming you have prepared the system image components, as outlined previously in the "Modular Image Overview and Preparation" section of this chapter, building a modular image is relatively easy. The Mac OS X v10.6 version of SIU includes upgraded Automator actions that can be used to build a NetRestore image that will restore a system image built from installation packages.

TIP ▶ Even if you don't plan to use the NetBoot service to deploy your modular system image, you can still use this SIU workflow to create a restorable system image. Once the NetRestore build is complete you can extract the built system image using the technique outlined previously in the "Modifying the Deployable System" section of this chapter.

Building a Modular NetRestore Image

To create a custom NetRestore image using installation packages:

1 Mount your source system volume.

The source system can be either Mac OS X v10.6.x or Mac OS X Server v10.6.x. Because you are building a new system image from scratch, the source can be the original installation media or a mounted disk image containing the original installation media.

2 Open /Applications/Server/System Image Utility.app.

SIU will open to the basic network disk image creation interface.

3 Click the Customize button, and then the Agree button.

SIU will change to the workflow creation view. The required primary actions, Define Image Source and Create Image, are already placed in the new workflow.

The Automator Library floating window also automatically opens to the list of all available SIU-related actions. Selecting an action from the list will display a brief description of the action below the list.

4   From the Define Image Source action, make sure that the appropriate Mac OS X or Mac OS X Server installation media is selected. If not, select the system source from the Source pop-up menu.

This source will provide the base system for your modular image.

5   Drag the Add Packages and Post-Install Scripts action from the Automator Library to the SIU workflow area. Make sure to drag this new action between the two default primary actions.

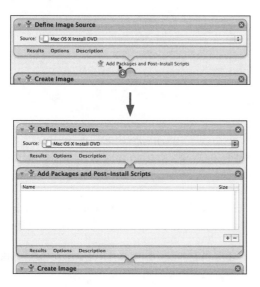

NOTE ▶ Post-install scripts are not supported for building NetRestore images.

6   Add your additional installation packages by clicking the small plus button to open a selection dialog or by dragging installers from the Finder.

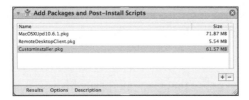

These packages will be installed on top of the base system in the order that you have added them to the listing. Unfortunately, you cannot reorder the installation list, so you must delete installers (using the minus button) if you want to rearrange the order.

7 At the top of the Create Image action window, make sure to select the NetRestore button.

TIP ▶ This technique can also be used to create custom NetBoot or NetInstall images. However, if your goal is to create a restorable system image, then you will want to stick with NetRestore.

8 Configure the remainder of the Create Image action according to your specifications. The following describes each option:

▶ Installed Volume is the name of the system image volume. Thus when this image is restored to a Mac, the Mac's system volume will take on this name.

▶ The Save To pop-up menu and Image Name define the location and the name of the resulting network disk folder.

▶ The Network Disk name will be displayed by any interface that allows you to select this image, including the Server Admin application and the Startup Disk preferences.

▶ Image Index is used by the NetBoot service for load balancing purposes, as covered in Chapter 5, "Deploying System Images." If you're not sure what number to use, simply leave the default setting, as this can be easily changed later.

▶   Description is extra text used to describe the contents of the network disk image. This will be displayed in Server Admin.

NOTE ▶ The goal of this section is to show you how to create a modular NetRestore image. At this point you have configured enough of a workflow to accomplish this goal. Should you want to create a more complex workflow you can certainly add more actions. Again, the majority of SIU-related actions are covered in Chapter 5, "Deploying System Images."

9   Optionally, once you have configured your modular image build workflow, click the Save button to save this workflow for future use.

Choosing this option will create a ".workflow" file that can be used in both SIU and Automator. This also places the workflow in the SIU Workflows list to the right for easy access.

Saving a workflow is extremely useful for future image modifications: for example, if you intend to change the contents of your source volume on a regular basis and you need to create updated system images based on your new system volume. You can also save workflows and move them to another Mac or share them with another administrator.

10   When you are ready to create a modular NetRestore image, click the Run button to initiate the creation process.

The build process takes from a few minutes to a few hours, depending on the size of the resulting system image and the speed of your hardware configuration. SIU will show a small spinning gear in the lower-right corner to indicate progress, and you can always click the Stop button to stop the progress. For a more detailed log of the creation process, you can choose View > Show Log.

TIP You may find it beneficial to increase the log level from the SIU preferences to gather more information during the build process.

Updating a Modular NetRestore Image

Here is where using the modular system workflow really pays off. To update your image, simply specify new or updated system source or installation packages and then have SIU build a new image for you. If you saved your previous SIU workflow, updates are even easier because you already have a starting point for your new build. This new image will be exactly the same as the previous system image for the items that you have not updated or changed. Thus, updating a modular system image generally requires much less work than updating a cloned system image.

Further, because in this workflow all your additions and updates take the form of installation packages, you can easily update systems that are already deployed. Using a tool such as Apple Remote Desktop you can distribute these new installation packages to your deployed systems. Once updated, your deployed systems should have nearly the same system configuration as your new modular system image.

What You've Learned

▶ When defining requirements for a system image, you must take into consideration user requirements, computer-specific requirements, software update requirements, and the pros and cons of using a unified system image.

▶ Mac OS X's managed preferences architecture is a more flexible alternative to including configuration settings in your system images.

▶ You can create a deployable Mac OS X system image by cloning a model system that you have already configured. The clone process can be performed manually with Disk Utility or automated with System Image Utility (SIU).

▶ You can use SIU to build a cleaner and easier-to-update system image by using prebuilt and custom installation packages.

References

You can check for new and updated Knowledge Base documents at www.apple.com/support.

Mac OS X Installation Troubleshooting

▶ HT2186, "Don't install older versions of Mac OS than what comes with your computer"

▶ HT2681, "What's a 'Computer-Specific Mac OS X Release?'"

▶ HT1159, "Mac OS X versions (builds) included with Intel-based Macs"

▶ TS1394, "Mac OS X: Troubleshooting installation and software updates"

▶ HT2956, "Troubleshooting Mac OS X installation from CD or DVD"

▶ HT2632, "Mac OS X: Troubleshooting the Mac OS X Installer"

Web Resources

▶ Apple System Imaging and Software Update Administration guide, http://images. apple.com/server/macosx/docs/System_Imaging_and_SW_Update_Admin_v10.6.pdf

▶ Mac OS X v10.6 system requirements, www.apple.com/macosx/specs.html

▶ Mac OS X Server v10.6 system requirements, www.apple.com/server/macosx/specs.html

▶ Apple Software Updates, www.apple.com/downloads/macosx/apple

▶ Apple Server Admin Tools v10.6 download, http://support.apple.com/kb/DL914

▶ DiskWarrior by Alsoft volume structure repair tool, www.alsoft.com/DiskWarrior/index.html

▶ Mac OS X automation resources, www.macosxautomation.com

▶ InstaDMG modular system image tool, www.afp548.com

▶ InstaDMG support forum, www.afp548.com/forum/index.php?forum=45

Review Quiz

1. What is the minimum version of Mac OS X supported by a new Mac computer?

2. What two methods can be used to create a Mac OS X v10.6 system disk image suitable for deployment?

3. What are the benefits of each system image creation method?

4. What is the underlying format of Mac OS X's preference management system?

5. What is a preference manifest?

6. What three methods can be used for creating a cloned system image?

7. Which files should be removed prior to creating a cloned system image?

8. What Mac OS X v10.6 utility is used to create network disk images? Where can this utility be found? What is the minimum version of Mac OS X supported by this utility?

9. What two sources can be used to create a network disk image?

10. What are the differences between NetBoot, NetInstall, and NetRestore images?

11. What is Automator? What is an Automator action? What is an Automator workflow?

12. How can Automator facilitate network disk image creation?

13. What is the primary SIU action required for creating network disk images? What other SIU action is almost always required?

14. Aside from SIU, how else can you access actions used to create network disk images?

15. What are the specific steps for building a modular system image using SIU?

Answers

1. The minimum version of Mac OS X supported by a new Mac computer is the version that it shipped with from the factory.

2. The two methods that can be used to create a Mac OS X v10.6 system disk image suitable for deployment are a cloned system image created by setting up a model computer and then copying the system to a disk image, and a modular system image built by applying multiple installation packages to a disk image.

3. Cloned system images offer an easier workflow for novice administrators and require less time to create the initial system image. Modular system images offer these benefits: system images are clean because they have never been booted; system images have no model-specific settings; Apple updates won't interfere with customizations because updates are always applied prior to customizations; this method decreases your workload when creating multiple system images that require unique software and configurations; this method decreases your workload when updating system images; multiple and updated system images are perfectly consistent for similar items every single time; all configurations are fully documented and easily audited; this method requires simplified testing for updates and image modifications; this method is easily automated; and this method is easily integrated with system maintenance workflows and third-party deployment tools.

4. Mac OS X's managed preferences system uses XML formatted key and value data stored in any source supported by Mac OS X directory services.

5. A preference manifest describes the contents of the customizable settings of an application or system process. Preference manifests can be imported into Workgroup Manager to provide a template for custom managed preferences settings.

6. Cloned system images can be created in the graphical interface using Disk Utility, in the command line using `diskutil` and `asr`, or by creating a NetRestore image with System Image Utility.

7. Before creating a cloned system image, you should remove user-specific files, computer-specific files, and cache files that could cause problems when deployed to other systems.

8. System Image Utility (SIU) in Mac OS X v10.6 is used to create Mac OS X v10.6 and Mac OS X Server v10.6 network disk images. The minimum version of Mac OS X supported is version 10.6. Mac OS X v10.5 is supported by SIU in Mac OS X v10.5.

9. Two sources for network disk images are the original Mac OS X installation media or nonbooted system volumes. Mounted disk images containing either are also supported, though SIU won't treat them any differently.

10. NetBoot images start up to a full version of Mac OS X, NetInstall images start up to the Mac OS X system installer, and NetRestore images start up to an installer that will restore a system image.

11. Automator is an application that allows you to automate repetitive application tasks. Automator actions present small graphical interfaces that enable you to perform a very specific automated task in a specific application. By combining multiple Automator actions into an ordered list, you can build an Automator workflow that can be used to perform a repetitive task.

12. SIU includes Automator actions that can be used to create custom workflow-generated network disk images, which can be used to automate system deployment tasks.

13. The primary required SIU action for creating a workflow-generated network disk image is Create Image, which must be the last action in the SIU workflow. The Define Image Source action must be the first SIU action for nearly every type of SIU workflow except any workflow that starts with the Define NetRestore Source action.

14. The Automator application also has access to the SIU actions. These actions can be found in the System section of the Automator action library. Using Automator to build workflows allows you to integrate SIU actions with other Automator actions.

15. Within SIU you can build a modular image by creating an Automator workflow that includes at a minimum: the Define Image Source action that specifies the source as the Mac OS X installation media; the Add Packages and Post-Install Scripts action that has been configured to install additional items; and finally the Create Image action that has been configured to create a NetRestore image.

5

Chapter **5**

Deploying System Images

This chapter focuses on the two main Apple system deployment technologies: Apple Software Restore and NetBoot. Apple Software Restore is a highly optimized volume duplication service that can quickly deploy an entire system to a Mac's internal drive in minutes, but there's a catch. Your Mac needs to already be running Mac OS X to take advantage of Apple Software Restore. This "chicken before the egg" situation can be remedied by providing a temporary Mac OS X system long enough to perform the system restoration. You can accomplish this with a locally attached system drive, but a much more flexible approach is to leverage a shared network operating system. Enter NetBoot.

Mac OS X Server has always been able to provide full network-based operating systems to Mac clients using NetBoot. The obvious advantage of NetBoot is that you can provide a unified operating system to all your deployed Macs without a physical delivery mechanism such as optical media or external drives. However, although you could choose to always use an entirely network-based operating system, this can be an inefficient use of your resources and doesn't provide optimal performance. After all, every Mac ships with a relatively large and fast internal drive.

Since then Apple has introduced NetInstall and NetRestore, which are network disk images optimized for network system deployment. With these new additions the NetBoot service fills the role of a complete deployment solution spectacularly by allowing you to configure a custom system, available from your network, that can perform your entire deployment workflow with little or no user interaction.

Understanding System Image Deployment

Deploying system images is, relative to creating them, quick and easy. This, of course, is the point of system deployment; your goal is to deploy this system image as quickly as possible to your computers.

In this section you will learn how to use the Apple Software Restore (ASR) system to restore system images to local volumes. The term "restore" is used here to mean the process by which you copy the contents of a system disk image to a bootable system volume. Note that this section focuses specifically on individual system restore techniques, which will be demonstrated as if you were restoring to a single volume. Scaling out these techniques to all your computers simply means repeating the restoration workflow over and over again for each computer. This type of automation is easily handled using a script or a remote management tool such as Apple Remote Desktop (ARD).

Apple Software Restore Fundamentals

The ASR process is essentially a highly optimized volume duplication system. When restoring locally, the *source* can be a disk image prepared for deployment or any mounted Mac OS–formatted volume, including volumes that reside on external drives, optical media, and nonprepared disk images. Thus, you could actually use the ASR restore mechanism to make perfect clones from one volume to another. The only source requirement is that the ASR restore process must be able to unmount and copy the volume. This limits you to source volumes that are not currently being used as a startup disk.

The restore *destination* volume can be any nonoptical storage device mounted locally to the Mac running the restore process. This includes any nonsystem volumes on a partitioned drive, volumes on external drives, and even volumes that reside in read/write disk images. The only destination requirement is that the ASR process must be able to unmount and replace the volume's contents. Again, this requirement is why you cannot restore to a volume that is currently being used as a startup disk.

The size of your restore destination is also a consideration. Obviously, the restore process works only if your destination volume is as large or larger than the source volume contents. If the destination volume is larger, the ASR process will simply leave the remaining volume space as is. The exception to this is when restoring at the device level. The ASR process can also restore or clone an entire storage device, including all partitions, to another device. This technique is rarely used because the ASR process will have to reformat the destination device with the exact same partition scheme as the source device. Thus, the destination device must always be as large or larger than the source device, and any extra space on the destination device will not be formatted.

ASR uses two methods for duplicating a volume. The most commonly used one is erase and copy. With this method the ASR process completely erases the destination volume and performs a very fast block-level copy. This method is often ten times faster than the alternative, and it always results in the "cleanest" system restore.

However, if you need to retain the contents of the destination volume, you can perform a file copy. With this method the ASR process copies the items one at a time, replacing any items on the destination volume with the items from the source volume. It's important to realize that the ASR process does not consider the age or version of individual items and will replace all items on the destination volume with a similar item from the source volume.

Finally, ASR can perform a verification of the restore. The verification process ensures that your restore or clone was fully completed without error to the destination. It does this by comparing the destination to the source. This verification adds to the amount of time it takes to complete the ASR restoration process, but it guarantees an error-free restoration or clone.

System Deployment Scenarios

Consider the three basic requirements for deploying a system using ASR; you must be running Mac OS X, the source volume must be unmountable, and the destination volume must be unmountable. Given this, there are a variety of deployment solutions that you can consider:

▶ Target disk mode "push"—If you have an additional Mac with built-in FireWire and a FireWire cable, you can place the destination Mac in FireWire target disk mode. Enable target disk mode either in the Startup Disk system preference or by holding down the T key during startup. Then plug the destination Mac into another Mac with access to your system image. You will be able to "push" restore the entire system image to the destination Mac in a matter of minutes.

▶ Large external system drive—If you don't have a spare Mac handy, you can install a copy of Mac OS X to an external FireWire or USB drive and simply start from the external drive. This drive would also contain your system images, which you would then restore to the internal drive of the Mac. Further, you can install additional administrative and maintenance tools on this external drive and create a portable Mac toolkit for all your local system administration needs.

▶ Small external system drive—The Mac OS X Install DVD includes the ASR restore mechanism and both Ethernet and AirPort networking drivers. Simply boot your Mac from the installation media and restore from a system image shared on a network server. Further, if you find carrying around the installation media inconvenient, you could clone the install media to a USB flash drive.

> **TIP** ▶ You can also use the install media to clone the internal system drive from one Mac, booted from the DVD, to the internal system drive of another Mac in target disk mode.

▶ Network Disk—The only solution that doesn't require any local system is to use a network disk image hosted from a NetBoot server. This solution is the most scalable, as you don't have to carry around any extra drives or media, and is the primary focus of this chapter.

Apple Predelivery Deployment for New Macs

As an alternative to deploying your custom system image to new Mac computers, you can have the Apple Custom Software Solutions (CSS) team do the work for you. The Apple CSS team can deploy a customer's system image to new Macs at the factory. They can also assist with a customer's asset tracking by applying custom asset tags at the factory and providing an asset report upon delivery.

This complimentary service is available for new Mac orders of 75 units or more. For orders between 75 and 200 units, the CSS team will accept a customer-submitted image for deployment. For orders of more than 200 units, the CSS team will work with the customer to create a modular system image deployment solution. This modular solution allows the customer to pick and choose software components for future new Macs using a dedicated website portal.

The CSS team will thoroughly test either system image type to make sure all software and configurations work properly. Once the customer signs off on a fully tested system image, he is given a custom Apple part number to order from. Any time the customer orders that part number, the CSS team will deploy the custom system image to the new Mac hardware at the factory before the computer is shipped.

> **MORE INFO** ▶ You can find out more about Apple CSS by contacting your Apple account executive or calling the general Apple sales number 1-800-MY-APPLE (800-692-7753) and asking to be connected with the appropriate sales account executive.

Restore System Images Locally

For very small deployments, or the occasional reimaging of a repaired computer, nothing beats the speed and simplicity of restoring your system image locally. Regardless of the equipment setup or local startup method you choose, you can access the Apple Software Restore (ASR) system from either the graphical interface using the Disk Utility application or at the command line using the asr tool.

Using ASR Locally from the Disk Utility Application

To use ASR locally from the Disk Utility application:

1   Open the Disk Utility application, select any storage item from the list on the left, and then click the Restore tab. The storage item you select from the list has no relation to the items you will choose for the restore process.

2   From the Finder or the Disk Utility item list, drag a source volume or prepared disk image to the Source field. You can also click the Image button to select a disk image from an Open browser dialog.

MORE INFO ▶ Note that for the source you can also specify a URI referencing a restore image hosted from a share. This supports images stored on a web server (http://) or a multicast ASR server (asr://). These network restore options will be covered later in the "Deploying Systems with NetInstall and NetRestore" section of this chapter.

3   From the Disk Utility item list, drag a destination volume to the Destination field.

4   Optionally, you can disable the Erase Destination option.

This feature is enabled by default because it uses a much faster block-level copy. However, if you can't completely erase the volume, ASR will use the slower file copy method.

NOTE ▶ ASR verification is enabled by default when using Disk Utility and cannot be disabled.

5   Once you have set the source and destination, click the Restore button to start the ASR process.

6   In the verification dialog box that appears, click Erase, and then authenticate as an administrative user.

The ASR system will unmount the destination and source volume if one was specified and begin the restore or clone process. Disk Utility will show you a progress indicator in the lower-right corner, and when ASR is complete will remount the destination volume. When a source volume, as opposed to a prepared disk image, is used, the source will be remounted as well.

Using ASR Locally from the Command Line

You can directly access the ASR system by using the asr command. The syntax is asr restore -source followed by the path to the source volume or prepared disk image, then -target followed by the path to the destination volume, and then any options such as -erase or -noverify.

In the following example, Michelle uses the asr command to restore a prepared disk image on her desktop, ModularSystem.dmg, to the Macintosh HD volume. Note that she has to run the asr command with root access and that she has specified the faster erase and block-level copy method. Also, because she chose the erase method, she was prompted to enter a "y" to validate her option; if she had entered the -noprompt option this safeguard would have been bypassed.

```
MyMac:~ michelle$ sudo asr restore -source Desktop/ModularSystem.dmg -target
/Volumes/Macintosh\ HD/ -erase
Password: (passowrd not shown)
 Validating target...done
 Validating source...done
 Erase contents of /dev/disk1s10 (/Volumes/Macintosh HD)? [ny]: y
 Erasing target device /dev/disk1s10...done
 Retrieving scan information...done
 Validating sizes...done
 Restoring ....10....20....30....40....50....60....70....80....90....100
 Verifying ....10....20....30....40....50....60....70....80....90....100
 Remounting target volume...done
```

Understanding the NetBoot Service

The NetBoot service essentially allows you to boot a Mac computer via the network using a system image hosted on another computer running Mac OS X Server. Multiple network clients can use this network disk image simultaneously, allowing you to deliver an identical operating system to all the computers you choose on your network, thus providing an ideal platform for system deployment tasks.

NetBoot Service Requirements

The requirements for NetBoot to function properly depend on the version of your network disk images and scale of your deployment. If your network disk images contain Mac OS X v10.6 or Mac OS X v10.6 Server, the client Macs must meet the minimum system requirements for that software. However, a Mac OS X v10.6 Server can host network disk images containing system software all the way back to Mac OS v9.2.

> **NOTE ▶** The Mac OS X v10.6 version of System Image Utility will not allow you to create a network disk image for previous versions of Mac OS.

The NetBoot service relies heavily on your computer's built-in firmware to facilitate network startup, so you must also make sure your Mac clients are updated to the latest firmware. The NetBoot service included with Mac OS X v10.6 Server supports older PowerPC-based computers as long as they have Macintosh firmware version 4.1.7 or later. To check the version of a computer's firmware locally, go to /Applications/Utilities/System Profiler; remotely, use the report-gathering feature of Apple Remote Desktop (ARD), as covered in Chapter 7, "System Maintenance."

To use NetBoot with any version of Mac OS X, client Macs must have a minimum of 512 MB of RAM and 100Base-T built-in Ethernet or faster network connections. At the time of this writing, there are a few exceptions to this rule. Some newer Mac computers, including the MacBook Air, have updated firmware that allows NetBoot service access using an external Apple USB Ethernet adapter or built-in AirPort. You can tell if your Mac supports NetBoot via AirPort if, when you start up holding down the Option key, you can select a wireless network to scan for network disks.

From an infrastructure perspective, there are no theoretical capacity limits for NetBoot at this time. Rather, NetBoot capacity planning is based on network speed and server performance. The total number of supportable NetBoot clients varies with network speeds and reliability. NetBoot deployments between 10 to 50 clients require 100Base-T-switched networking. Gigabit Ethernet is required to use the NetBoot service with 50 or more, although Apple has no official test results for configurations beyond 50 clients.

> **NOTE** ▶ Apple does not support the use of multiple bonded Ethernet ports on NetBoot clients.

Finally, the reliability and performance of your NetBoot deployment is directly affected by your network and NetBoot server configuration. This topic is covered in the "Optimizing NetBoot Performance" section later in this chapter.

Network Disk Image Contents

As covered in Chapter 4, "Creating System Images," the NetBoot service uses network disk images created with the System Image Utility (SIU) application. Network disk images are similar to regular system disk images but with a few key differences. Network disk images are actually bundles, which contain a system image file along with the additional items required by the NetBoot service. These network disk image bundles are easily identified by the .nbi filename extension.

The contents of a Mac OS X v10.6 network disk image bundle include:

▶ A NetBoot property list file named NBImageInfo.plist that contains most of the configuration settings for the network disk image. This file is created and modified using the server administration tools, but as with any property list file, you can also manually edit this file. This file is detailed in the "Monitoring and Troubleshooting the NetBoot Service" section later in this chapter.

▶ A read/write disk image containing the full system volume that will be used by the NetBoot service clients. This disk image is usually named "NetBoot.dmg" for standard NetBoot images or "NetInstall.dmg" for NetInstall or NetRestore images. However, it can be named anything as specified by the NBImageInfo.plist file. By default, standard NetBoot system images can be easily modified by simply mounting the volume and making changes.

> **NOTE ▶** Never modify an active network disk system image. Also, you should not apply full system "point" updates to a network disk system image, because that will not update the NetBoot startup files that are saved outside the system image volume.

▶ A folder named i386 containing the fundamental core system files required to initiate the Mac OS X startup process on Intel-based Macs. This folder includes the system booter, the 32-bit Mac OS X kernel "mach.macosx," and a 32-bit driver cache "mach.macosx.mkext." The "x86_64" folder contains similar items for booting Mac OS X in 64-bit kernel mode.

▶ Older network disk images will have a folder named ppc, containing the fundamental core system files required to initiate the Mac OS X startup process on PowerPC-based Macs. This folder contains items similar to those in the i386 folder but specific to PowerPC-based Macs. If there are no folders, then the image is assumed to be an older image for PowerPC-based Macs.

NetBoot Startup Process

When a client computer is tasked with starting from a network disk image, it performs a number of steps that are considerably different from the standard Mac OS X startup routine:

1. The client places a request for TCP/IP address information. When a Mac NetBoot client is turned on or restarted, it requests TCP/IP address information from a Dynamic Host Configuration Protocol (DHCP) server, via UDP port 67.

    NOTE ▶ The server providing the DHCP service can be the same server providing the NetBoot service, but the two do not have to be provided by the same device.

2. After receiving TCP/IP address information, the NetBoot client sends out a request for startup software using the Boot Service Discovery Protocol (BSPD), via UDP ports 67. The NetBoot server responds to the client with the information necessary to initiate the boot process.

3. The NetBoot server delivers the core system files (booter and kernel files) to the client using Trivial File Transfer Protocol (TFTP) via UDP port 69.

4. Once the client has started the core system, it can initiate a network mount and load the remainder of the operating system from the network disk image. The images can be served using Hypertext Transfer Protocol (HTTP) via TCP port 80 or network file system (NFS) via various TCP/UDP ports.

NOTE ▶ Mac OS 9 NetBoot images are shared using the Apple File Protocol (AFP) via TCP port 548.

After Mac OS X is started from the network disk image, the client again requests TCP/IP address information from the DHCP server. Depending on the type of DHCP server used, the NetBoot client might receive an IP address different from the one received in the first step.

When you start a client computer from a network disk image, the client computer uses a read-only version of the original system volume. Users cannot store documents or preserve preferences on this system volume because it's mounted as a read-only volume. When the Mac needs to write anything back to its startup volume, the NetBoot service automatically redirects the written data to the client's shadow files (covered in the following section). Data in shadow files is only retained for the duration of a NetBoot session. By using these temporary shadow files, the NetBoot service guarantees that your Macs always start from a clean image.

NetBoot Shadow Files and Diskless Mode

Many clients can read from the same network disk image, but when a client system needs to write anything (such as print spools, browser caches, and other temporary files) back to its startup volume, the NetBoot service automatically redirects the written data to the client's *shadow file*. These shadow files are separate from regular system and application software files, and they preserve the unique identity of each client during the entire time the client is running off a network disk image. The NetBoot service also transparently maintains changed user data in the shadow files, while reading any unchanged data from the system image. The shadow files are re-created at each startup, so any changes that the user makes to the startup volume are lost at restart.

This behavior preserves the condition of the environment the administrator set up when creating the network disk image, which is ideal in lab and kiosk situations where you want to ensure that users never alter the startup volume. If you're using the NetBoot service for deployment purposes only, this is also an ideal approach, as your NetBoot system is only there to act as a conduit for your deployment mechanism and shouldn't be modified by the client computer.

This behavior has other important implications, however. For example, if a user saves a document to the startup volume, after a restart that document is gone. However, this potential problem can be remedied with network-based user accounts; then when network-based users log in, they can store documents and preserve preferences in their network home folders.

The shadow files' default location also presents a problem in some NetBoot deployment scenarios. By default, for the best performance, the NetBoot shadow files are stored on the client computer's local internal drive in /private/var/netboot/.com.apple.NetBootX. Because this folder, and the volume it resides on, are used by the NetBoot system, you cannot perform any meaningful system deployment tasks on the computer's local internal drive.

This is why NetInstall and NetRestore images use virtual RAM disks to store temporary shadow files. This leaves the Mac's local drive free for deployment tasks. To resolve this issue for standard NetBoot images, the NetBoot service supports a diskless booting mode wherein the shadow files are stored on an AFP share point hosted from the NetBoot server. The shadow file share is named NetBootClients*n* in the /Library/NetBoot folder on your NetBoot server, where *n* is the number of the share point as configured by the Server Admin tool.

NOTE ▶ Diskless booting with standard NetBoot images requires the use of AFP share points, which can present a problem if you purchased the ten-client version of Mac OS X Server, because your license restricts you to supporting no more than ten simultaneous AFP connections.

NOTE ▶ Diskless NetBoot can present a denial-of-service vulnerability, as the NetBoot server must have a guest-writeable AFP share point open. An attacker can fill this share point with large files to consume all available disk space and make the server unusable. To partially mitigate this problem, configure the NetBoot service so that the client data is stored on a volume other than the boot volume.

With diskless booting enabled, standard NetBoot images can operate client computers that are literally diskless. This gives you full access to the computer's local internal drive, allowing you to perform deployment, maintenance, or recovery tasks. Further, you can individually select the diskless booting option for each standard NetBoot image, as covered in the "Configuring NetBoot Images" section later in this chapter.

Configuring the NetBoot Service

In this section you will learn how to configure the NetBoot service on a computer with Mac OS X v10.6 Server. These instructions assume you have already installed the server system software, completed the initial server setup, and properly set up the network configuration. They also assume that the DHCP service is available on your network, either from another network device or this Mac server.

Optimizing NetBoot Performance

The NetBoot service, and network-based system deployment in general, is among the most demanding services you can subject your network and servers to. Therefore, before setting up your NetBoot server, you should carefully consider the configuration factors that will affect the overall performance of your NetBoot service.

There are no theoretical client limits for the NetBoot service at this time. Rather, NetBoot performance, and thus useful client capacity, is based on network speed and server configuration. Obviously, the more clients you intend to simultaneously use the NetBoot service, the more resources you will need to devote to hosting NetBoot services. An "underpowered" NetBoot deployment will at best yield consistently poor performance and at worst simply not work at all.

Optimizing Network Performance

Though the NetBoot service supports 100Base-T Ethernet connections for the client computers, an entirely Gigabit Ethernet network should be used for all NetBoot server connections for the best performance.

Apple Xserve, PowerMac, and Mac Pro computers all support multiple Ethernet connections either built in or via additional Ethernet adapters. Thus, to enhance NetBoot service performance, you could attach each Ethernet port on your NetBoot server to separate subnets on your network. Or if you want to use only a single IP address for your NetBoot server, Mac OS X Server supports bonded Ethernet connections using IEEE 802.3ad link aggregation. This setup also requires network switches that support the IEEE 802.3ad standard, but it enables you to effectively multiply the bandwidth of your NetBoot server while maintaining a single IP address.

Optimizing Server Performance

For the best NetBoot performance, you should avoid running other nonrelated services on your NetBoot servers so the NetBoot service won't have to contend with other services sapping resources from your server.

Additionally, the two factors that most affect the NetBoot performance, from a server hardware perspective, are amount of RAM and drive performance. Mac OS X Server will cache as much of the network disk image in system memory as possible, so the more RAM you install in your server, the better.

Further, the drives containing the network disk images can be a limiting factor, so the faster the speed of the drive, the better. At the very least, you should consider placing your network disk images on a different drive than the startup drive. You can also spread the NetBoot workload across multiple drives; for instance, you can use a RAID array to increase drive performance. For even larger deployments you could use Storage Area Network (SAN) hardware with Apple Xsan to provide high-performance shared storage for multiple NetBoot servers. This approach takes advantage of the built-in load-balancing features of the NetBoot service, covered in the following section.

Using NetBoot Service Load Balancing

The NetBoot service includes demand-based load-balancing. This allows you to spread the NetBoot service load across multiple servers, thus providing increased NetBoot performance. Adding more NetBoot servers increases performance more than adding more fast storage to a single server does; however, the latter solution is much less expensive.

> **NOTE ▶** Hosting multiple identical network disk images on the same server does not improve performance as the NetBoot service ignores duplicate images on the same server

> **NOTE ▶** Hosting your network disk images on another partition of the system drive does not improve, and can even reduce, performance.

The goal of load balancing is to make your network disk images available from as many servers as possible. Each network disk image has an image ID, or index value, which client computers use to identify images hosted from NetBoot shares. When a client lists the available network disk images in the Startup Disk preferences, if multiple hosted images have the same index number, the client assumes that the images are identical and displays only one entry. During the startup process, the client will attempt to connect to the least busy NetBoot server to get the best performance.

If a network disk image will be hosted on only a single server, it should be assigned an index value between 1 and 4095. If a network disk image will be hosted on multiple servers, it should be assigned a value between 4096 and 65535. In System Image Utility, when a basic network disk image is created, the specific index number is chosen automatically for you.

> **TIP** You can change the index number of a network disk image in the Server Admin application or when creating a custom network disk image using the System Image Utility application. Techniques for both actions are covered later in this chapter.

If you will be using a large number of diskless NetBoot clients, your NetBoot servers will also have to deal with the additional AFP overhead required for saving the client shadow files. The easiest way to boost performance in this situation is to configure your NetBoot servers to host the client shadow files on a separate drive from the network disk images.

Configuring NetBoot General Settings

Despite the complexity of the NetBoot service, configuring this service on your Mac server is relatively easy. Like all other Mac OS X Server services, NetBoot is configured from the Server Admin application. Server Admin is also located in the /Applications/Server folder on your Mac OS X v10.6 Server computer. In addition, this application can be installed as part of the Server Admin Tools v10.6 on any Mac OS X v10.6 computer.

To configure NetBoot general service settings:

1 Open /Applications/Server/Server Admin, and then connect to your server.

2 If the NetBoot service isn't visible in the left column, you need to add it and the other associated services:

▶ Click the Add (+) button, and then choose Add Service from the pop-up menu.

▶ In the Services pane that appears, make sure the AFP, DHCP, NetBoot, and NFS checkboxes are enabled for configuration, and then click Save.

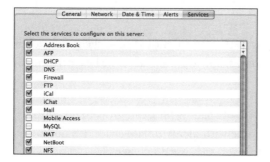

3 In the left column of the Server Admin window, select the NetBoot service, and then click the Settings button in the toolbar.

4 Click the General tab to configure the primary NetBoot service settings.

5 Enable at least one network interface port to host the NetBoot service.

The list of available ports is generated based on the server's current network preferences. If you haven't already configured the appropriate network settings, quit Server Admin without saving and properly configure the server from the Network system preference. Returning to the NetBoot settings will refresh the list of available ports.

6 Enable at least one Images volume to host the network disk images, and enable one Client Data volume to host the diskless shadow files.

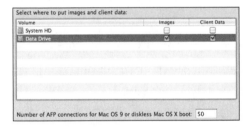

Even if you don't plan on using diskless NetBoot, you must select a client data volume. You can use the same volume for both tasks, but you will realize the best performance by separating the two.

NOTE ▶ NetBoot client data, in the form of shadow files, can grow to be quite large, so make sure to select a client data volume with plenty of free space. It's not uncommon to see shadow files of 1 GB or more for each NetBoot client.

7 Optionally, enter a number to limit or increase the number of AFP connections for Mac OS 9 or diskless NetBoot operations.

The default setting is 50 AFP connections, which can be easily handled by a dedicated Xserve or Mac Pro computer. However, for more taxed server computers you may want to set a lower value, which will force client Macs to another NetBoot server if the value is reached, or if no other server is available, it will prevent the clients from starting at all.

8   When you have made your selections, click Save, but do not click the Start NetBoot button yet.

The Server Admin will now automatically configure all the appropriate NetBoot share points based on your selected volumes. However, these share points are empty by default. You will need to copy your network disk images into the appropriate locations and configure the image settings, as described next.

Configuring NetBoot Images

In the preceding section, you configured the general NetBoot service settings, which should have created the appropriate NetBoot share points. You can verify your NetBoot configuration by viewing your server's share points in Server Admin:

1   In the left column of the Server Admin window, select your server name.

2   In the toolbar, click the File Sharing button.

3   Click the Share Points button.

For every volume that you selected to host network disk images, a shared folder is created on that volume at /Library/NetBoot/NetBootSPn, where n is a number assigned automatically based on the volume order in Server Admin. For every volume that you selected to host NetBoot client data, or shadow files, a shared folder is created on that volume at /Library/NetBoot/NetBootClients$n$, where again n is an automatically assigned number.

To host your network disk images on your servers, you must first copy the images to the appropriate NetBoot share points. You can use the Finder or the command line to copy your network disk image bundles to the correct locations. If you're copying network disk images from a client to your server, it's best to use an AFP connection. Remember that if you're going to use multiple NetBoot share points or servers, you will need to copy your network disk images into each NetBootSPn folder on all configured volumes and servers.

NOTE ▶ Make sure to copy the entire network disk image bundle to each share point.

Although you can attempt to host as many network disk images as you want, Mac OS X v10.6 Server is limited based on the length of image names. This is because the UDP packet sent to clients for NetBoot service discovery has a limited size. If you are using net-work disks with long names, then you will be limited to less available network disks. Thus, using shorter names allows you to host more network disk images.

In Server Admin each image can be individually enabled, allowing client computers to use the image, or each image can be disabled, preventing client computers from accessing the image. Although you can host several images, you must specify one of the network disk images as the default image. When you press the N key on a client computer at startup, if the client has never started from that NetBoot server before, the server will provide the selected default image to start the client.

After you have copied your network disk images to the NetBoot share points, you can configure and enable the images:

1 Open Server Admin, and then connect to your server.

2 Select the NetBoot service from the left column, and then click the Settings button in the toolbar.

3 Click the Images tab to configure your network disk images.

   Server Admin scans all the NetBoot share points and creates a list of available network disk images. The Image Name, Description, Index value, Architecture, Protocol, and Description were originally set in System Image Utility.

4 To make an image available to your clients, select the Enable checkbox.

5   Optionally, you can make any single image the default image by selecting the appropriate button.

Only one image can be the default network disk image.

NOTE ▶ If you're going to set a default image, make sure to set it similarly on every NetBoot server.

NOTE ▶ Use caution when setting a NetInstall or NetRestore image as your default image, as users may accidentally access this image. Depending on what your network disk image is configured to do, a user may end up erasing important data.

6   Optionally, you can set any standard NetBoot image to use diskless mode. Remember, NetInstall and NetRestore images don't need diskless mode, so the option will be grayed out.

7   Optionally, you can change a network disk image's Index value by double-clicking it in the image list.

Remember, images with an index value between 4096 and 65535 will appear only once to client Macs, even when hosted from multiple NetBoot servers.

8   Optionally, from the Architecture pop-up menu, you can limit a network disk image to either PowerPC- or Intel-based Macs. By default, all Mac OS X v10.6 images only support Intel-based Macs.

9   Optionally, from the Protocol pop-up menu, you can set a Mac OS X network disk image to be hosted using either the NFS or HTTP protocol. You cannot adjust Mac OS 9 network disk images in this respect, because they must use the AFP protocol.

NFS continues to be the default, and the preferred method, for Mac OS X network disk images. HTTP is an alternative that enables you to serve disk images without having to reconfigure your firewall to allow NFS traffic.

10   After you have made your selections, click Save, but do not click the Start NetBoot button yet.

At this point your server should be ready to start hosting the NetBoot service, as covered in the next section.

Starting the NetBoot Service

After you have configured your server's general NetBoot settings and network disk image settings, you can start the NetBoot service.

1   Click the Start NetBoot button.

Server Admin automatically configures and starts all services required by your NetBoot configuration, even those services that you would normally configure separately. At the very least, your NetBoot server will respond to BSPD queries via the DHCP service. Depending on your enabled NetBoot images, your server will also start NFS, AFP, and HTTP services.

2   To verify that these services are running, select the NetBoot service, and then click the Overview button in the toolbar.

You should be able to make a change to your server's NetBoot configuration without restarting the service. However, if the settings don't appear to take, you may need to stop the NetBoot service, make and save your changes, and then restart it. This will ensure that all the appropriate services have been reset based on your new configuration.

Stopping the NetBoot service will never disable NFS, AFP, or HTTP services. This is a precautionary measure should you be hosting other resources from these related services on the same server. Stopping the NetBoot service will disable only the BSPD service, so clients still won't be able to start from your server; however, the NetBoot shares will remain available on the network. Thus, you will have to manually stop all these services, or disable the shares from the NetBoot general settings, should you want to completely disable the NetBoot shares.

> **NOTE ▶** It's always a wise choice to thoroughly test your network disk images on a private network before you make them available to the general network population. You can also apply NetBoot filters, as covered in the following section, to prevent unwanted access to the new images before they have been fully tested.

Configuring NetBoot Filter Settings

NetBoot filtering removes the risk of accidentally allowing non-NetBoot clients to access unlicensed applications or to perform an unnecessary installation. By maintaining accurate filter settings, you can seamlessly integrate NetBoot into traditional network configurations without having to worry about accidental use. Furthermore, Mac OS X v10.5 Server introduced the ability to set NetBoot filters on a per-image basis. Per-image filtering can be particularly useful if you have one server for multiple departments. Each department can have its own network disk image, and you can use per-image filters to limit which departments can access which image.

Mac OS X v10.6 Server provides three types of network disk filtering:

▶ General NetBoot and DHCP filtering—From the NetBoot Filter pane, you can define an allow or deny list for all NetBoot and DHCP requests. This filter identifies a specific Mac based on its built-in Ethernet, or MAC, address.

▶ Per-image model property filtering—For each network disk image, you can define an allow list for specific Mac models. This filter identifies a specific model of Mac based on its system identifier.

▶ Per-image hardware address filtering—For each network disk image, you can define an allow or deny list. This filter also identifies a specific Mac based on its built-in Ethernet or hardware address.

Configuring NetBoot and DHCP Filtering

To configure general NetBoot and DHCP filtering:

1 Open Server Admin, and then connect to your server.

2 Select the NetBoot service from the left column, and then click the Settings button in the toolbar.

3 Click the Filters tab.

4 Select the "Enable NetBoot/DHCP filtering" checkbox, and then choose the appropriate button to define an allow or deny list.

5   Add Ethernet hardware addresses to the list in any of these ways:

▶   Manually add or delete hardware address entries from the list using the Add (+) or Delete (–) buttons at the bottom of the list.

▶   Let Server Admin attempt to resolve a computer's hardware address from its host name. Enter a host name, and then click the Find button; if the hardware address is resolved, click the Add (+) button to add it to your filter list.

▶   Import a text file containing a tab-delimited list of hardware addresses. Click the Choose button to select the text file, and then click the Extract button to import the addresses into the filter list.

6   Once you have defined your list, click Save, and then restart the NetBoot service if it were running while you were making changes.

Configuring Per-Image NetBoot Filtering

To configure per-image NetBoot filtering:

1   Open Server Admin, and then connect to your server.

2   Select the NetBoot service from the left column, and then click the Settings button in the toolbar.

3   Click the Images tab.

4 Select a network disk image from the list, and then click the small pencil button at the bottom of the images pane.

A dialog appears, allowing you to set the Mac model or Ethernet hardware address filtering.

5 To filter based on the Mac model, click the "Allow only computers below" button. From the Model list, select checkboxes next to the Mac computer models that will be allowed to access the selected network disk image.

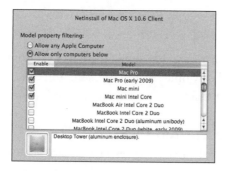

NOTE ► All Mac OS X v10.6 network disk images are set to allow only Intel-based Macs to boot from the images.

6 To filter based on Ethernet hardware addresses, select the appropriate button to define an allow or deny list, and then add Ethernet hardware addresses to the list in either of the following ways:

► Manually add or delete hardware address entries from the list using the Add (+) or Delete (–) buttons at the right of the list.

► Import a text file containing a tab-delimited list of hardware addresses. Click the Select button (...) to the right of the list, and then select the text file.

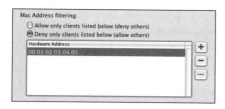

7 Once you have defined your per-image filters, click OK to dismiss the dialog, and then click Save. Restart the NetBoot service if it was running while you were making changes.

The easiest way to test your NetBoot filters is to use the Startup Disk system preference on your blocked or allowed Mac clients, as covered in the next section. If a Mac has been blocked due to a NetBoot filter setting, the image will not appear as an option in the Startup Disk preferences.

Configuring Clients to NetBoot

Supported Mac models already include built-in firmware that allows them to start from your NetBoot service, so you don't need to install any other special software. You can choose from several methods to make your client Macs start from your NetBoot service.

Setting a Network Disk Image as the Startup Disk

The most familiar method is to open the Startup Disk preferences on a local Mac client. Every time you open this, it will send out a BSPD request and automatically discover any available network disk images. This interface will show all three image types—NetBoot, NetInstall, and NetRestore images—with unique icons to help users differentiate between the three types of images. With the desired network disk image selected, you can reboot the computer. The computer then attempts to use the selected network disk image on every subsequent startup. However, a network disk images can be designed to automatically change the startup disk back to internal system volume, which is the case for successfully completing a NetInstall or NetRestore.

If you need to change the startup disk for multiple Mac clients, you can use Apple
Remote Desktop (ARD). Within the Remote Desktop administrator application, select a
group of Macs, and then choose Manage > Set Startup Disk. The Set Startup Disk interface will automatically discover available network disk images and present them in a list.
Select the desired network disk image, and then click the Set button to have ARD send
that setting to the specified Mac clients. Similar to using the Startup Disk preferences,
the computer will attempt to use the selected network disk image on every subsequent
startup until reconfigured.

When your Mac has been configured to start from a NetBoot server, during startup
you will see a blinking globe icon indicating that it's attempting to establish a connection to the NetBoot server. Once the Mac has connected to the server and has begun
the Mac OS X startup process, you will see the dark gray Apple logo in the center of the
screen. At the bottom of the screen, you will also see a dark gray spinning globe logo indicating that the NetBoot startup process is continuing.

Selecting NetBoot at Startup

You can temporarily select the default network disk image for a local Mac during startup:

▶ While starting a Mac, hold down the N key or Option-N key combination on the
   keyboard. Holding down the N key will connect the last booted network disk image
   (if previously selected), while holding down Option-N will always boot to the default
   network disk image. Your client computer will then boot from the default network
   disk image hosted by the NetBoot server. This method allows you to use NetBoot

for a single startup. Subsequent restarts will return the computer to the previously selected startup state, unless the startup disk was changed while the client was running from the network disk image.

▶   While starting a Mac, hold down the Option key on the keyboard. This invokes the Startup Manager, which presents an icon list of available system folders, as well as a globe icon for NetBoot. Click the globe icon, and then click the advance arrow to begin the NetBoot process. The default network disk image will appear, set for only a single startup.

> **NOTE ▶** At the time of this writing, some newer Intel Macs have the ability to select a specific network disk from the firmware Startup Manager. This feature is not widespread at the moment and varies from Mac model to model.

Accessing NetBoot Across Subnets

For larger networks you may need to set a Mac client to access a NetBoot server on a different subnet or network. BSDP requests, like DHCP requests, are not normally broadcast beyond the local subnet, so if you're regularly going to be accessing NetBoot services across subnets, your network administrator will need to forward BSDP broadcast traffic between subnets. This is the same configuration for using DHCP across your network.

You can also specify a particular NetBoot server and image. However, when you specify a specific server, the NetBoot service cannot automatically load balance demand. Once you set a Mac client for a specific NetBoot server and image, it will always attempt to start from that image no matter how busy the server is. For this reason you will usually be best served by forwarding BSDP broadcast traffic.

However, if modifying your network configuration is not possible, you can specify a specific NetBoot server and image using any one of the following methods:

▶   At the command line on a local Mac enter the `bless` command to set a specific NetBoot server. For example, if you were going to set a Mac to start from the default image on the NetBoot server atv10.1.17.1 you would enter:

```
sudo bless --netboot --server bsdp://10.1.17.1
```

> **MORE INFO ▶** You can use the `bless` command to set a specific network disk image on Intel-based Macs. To find out more about this command, read the built-in manual page at the command line. Mike Bombich also hosts an excellent article about use of this command for NetBoot operations across subnets at www.bombich.com/mactips/nbas.html.

▶ Use ARD to set a specific NetBoot server and image for multiple Mac clients. From the Remote Desktop administrator application, open the Set Startup Disk interface and click the Custom Volume entry. This reveals a dialog allowing you to enter a specific server IP address in the Server Address field and a specific network disk image name in the Network Volume field. You must enter the image name exactly as it appears in the network disk Images list in Server Admin.

▶ Use the third-party NetBoot Across Subnets application from Bombich Software. Again, you can find out more about this at www.bombich.com/mactips/nbas.html.

▶ Enable *bootpd* service relay from a Mac system on local networks. Any Mac OS X system can be configured to relay *bootpd* request across subnets. This allows you to host all your network disk images on a central server, then use relay services to direct all requests from remote networks to this server. For more information read the *bootpd* manual page.

NetBoot Startup Caveats

Even after you set a Mac to start from a NetBoot server, several factors can upset the process:

▶ If no network connection exists, a NetBoot client will eventually time out and attempt to start from the local drive. To prevent this, keep local drives free of system software and deny users physical access to the Ethernet ports on a computer.

▶ Any administrative user with access to the Startup Disk preferences can choose a different startup disk. To prevent this, allow only normal user accounts or disallow the Startup Disk preferences using managed preference settings.

▶ By default, any user can subvert the selected startup disk by holding down one of the startup modifier keys. To block this action, set a firmware password on each Mac client.

▶ A user could start up from another system volume, such as the Mac OS X Install DVD, and change the startup disk. A user could also reset the non-volatile memory (NVRAM), which resets the configured startup disk, requiring you to reselect the network disk image. Again, to block this action set a firmware password.

Monitoring and Troubleshooting the NetBoot Service

As one of the more established Mac OS X services, NetBoot is generally highly reliable, and most NetBoot issues stem from improper configuration. When troubleshooting is needed it starts, as usual, with collecting information through monitoring mechanisms.

Monitoring the NetBoot Service

You can monitor NetBoot client usage with Server Admin. With the NetBoot service selected, click the Clients button in the toolbar to reveal a list of client computers that have booted from the server. Note that this is a cumulative list, or a list of all the clients that have connected to the server, not just a list of currently connected computers. By selecting a given computer in the list, you can also see additional information about that client, such as its system type, client name, the name and index of the network disk image it started up from, and the last time it booted.

Additionally, you can monitor the current NetBoot service connections by selecting the Connections icon in the toolbar. The connections list will also show real-time status of any NetInstall and NetRestore images. It's important to note, however, this list shows all currently running Macs that have started from any local NetBoot server, including other servers you may not be monitoring. In other words, if you have more than one active NetBoot server on a local network, the Connections pane will show all Mac clients that are currently using NetBoot, even if they are not using the server that you are currently monitoring.

Finally, the NetBoot logs can be useful when monitoring the progress of the NetBoot service in action. You can also access the NetBoot service logs from Server Admin by selecting the NetBoot service, and then clicking the Log button in the toolbar.

Troubleshooting the NetBoot Service

The NetBoot service process is fairly straightforward. If a client does not successfully start from a NetBoot server, you can troubleshoot the issue in the following ways:

▶ Rule out the network. Start the client Mac normally, or use another Mac to verify that the computers can receive DHCP information and that you can see the network disk volumes from the Startup Disk preferences.

▶ Press and hold the Option key as you boot the client, which will indicate if you have a firmware password configured for the computer. If so, the use of the N key and Option-N key combination will be disabled at startup.

▶ Check the disk space on the server. Shadow files and disk images may be filling the server's disk space. You may want to add more or bigger drives to accommodate these files.

▶ Check for NetBoot service filters. Do you have filters enabled for IP address, hardware address, and model type? If you do, you should temporarily disable the filters and test to see if they are blocking access to Macs on which you want to use NetBoot.

▶ Check your server firewall configuration. The NetBoot service requires that a combination of BSDP/DHCP, TFTP, NFS, AFP, and HTTP ports be open. Temporarily disabling the firewall or adding a rule to allow all traffic from the subnet from which you're trying to use NetBoot will reveal whether you have a firewall configuration problem.

▶ On the NetBoot server, the underlying process that provides NetBoot service communication is bootpd, so you can check the server logs for bootpd messages. These logs can also identify whether you mistyped an Ethernet hardware address or selected the wrong type of hardware for a filter.

▶ The NetBoot and DHCP services are both provided by the bootpd daemon process. To completely stop and restart the daemon you need to stop both services.

▶ Check the NetBoot service configuration files. The primary NetBoot configuration file is /etc/bootpd.plist. This file contains general NetBoot and DHCP service settings. Each network disk image also contains a NBImageInfo.plist file that contains information specific to that image. The format and contents of both configuration files are well documented in the built-in `bootpd` manual page accessed at the command line. Further, both files can be viewed and edited with a normal text editor or the Property List Editor application included with the Xcode Tools.

▶ Move aside or delete the DHCP and NetBoot cache files in /var/db/dhcpd_clients and /var/db/bsdpd_clients, which can become corrupted. If one or both of these files are removed they will be automatically re-created. Static DHCP reservations and NetBoot filtering by MAC address are kept in these files so you should record the data in order to reconfigure the services after deleting the cache files.

Deploying Systems with NetInstall and NetRestore

Before reading the following sections, you should be familiar with the techniques covered in Chapter 4, "Creating System Images." The previous chapter provides an introduction to creating NetInstall and NetRestore images using System Image Utility (SIU). The remainder of Chapter 5 focuses on understanding and customizing the deployment mechanisms used by these images.

Understanding NetInstall and NetRestore

NetInstall and NetRestore network disk images, when hosted from a NetBoot server, provide a total network deployment solution. These images include a small system to start up the Mac and then deploy a standard or customized Mac OS X system to the Mac's local drive, but they differ in technique. NetInstall images leverage the Mac OS X installer technology, whereas NetRestore images use Apple Software Restore (ASR). If flexibility is your priority, then using a NetInstall image is the better choice as you can pick and choose components during the system installation. On the other hand, if deployment time is your priority, then using a NetRestore image is the better choice, as system restores are faster than installations.

When a Mac starts up from a NetInstall image the user experience is identical to the Mac OS X installer interface. With a few clicks you can be on your way to installing a system to the local Mac's drive. Alternately, you can customize the packages you wish to install or use any of the utilities built in to the standard Mac OS X installer system. The resulting installed system is based on the system source and customizations selected when the image was built using SIU, and optionally by the custom install options selected by the user.

When a Mac starts up from a NetRestore image, again the user experience is similar to the Mac OS X installer interface. However, you will not be able to pick and choose individual packages. Instead an entire system image will be restored to the local Mac's drive. Again, the advantage is that a system restore is much quicker than a system installation. From a NetRestore image you will also be able to access the utilities built in to the standard Mac OS X installer media.

TIP You can fully automate the NetInstall and NetRestore images using the Enable Automated Installation action covered in the "Using SIU Workflow Actions" section later in this chapter.

TIP When complete, both the NetInstall and NetRestore deployment processes automatically restart the target Mac using the newly installed or restored system volume.

When using a basic NetRestore image, the image that will be restored to the local Mac is based on the system source selected when the image was built in SIU. Although you can't pick individual packages using a NetRestore image, you can create a custom NetRestore image that allows you to pick from a list of prepared system images that can be hosted from other network shares. The next two sections explain how to take advantage of a custom NetRestore image that can be used to pull system images from a variety of external sources.

Using ASR with Network Sources

The ASR system can restore from system images shared over a network connection. You can choose among several methodologies, including both unicast and multicast network protocols. Supported unicast network protocols include AFP, NFS, SMB, and HTTP. The only supported multicast protocol is the proprietary ASR multicast protocol.

A NetRestore image provides an easy-to-use interface for ASR but is a bit more limited. Basic NetRestore images use a single restore image hosted from a NetBoot service NFS or HTTP share. On the other hand, custom NetRestore "shell" images can access multiple restore sources from any number of HTTP shares or an ASR multicast.

Unicast network protocols remain the dominant file-sharing protocols because most users require different information at different times. Unicast simply means there is a single connection between the computer sharing the resource and the computer accessing the resource. For many network deployments, unicast solutions are appropriate and easier to set up than multicast solutions.

You can restore an ASR image from any AFP, NFS, or SMB share point. However, if you want to use a custom share point as a source for ASR images, you will have to do so from a local system or a standard NetBoot image. Basically, once you have mounted the share point, you use exactly the same methods as you would with a locally stored disk image. Simply drag the disk image file into the Restore interface in Disk Utility, or specify the appropriate file-system path when using the asr command. You would have to build custom scripts or use third-party tools to automate this solution.

Both standalone ASR and custom NetRestore images can directly access a restore image from an HTTP, or web, server. The transfer mechanism is still unicast, but many web servers have been highly optimized for multiple clients and can scale to provide tremendous throughput when accepting connections from multiple clients. The implementation process is as simple as placing your restore images on a web server of your choice, and then entering the URI as the source when using Disk Utility, the asr command, or a custom NetRestore "shell" image.

> **TIP** The ASR system also supports secure HTTPS connections.

Create a Custom NetRestore "Shell" Image

A so-called NetRestore "shell" image differs from a standard NetRestore image in that it contains no built-in system image. Instead, you configure one or more custom URLs that reference restore images hosted from either an HTTP website or an ASR multicast server. The idea is that the NetRestore "shell" provides a mechanism to start up the Mac and run the restore, while the images are being provided by another service. This allows you to build a single NetRestore image where you can easily select from multiple external restore images. This not only reduces the number of network disk images you have to build, it's also more flexible by allowing you to easily change restore image sources.

Configure Restore Sources

To make your restore images available for a NetRestore "shell" image either place them on an unrestricted (no authentication required) web server or configure an ASR multicast stream as covered in the "Configuring ASR Network Multicast" section later in this chapter. If you choose to go with images hosted from a web server, you should temporarily enable folder listings on the website. This makes it much easier to verify that the image is available and has the correct URI.

NetRestore supports both manually configured restore sources and automatically discovered restore sources. Manually configured restore sources are static URLs saved as part of the NetRestore image. You can set these URLs when the NetRestore image is built, as covered in the "Build NetRestore 'Shell'" section next in this chapter, or you can set these URLs afterward as covered in the "Modify NetRestore Settings" section.

The Bonjour network discovery service facilitates automatically discovered images sources. The advantage here is that you don't have to manually configure these sources as part of the NetRestore images. When you enable an ASR multicast image, the server automatically registers with Bonjour to advertise the availability of the image. Thus, when your Mac is running from NetRestore, the ASR multicast source will automatically appear in the list of available images to restore from.

Web servers, on the other hand, don't automatically register with Bonjour in a manner that NetRestore can recognize. However, you can use the dns-sd command on any Mac OS X computer to advertise the availability of web-based NetRestore sources. The following example shows how to register a URI that can be discovered by NetRestore on a local network. In this example the NetRestore interface will show "Bonjour-discovered HTTP Source" in the list, which references a source at the URI www.pretendco.com/asr/imagefile.dmg.

```
dns-sd -R "Bonjour HTTP Source" _netrestore._tcp . 9 desc="Bonjour-discovered HTTP
Source" src="http://www.pretendco.com/asr/imagefile.dmg"
```

This dns-sd command must remain running for the Bonjour source to be advertised. If you kill this process, or close the Terminal window where you entered the command, then the advertised source will disappear. Thus, if you want this to be a permanently enabled Bonjour source you need to configure a Launch Daemon for this command, as covered in Chapter 6, "Postimaging Deployment Considerations."

Build NetRestore "Shell"

To build a custom NetRestore "shell" image you need to make a simple SIU workflow using the Define NetRestore Source action. This action, along with NetRestore images in general, is new with Mac OS X v10.6 Server.

Unlike with other SIU workflows, when you use the Define NetRestore Source action you do not have to select a system source. Instead this action will copy components from the Mac's currently running system to create the NetRestore system. Thus, it's recommended that you build this image from a Mac OS X Server. Doing so will create a NetRestore system that when booted can be remotely accessed via screen sharing (VNC) and remote login (SSH). NetRestore "shell" images created on a Mac OS X client computer will still work, they just won't have these remote access features enabled.

To create a custom NetRestore "shell" image:

1   Open /Applications/Server/System Image Utility.app.

    SIU will open to the basic network disk image creation interface. If no system sources were found, SIU will warn you.

2   In the bottom left-hand corner of the SIU window click the plus button, and from the pop-up menu select Create New Workflow.

3   Agree to the license agreement and SIU will change to the workflow creation view.

4 Delete the Define Image Source action by clicking the close button in the top right-hand corner of the action window. This action is not needed for a NetRestore "shell" image.

5 Drag the Define NetRestore Source action from the Automator Library to the SIU workflow area. Make sure to drag this new action above the Create Image action.

6 To add manual restore sources, in the Define NetRestore Source action, click the small plus button and enter a URI and description for the source.

If you only define a single source and no other options, then the selection interface will be skipped when your Macs start up from this NetRestore image. In this case you will simply choose the destination drive and the restore will commence.

7 Optionally, you can configure the remainder of the Define NetRestore Source action according to your needs:

▶ Enabling browsing for ASR multicast streams will allow you to select these streams via Bonjour.

▶ Enabling other NetRestore sources will allow you to select manually advertised Bonjour sources as covered in the previous section, "Configure Restore Sources."

▶ Enabling manual source entry will allow you to manually enter a URI at the NetRestore selection screen.

8 At the top of the Create Image action window, make sure to select the NetRestore button.

9 Configure the remainder of the Create Image action according to your specifications. The following describes each option:

▶ The Installed Volume name is the name of the system image volume. Thus when this image is restored to Mac, the Mac's system volume will take on this name.

▶ The Save To pop-up menu and Image Name define the location and the name of the resulting network disk folder.

▶ The Network Disk name will be displayed by any interface that allows you to select this image, including the Server Admin application and the Startup Disk preferences.

▶ The Image Index is used by the NetBoot service for load balancing purposes, as covered previously in this chapter. If you're not sure what number to use, simply leave the default setting, as this can be easily changed later.

▶ The Description is extra text used to describe the contents of the network disk image. This will be displayed in Server Admin.

NOTE ▶ The goal of this section is to show you how to create a NetRestore "shell" image. At this point you have configured enough of a workflow to accomplish this. Should you want to create a more complex workflow you can certainly add more actions.

10 Optionally, once you have configured the SIU workflow settings, click the Save button to save this workflow for future use.

11 When you are ready to create the NetRestore "shell" image, click the Run button to initiate the creation process.

The build process should only take a few minutes as the NetRestore "shell" image is under 2 GB in size. SIU will show a small spinning gear in the lower-right corner to indicate progress, and you can always click the Stop button to stop the progress. For a more detailed log of the creation process, you can choose View > Show Log.

Modify NetRestore Settings

Once you have built a custom NetRestore "shell" image you can easily modify the restore source settings without having to build a new image. Start by mounting the read/write NetInstall.dmg image inside the NetRestore .nbi folder. Remember, the system image used by NetRestore images is still called "NetInstall." When the NetInstall volume mounts navigate to and open /Volumes/NetInstall/System/Installation/Packages/InstallPreferences.plist.

NOTE ▶ Never modify a network disk image that is currently in use by the NetBoot service.

If you have the Xcode developer tools installed, then this property list file should open in Property List Editor. As you can see in the following screen shot, the manual restore sources are inside a "restoreSourcesArray". From Property List Editor simply double-click to modify any source attributes. You can also use Copy and Paste to add new static sources to the list. When you are done modifying these settings make sure to save the property list file and unmount the NetInstall volume.

Configuring ASR Network Multicast

With ASR network multicast you can share a prepared disk image over the network without setting up any other services. The ASR system can provide increased network performance by transmitting the disk image data via a multicast network protocol. Using a multicast protocol allows you to simultaneously restore a prepared disk image to 100 or 1,000 computers in roughly the same amount of time it would take to restore it for 1 computer.

NOTE ▶ ASR multicast is supported only on wired Ethernet networks.

This feat is accomplished by a single Mac, hosting the prepared disk image, broadcasting the disk image data to the network in a continuous loop. Other Macs on the network can "hook in" to this data stream and start restoring to a local volume. Because the data stream is on a continuous loop, it doesn't matter where in the stream the destination Macs start their restore process because they can simply wait for the appropriate data to come around again until the entire image is restored. Also, if any network packets are missed by the destination Macs, they simply wait for those packets to come around again.

Therefore, if you have an ASR multicast stream running and you use a remote management tool such as ARD to kick off the restore process at the exact same time on all your deployed systems, they will all finish in roughly the same amount of time it would take you to restore a single Mac. If you were using a unicast network protocol and attempted the same thing, your server and network would slow to a crawl, as each Mac would attempt to initiate an individual connection to your server hosting the image.

The only caveats here, and they are big ones, is that your network hardware must support multicast protocols, and the ASR multicast stream can seriously degrade your network's performance for other protocols. For these reasons ASR multicast streams should never be attempted during operational hours on your general use network. In many cases during an initial sitewide deployment, a preparation area is set up with a dedicated closed network running a looping ASR multicast stream. The computers are then brought into this area to be imaged and deployed when the imaging is complete.

Configuring a Multicast ASR Stream

To set up an ASR multicast stream, all you need is a Mac OS X or Mac OS X Server computer connected to your wired Ethernet network, a copy of the system image you wish to deploy, and an ASR service configuration property list file. This configuration file is an XML-formatted text document that specifies the network settings for the ASR multicast stream. There are two key/value pairs required by this file:

▶ Multicast Address—This is the multicast address for the data stream. This address can be anywhere between 224.0.0.0 and 239.255.255.255, but you should consult with your network administrator for an appropriate address.

▶ Data Rate—This is the desired data rate in bytes per second. For example, entering *5000000* would indicate that you want a stream of 5 megabits per second (Mbit/s).

Finding the correct data rate may take some experimenting, as data rates that are too high will yield high network packet loss, slowing the restore operation or causing it to fail.

Other variables to take into consideration include network speed, other network traffic, computer processor speed, and destination drive speed. Generally, you can expect successful data rates between 2 Mbit/s and 20 Mbit/s. A good rule of thumb is to start with 6 Mbit/s on 100 megabit networks and 12 Mbit/s on gigabit networks, then make adjustments based on feedback from the asr restore process.

> **NOTE ▶** Choosing to deploy a compressed system image can also affect restore performance; slower Macs cannot decompress the data as quickly as faster Macs. You will have to experiment with different data rates and compression to determine the best combination for your scenario.

You can further fine-tune your ASR multicast stream by including the following optional keys:

▶ DNS Service Discovery—This value determines if the server should be advertised via Bonjour network discovery. This setting defaults to true if not specified

▶ Client Data Rate—This is the data rate at which the slowest client can write data to its target disk.

▶ Multicast TTL—This value indicates time to live on the multicast packets.

▶ Port—Use this value to indicate a custom port used in the initial client-server handshake.

You can create the ASR multicast stream configuration file using any text editor, the Property List Editor application, or the defaults command. The quickest way to get started is to use the defaults command. In the following example, Michelle uses defaults write to create a new ASR service configuration file named asrconfig.plist to her Documents folder. As you can see, she chooses a data rate of 6 Mbit/s and a multicast address of 244.0.0.10.

```
MyMac:~ michelle$ defaults write ~/Documents/asrconfig "Data Rate" -int 6000000
MyMac:~ michelle$ defaults write ~/Documents/asrconfig "Multicast Address" 224.0.0.10
```

Starting a Multicast ASR Stream

Once the ASR multicast stream configuration file is created, you can use the asr command to start the multicast stream. Continuing the previous example, Michelle uses asr -server followed by the path to the configuration file she just created, and then -source followed by the path to the prepared disk image that will be streamed to the destination Macs. Notice that she must use root access to start the ASR multicast stream.

```
MyMac:~ michelle$ sudo asr -server Documents/asrconfig.plist -source
/Volumes/Storage/ModularSystem.dmg
Password: (password not shown)
Ready to start accepting clients
Starting stream Wed Apr 15 18:29:29 2008
Starting stream Wed Apr 15 18:41:37 2008
```

The stream will not start until the first client makes the connection, as indicated by the asr command's output of "Starting stream..." on the Mac hosting the stream. This stream will continue to loop, as indicated by each entry of "Starting stream..." The stream loop will continue indefinitely until it is killed either by a `sudo killall asr` command issued from another command-line session or by the Command-period keyboard combination entered at the terminal.

Restoring from a Multicast ASR Stream

Restoring from an ASR multicast stream is just as easy as restoring from any other source. The only change is that you specify the URI for the Mac hosting the ASR multicast stream as the source image. When booted from a NetRestore image, the ASR multicast stream can also be discovered automatically via Bonjour.

The following example illustrates what Michelle would use at the command line to restore from an ASR multicast stream hosted on a Mac at IP address 10.1.0.50 to a local destination volume.

```
MyMac:~ michelle$ sudo asr restore -source asr://10.1.0.50 -target /Volumes/
Macintosh\ HD/ -erase
```

Using SIU Workflow Actions

Earlier sections in this reference guide have covered the primary SIU workflow concepts. An introduction to building SIU workflows, including coverage of the Define Image Source and Create Image actions, is available in Chapter 4, "Creating System Images." The Define NetRestore Source action, used for creating NetRestore "shell" images, is covered previously in this chapter.

This section will detail use of the remaining optional SIU actions. Perhaps most important is to recognize when a SIU action is appropriate. Some combinations of SIU actions simply aren't appropriate given your selected system source (installation media or system volume) and resulting image type (NetBoot, NetInstall, or NetRestore).

The following table shows which SIU actions are appropriate to use with these network disk choices. In this table, the Mac OS X Install DVD icon indicates the source is installation media while the drive icon indicates the source is a system volume. The one exception is the Define NetRestore Source action, which uses the Mac's current running system volume as the source, as indicated by the System folder icon.

SIU Automator Action:	NetBoot	NetInstall	NetRestore
Define Image Source (often required)	🖳⬇	⬇	🖳⬇
Create Image (required)	🖳⬇	⬇	🖳⬇
Add Packages and Post-Install Scripts	⬇	⬇	🖳⬇ *
Customize Package Selection	⬇	⬇	⬇
Add User Account	⬇	Not Applicable	⬇
Apply System Configuration Settings	🖳⬇	⬇ *	🖳⬇ *
Enable Automated Installation	Not Applicable	⬇	🖳⬇ *
Partition Disk	Not Applicable	⬇	🖳⬇
Filter Clients by MAC Address	🖳⬇	⬇	🖳⬇
Filter Computer Models	🖳⬇	⬇	🖳⬇
Define NetRestore Source	Not Applicable	Not Applicable	🗂

NOTE ▶ The asterisks in this table indicate known issues (aka bugs) at the time of this writing.

Actions for Installation Packages

Two optional actions allow you to customize the installation packages used to build network disk images.

Add Packages and Post-Install Scripts

The Add Packages and Post-Install Scripts action can be placed anywhere between the two primary SIU actions. When starting with installation media as your source, this allows you to build custom "fresh" modular system images that have never been booted and thus contain no problematic computer-specific files, as covered in Chapter 4, "Creating System Images."

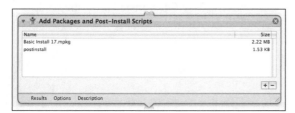

For NetBoot, the installation packages and scripts are installed directly to the network disk image as it's being built by SIU. For NetRestore, the installation packages are installed directly to the restore disk image as it's being built by SIU, but the scripts will be applied to the target Mac after the system has been restored. For NetInstall images, the installation packages and scripts are applied to a target Mac while it is running the installer when booted from the NetInstall image. The items are installed to the target Mac immediately after Mac OS X is installed.

> **NOTE ▶** The NetInstall and NetRestore systems run a very limited version of Mac OS X that does not include many system resources that may be used by scripts. For example, this system does not include the `dscl` command-line tool, so scripts that access this command will not run properly.

The order in the list will dictate the order in which the items are run. Unfortunately, you cannot reorder the installation list, so you must delete installers (using the minus button) if you want to rearrange the order.

However, if you have already created a NetInstall image using this action, you can modify the installation behavior and even add new installation packages without rebuilding the image. Once you have mounted the NetInstall.dmg system image, navigate to the /Volumes/NetInstall/System/Installation/Packages/ folder. All the installation packages are stored in this folder, including any scripts you have added, which are converted into installation packages that bear a similar name to the original script. The postsystem installation order is determined by an XML-formatted text file also in this folder named OSInstall.collection. Simply edit this file to adjust the installation order or install additional packages.

Customize Package Selection

The Customize Package Selection action can be placed after either the Define Image Source action or an Add Packages and Post-Install Scripts action. If both are used in your workflow, the Customized Packages action should be placed after both installation actions. This action only works properly if the system source is Mac OS X installation media.

When placed in your workflow, this action will look through all previous installation packages in your workflow, and then present a list of all the available installation choices. Use the Default column to select the items you want to install by default. For NetBoot and NetRestore images, these settings are applied by SIU during the image build process. For NetInstall images, these settings apply when the target Mac is running the install while booted from the NetInstall image.

The Visible column only affects NetInstall images. The selections here will determine which choices a user can see when he has elected to perform a custom install when booted from the NetInstall image. If you deselect an item in the Visible column, the user will not be given the choice, so if you want to force an item to be installed, select the checkbox in the Default column and deselect the checkbox in the Visible column.

If you have already created a NetInstall image using this action, you can modify the installation behavior without rebuilding the image. Once you have mounted the NetInstall.dmg system image, locate the /Volumes/NetInstall/var/db/MacOSXInstaller.choiceChanges file. This XML-formatted text file includes the installation choices set by this action. Simply edit this file to adjust the installation selection.

Actions for System Settings

Two optional actions apply various system settings to the network disk image.

Add User Account

The Add User Account action works only for NetBoot or NetRestore images. It's also the only action that can be used multiple times in a single workflow. This action will add new local users to the NetBoot system image or the NetRestore restore image. This action is essentially necessary if your source is installation media, as you must create at least one local user to administer Mac OS X systems. Further, this action will prevent the Setup Assistant from running by removing the .AppleSetupDone file on the resulting image. If your source is a system volume that you have already configured, this action can still be used to create additional users, but it's not required.

> **TIP** ▶ To create users with NetInstall images, build an installation package that creates the users and then use the Add Packages and Post-Install Scripts action to add the user creation package.

Apply System Configuration Settings

The Apply System Configuration Settings action automates tasks that are difficult to script by hand. It can be used to configure a variety of settings on the target Mac. For NetBoot images, these system settings are applied every time the client computers start up from the NetBoot image. For NetInstall and NetRestore images, these settings are applied by the target Mac on the first startup of the newly installed or restored system.

▶ From the Apply System Configuration Settings action you can:

▶ Apply directory service settings to the target Mac based on the Directory Service settings of the Mac currently running SIU. Thus, this action requires that you have already configured the directory services on the Mac currently running SIU. This action will work with both Active Directory and LDAP services, including authenticated and nonauthenticated bindings. Optionally, if you're using custom binding authentication per computer, you can configure multiple bind settings using the Ethernet Address field to specify each computer.

▶ You can apply computer name and local hostname settings for the target Macs based on a properly formatted text file containing this information. This text file must contain entries for every client Mac that will use this network disk image. Each client entry in the file is indicated by a new line or a carriage return. The format for the client entry is tab-delimited with the following items: the computer's Ethernet address; the computer's hostname, or if you don't want to assign hostnames, use the word "-automatic-"; the computer's sharing (the name seen in the Sharing preferences); and finally the computer's Bonjour name.

▶ Alternatively, you can have the system automatically generate a unique computer name based on a name you enter, followed by the computer's MAC address.

> **NOTE** ▶ Choose only one of the two computer-naming options.

▶ You can have the NetInstall system automatically change all ByHost preferences to match the client computer. ByHost settings are normally computer-specific based on the preference file's name, but this action will change the name to reflect the client Mac.

> **MORE INFO** ▶ ByHost preference details are covered in Chapter 6, "Postimaging Deployment Considerations."

Actions for Additional Install Options

Two optional actions allow you to automate other installation actions that might take place during a NetInstall or NetRestore operation. These actions don't work with NetBoot images.

Partition Disk

The Partition Disk action, presented with an interface similar to the Disk Utility application, will automatically partition or reformat a specific local volume on the target Mac before the installation process begins. Note that this action requires that you enter the exact name of the local volume, which is Macintosh HD by default.

> **NOTE** ▶ This action will erase any data on the specified volume, so use it with extreme caution.

If you have already created a NetInstall or NetRestore image using this action, you can modify the partitioning behavior without rebuilding the image. Once you have mounted the NetInstall.dmg system image, locate the /Volumes/NetInstall/System/PartitionInfo. plist file. This XML-formatted text file includes the partitioning choices set by this action. Simply edit this file to adjust the partitioning configuration.

Enable Automated Installation

The Enable Automated Installation action will automate the NetInstall or NetRestore process to limit the interaction needed from a user at the target Mac. In fact, selecting the Named button and entering the exact name of the local target volume eliminates the need for any more user input on the target Mac; simply selecting the network disk image and restarting the target Mac will be the only interaction required to complete the entire process.

Keep in mind that great responsibility comes with this action. Because an automatic install or restore operation can be configured to erase the contents of the local drive, data loss can occur. You must control access to this type of network disk image and you must communicate to those with access to these images the implications of using them. Always instruct users to back up critical data before using automated NetInstall or NetRestore images.

> **NOTE ▶** Images that normal users could accidentally select should be limited to standard NetBoot images or nonautomated NetInstall or NetRestore images. Remember to set the default network disk image on every NetBoot server.

If you have already created a NetInstall or NetRestore image using this action, you can modify the automation behavior without rebuilding the image. Once you have mounted the NetInstall.dmg system image, locate the /Volumes/NetInstall/etc/minstallconfig.xml file. This XML-formatted text file includes the automation choices set by this action. Simply edit this file to adjust the automatic install or restore configuration.

Actions for Filtering

Two optional actions apply NetBoot service filter settings to prevent accidental access to the network disk images. These two optional actions work with all network disk images. Further, both of these actions simply modify the NBImageInfo.plist file inside the network disk image folder. You can modify this XML-formatted file using Property List Editor or the Server Admin application without having to rebuild a network disk image built using these actions.

Filter Clients by MAC Address

The Filter Clients by MAC Address action preconfigures the per-image network disk filter settings that you can access from the Images pane of Server Admin. This action is configured similarly to the MAC address filtering covered in the "Configuring Per-Image NetBoot Filtering" section earlier in this chapter.

Filter Computer Models

The Filter Computer Models action also preconfigures the per-image network disk filter settings that you can access from the Images pane of Server Admin. This action is configured similarly to the model property filtering covered in the "Configuring Per-Image NetBoot Filtering" section earlier in this chapter.

NOTE ▶ All Mac OS X v10.6 network disk images include a preconfigured model property filter that only allows Intel-based Macs to access the image.

Third-Party System Deployment Tools

The system image and deployment tools built into Mac OS X v10.6 fulfill the installation deployment needs for many administrators. However, you may find some third-party installation tools more appropriate for your deployment needs. For instance, Mac OS X does not include any built-in support for creating system images of a Mac Boot Camp partition containing the Windows operating system.

Free or Open-Source System Imaging Tools

The following tools are free, open source, or both. Although free is an attractive price, it often means you're on your own for support. However, most of these tools have online documentation and/or helpful forums. The URLs for all of them are listed in the "References" section.

▶ DeployStudio—DeployStudio leverages all the built-in Mac OS X deployment technologies; NetBoot, installation, and ASR. On top of this Deploy Studio provides a suite of client and server tools that help you develop highly customizable deployment workflows. Recently, DeployStudio has branched out to provide additional support for Boot Camp on Mac systems and even Windows on standard PC systems.

▶ InstaDMG—InstaDMG by AFP548 is a series of reference UNIX scripts and documentation that will help you automate the modular system image build process. InstaDMG is a free tool and has a loyal following and a fabulous user forum community that is working hard to improve the quality of the InstaDMG project.

▶ PKGImage—PKGImage by Apple-Scripts.com is a graphical modular system image build tool that is based on AppleScripts. This tool offers a simple graphical interface and some nice prebuilt configuration scripts. PKGImage is also a free tool.

▶ PSU Blast Image Config—This tool by the IT staff at Penn State University is a highly optimized system deployment tool that leverages ASR. It also includes automated configuration for many common deployment tasks.

▶ Winclone—This simple graphical tool by Twocanoes can create deployable Boot Camp system images. Winclone is a free tool with great documentation on the developer's website.

Third-Party Management Suites

Several commercial suites are available that provide sophisticated system deployment mechanisms along with a variety of advanced management features. Because these are commercial tools they also come with the advantage of technical support should you need it.

Solutions that fall into this category include the Casper Suite by JAMF, KACE systems management appliances, the FileWave suite, the LANDesk suite, and the LANrev suite. These solutions go beyond system image deployment and are covered in a bit more detail in Chapter 7, "System Maintenance."

What You've Learned

▶ You can leverage the NetBoot service to provide a network-based system deployment solution.

▶ You can easily create simple NetBoot and NetInstall images using the System Image Utility.

▶ You know the appropriate steps required to configure the NetBoot service on a Mac OS X Server, and you can configure Mac clients to start up from this service.

▶ You can create custom NetBoot and NetInstall images by using Automator workflows in System Image Utility.

▶ A variety of third-party tools are available that can also be used to deliver system images via the network.

References

You can check for new and updated Knowledge Base documents at www.apple.com/support.

NetBoot / Firmware Issues

▶ HT3115, "Working with architecture-specific NetBoot images"

▶ HT1237, "EFI and SMC firmware updates for Intel-based Macs"

▶ HT1395, "Mac OS X: Available firmware updates"

▶ HT1310, "Startup Manager: How to select a startup volume"

▶ HT1533, "Startup key combinations for Intel-based Macs"

▶ HT1343, "Mac OS X keyboard shortcuts"

Web Resources

▶ The Apple System Imaging and Software Update Administration guide, http://images.apple.com/server/macosx/docs/System_Imaging_and_SW_Update_Admin_v10.6.pdf

▶ Apple Server Admin Tools 10.6 download, http://support.apple.com/kb/DL914

▶ NetBoot Across Subnets by Bombich Software, www.bombich.com/software/nbas.html

▶ NetBoot Across Subnets article, www.bombich.com/mactips/nbas.html

▶ Multicast ASR data rate recommendations, www.bombich.com/mactips/multicast.html

▶ Proton Pack Server at AFP548.com—multicast ASR configuration tool, www.afp548.com

▶ DeployStudio—system and software deployment tool, www.deploystudio.com/Home.html

▶ InstaDMG at AFP548.com—modular system image tool, www.afp548.com

▶ PKGImage by Apple-Scripts.com—modular system image tool, www.apple-scripts.com/?page_id=27

▶ PSU Blast Image Config—system deployment tool, http://clc.its.psu.edu/Labs/Mac/Resources/blastimageconfig/default.aspx

▶ Winclone by Twocanoes Software—Boot Camp cloned system image tool, www.twocanoes.com/winclone

Review Quiz

1. How can the Apple Custom Software Solutions (CSS) help with your deployment?

2. What are the minimum network requirements to use NetBoot on a Mac client computer?

3. What are the primary steps involved in starting from the NetBoot service?

4. What are NetBoot shadow files and how do they relate to NetBoot diskless mode?

5. How does the NetBoot image ID, or index value, affect the NetBoot service?

6. On a Mac OS X Server computer, where should the network disk images be stored in order to be recognized by the NetBoot service?

7. What do you configure to allow a client computer to access the NetBoot service across subnets?

8. What does the Define NetRestore Source action do?

9. How can Apple Software Restore (ASR) be used to restore a system image to multiple computers simultaneously?

10. What do you enter at the command line to start an ASR restore or clone?

Answers

1. The Apple CSS team can build and test a customized system image based on your deployment specifications. This custom system image can be deployed to new Macs "at the factory" before they are delivered to you.

2. The NetBoot service requires client Macs with a built-in Ethernet connection. A few newer Macs, including the MacBook Air, can access the NetBoot service using their built-in AirPort card or an external Apple USB Ethernet adapter.

3. The primary steps to start a Mac client from the NetBoot service are:

   a. The client places a request for TCP/IP address information using the Dynamic Host Configuration Protocol (DHCP).

   b. After the client receives TCP/IP address information, it sends out a request for startup software using the Boot Service Discovery Protocol (BSPD), and the NetBoot server responds with startup instructions.

   c. The NetBoot server delivers the core system files to the client using Trivial File Transfer Protocol (TFTP).

   d. After the client has started the core system, it can initiate a network mount and load the remainder of the operating system from the NetBoot disk image using either the Hypertext Transfer Protocol (HTTP) or network file system (NFS).

4. NetBoot shadow files are used by the Mac client for temporary storage while it is operating from the read-only NetBoot system image. NetBoot diskless mode allows these files to be stored on the NetBoot server; this disables NetBoot caching on the Mac's local drive so you can perform administration tasks.

5. The NetBoot image ID, or index value, is used by Mac clients to determine whether the NetBoot image is hosted on multiple servers. Index values between 1 and 4095 indicate the NetBoot image is only available on a single server; values between 4096 to 65535 indicate that the image could be available on multiple servers.

6. The NetBoot service will look for network disk images in the /Library/NetBoot/ NetBootSP*n* folders on every volume that has been configured to host the images.

7. The recommended solution to providing NetBoot services across networks or subnets is to pass BSDP broadcast traffic between networks. A network system administrator can implement this configuration. However, you can set a specific NetBoot image on a Mac client locally using the `bless` command or remotely using ARD.

8. The Define NetRestore Source action will create a NetRestore image that can restore system images from other network sources including web servers and multicast ASR streams.

9. A Mac can be configured to host a multicast ASR stream that can be simultaneously accessed by multiple computers to restore a system image to a local volume.

10. To start an ASR restore or clone, at the command line enter `sudo asr -source` followed by the path to the source volume or prepared disk image, and then `-target` followed by the path to the destination target, and then any options that you want to specify.

6

Chapter Files	Deployment Planning Template.pdf, available at www.peachpit.com/acsa.deployment
Time	This chapter takes approximately 3 hours to complete.
Goals	Learn which items must be configured after a Mac OS X system image has been deployed
	Use Apple Remote Desktop and command-line tools to apply changes after a system has been deployed
	Automate postimaging configuration tasks using scripts
	Use the automatic server setup system to automate the initial configuration of Mac OS X Server computers

Chapter **6**

Postimaging Deployment Considerations

You have seen that creating a standard system image is the most effective way to deploy Mac OS X systems. Nearly all software and configuration settings can be stored in a single image, which in minutes can be pushed out to your deployed Macs, essentially ensuring identical performance and reliability from your Macs.

However, in a modern networked computing environment, you do not want every system to have a 100 percent identical configuration. At the least, each Mac needs its own IP address and computer name, and you may need to configure many other settings uniquely on each Mac after you deploy a unified system image.

This chapter covers settings that will need to be changed after you deploy a system image for both Mac OS X and Mac OS X Server systems. The chapter first covers techniques for postimaging configuration of Mac client computers, and then discusses techniques for configuration of Mac servers, including the automatic setup feature of the Mac OS X Server system.

Understanding Postimaging Client Configuration

After you restore a unified Mac OS X system image, you must configure certain settings uniquely for each Mac. The number of items you have to configure after system imaging is directly dependent on the goal of your final system configuration. Generally the more features and management settings your deployment requires, the more sophisticated your postimaging tasks will be. Also, the amount of configuration that went into your system image, whether it be a cloned or a modular one, will affect postimaging tasks.

This section introduces you to tools that can facilitate common postimaging tasks, regardless of the complexity of your postimaging configuration needs. Specifically, it covers postimaging techniques that can be used to set the following items, all of which should have unique configurations on each Mac client:

▶ Network settings—Each Mac must have a unique IP address, a unique computer name, and a unique host name.

▶ Directory service settings—In most cases each Mac must have unique settings that bind the computer to a directory server.

▶ Computer-specific preferences—Certain preferences are, by default, specific to a single computer.

▶ Software serial or license numbers—Some additional software titles require unique serial numbers or licensing numbers to operate.

▶ Firmware—The firmware built in to every Mac is unique to that computer. The system software does not contain any firmware settings, so firmware changes must be handled separately for each Mac client.

Once you know which postimaging tasks must be applied to your systems, you can use either of two general techniques to efficiently deploy these tasks on multiple systems: You can use Apple Remote Desktop (ARD) to remotely perform your postimaging tasks, or you can include, as part of your system image, local automated scripts to perform your postimaging tasks.

Configuration via ARD

In other chapters you have seen how ARD can be used to remotely monitor and administer Mac systems. This capability makes ARD an ideal tool for applying settings after a Mac has received a new system image. There are, however, a few caveats to using ARD for this purpose.

The systems you wish to manage must:

▶   Have Remote Management enabled with access for a system administrator account. This setting should be included with the system image. If your reimaging Mac systems were previously managed with ARD, it's best to use similar settings to the previous system's so the Remote Desktop application can reconnect automatically.

▶   Have networking enabled with valid and unique TCP/IP addresses. This requirement is easily handled via DHCP if the Macs have a fresh system image. Again, if you're reimaging Mac systems, it's best if they retain their previously used IP address so the Remote Desktop application can reconnect automatically.

▶   Be identified by their current network names. If a name hasn't been set it will make it very difficult for you to identify specific systems using Remote Desktop. However, if you are reimaging Mac systems that have been previously configured in a computer list saved by Remote Desktop, then the application will attempt to reconnect to the clients based on the saved information. Remote Desktop will try to reconnect using the Mac's previously used IP address or host name.

Thus, if you plan to use ARD for configuration of Mac systems that have not been previously managed with Remote Desktop, you will need to give each computer a unique IP address or computer name so that you can easily locate specific computers on the network. You can provide computer names for newly imaged systems by building a custom network disk image using System Image Utility, as covered in Chapter 5, "Deploying System Images." Alternately, you can configure a custom solution that names the Mac at first startup using either your own scripting tools or a third-party deployment tool.

> **MORE INFO** ▶ See Chapter 2, "Deploying Individual Items and Containers," for an introduction to enabling and configuring ARD for new systems. Also, the "Configuring ARD Remote Management Settings" section later in this chapter offers advanced solutions for configuring ARD.

Using ARD Management Features

Assuming you have access to your deployed Macs from the Remote Desktop administrator application, you can easily apply some commonly used settings to those systems.

1   While in Remote Desktop, select the Macs you wish to manage.

2   Choose a task from the Manage menu.

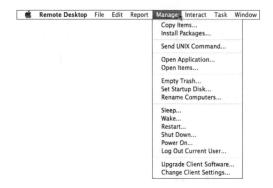

As you can see from the Manage menu in Remote Desktop, you can perform a variety of configuration tasks on targeted Macs:

▶   Deploy individual items, as covered previously in Chapter 2, "Deploying Individual Items and Containers."

NOTE ▶ Remember that some settings can be deployed simply by replacing the appropriate configuration or preference file.

▶   Deploy installation packages, as covered previously in Chapter 3, "Deploying with Installation Packages."

NOTE ▶ Remember that nearly any configuration can be deployed via an installation package.

▶   Send UNIX commands, which will be covered in the next section.

▶   Forcibly open specific applications or items.

▶   Forcibly empty the Trash for all users.

▶   Set the system startup disk, as covered previously in Chapter 5, "Deploying System Images."

▶   Set a new computer name. This dialog allows you to set a specific name for a single computer or set a similar name with a number appended for multiple comput-ers. This is an especially useful feature if you have reimaged Mac computers but you didn't provide an automated method for assigning specific computer names. Again, the Remote Desktop application will attempt to reconnect to any Mac saved to a computer list, even if it's not using the same computer name as used previously.

▶ Forcibly set various power states for the computer hardware, or forcibly log out the current user. Forced settings do not allow the current user to interrupt the change, thus preventing the user from being able to save any changes to open documents.

▶ Upgrade the ARD Remote Management client software or change its access settings.

Using the ARD Send UNIX Command

Mac OS X is a UNIX operating system at its core, so nearly any management task can be accomplished via a UNIX command. However, although you can access an individual remote computer's command line via SSH, unless you write a sophisticated script you cannot easily use SSH to send commands to multiple computers simultaneously.

The most powerful management feature of ARD is the ability to send individual or multiple UNIX commands to all your deployed systems nearly simultaneously. Almost any command that can be used locally on a Mac computer can be sent remotely using the ARD Send UNIX Command feature. The only commands that don't work with this feature are interactive commands that require user feedback after the initial command entry. However, most commands with interactive modes also support standard input from a single command-line entry by using the appropriate options, as described in the manual page for that command.

MORE INFO ▶ The following sections in this chapter give examples of command-line tools that can be used to accomplish many common postimaging tasks.

To send UNIX commands with ARD:

1 Open the /Applications/Remote Desktop application, and then authenticate if necessary.

2 From a computer list in the sidebar, locate and select the target Macs to which you will be deploying the items. From the toolbar click the UNIX button or choose Manage > Send UNIX Command.

An untitled ARD Send UNIX Command window opens, allowing you to enter the desired commands and set a few command options.

TIP The Template pop-up menu in the upper right-hand corner includes dozens of useful UNIX command examples. Note that from the Template's menu you can also assign your own UNIX command templates for future use.

3 Enter your full UNIX command string in the provided space.

You can enter multiple commands as long as you separate them with carriage returns. In fact you can copy and paste the text of full script files into the space provided.

The command text you see in the example screen shot is used to return the computer's UUID, which is used by ByHost preference settings. This is covered in detail in the "Modifying Preference Configurations" section later in this chapter.

4 Below the command entry area, select your command settings.

When sending commands that modify system settings, you should always run the command as the system administrator user, root.

In most cases you should also choose to display the command results so you can see the full progress of the command. If this option is not selected and the command is successful, the task will simply complete. However, if the command fails, it will always return a failure message.

5 At the bottom of the UNIX command window, check the status of any selected Macs. Your command will not run on any Mac computers that are in sleep mode or otherwise unresponsive.

To resolve unreachable connections, don't close the Send UNIX Command window. Instead return to the main Remote Desktop window and attempt to wake or reconnect to the unreachable Macs.

6 Once you are satisfied with the command settings, click Send.

If you chose to display the command results, a new window opens showing the command progress on each targeted Mac. A green checkmark icon appears next to the Mac clients when the command(s) have completed successfully.

TIP ▶ Don't forget about the Schedule and Save buttons—two important time-saving features at the bottom of the ARD Send UNIX Command window. The Save button allows you to place a shortcut of this task in the Remote Desktop sidebar; the Schedule button allows you to set a specific time for the UNIX command(s) to take place.

System Configuration via Command Line

Mac OS X includes nice graphical interfaces for configuring most system settings. However, manually configuring Mac OS X postimaging settings for large groups of deployed Macs via these interfaces requires far too much time for deployment purposes.

Instead, postimaging tasks are best handled using command-line equivalents. As you saw in the previous section, you can use ARD to send commands to multiple Macs simultaneously. You can also write UNIX command scripts and include them with an installation package or set them to provide automated postimaging configuration, covered in the "Automating Configuration Tasks with launchd" and "Automating Configuration Tasks with loginwindow" sections later in this chapter.

No matter how you choose to implement UNIX commands in your postimaging configuration, you need to know which commands to use. This section introduces some of the primary commands that can be used to set Mac OS X system settings, including the systemsetup, networksetup, kickstart, dscl, and nvram commands.

MORE INFO ▶ Several command-line tools are covered in this section, but you can also find more information in the Apple Mac OS X Server Command-Line Administration guide, available at http://images.apple.com/server/macosx/docs/Command_Line_Admin_v10.6.pdf. Despite the title, this guide covers tools that work for both Mac servers and clients.

Configuring General System Settings

The primary command for configuring general Mac OS X system settings is the systemsetup command. This command can be used to configure a variety of system settings. Some of its capabilities include:

▶ Configuring date, time, time zone, and network time server settings

▶ Configuring energy saver settings including automatic sleep and wake schedules

▶ Enabling or disabling Remote Login (SSH) and Remote Apple Events

▶ Setting the computer name

▶ Setting the startup disk

For quick access to all the system configuration options available through the `systemsetup` command, enter `systemsetup -help` at the command line. The command options are clearly explained, and in general, easy to use. For example, the following command will set the computer name to Pretendco Tower. Note that you are required to use `sudo` to invoke system administrator access.

```
sudo systemsetup -setcomputername "Pretendco Tower"
```

Configuring Network Settings

Every Mac OS X system requires three unique network settings:

▶ IP address—The easiest way to deal with unique IP addresses is by implementing DHCP, which can be used to automatically assign IP addresses. It's important to note that DHCP can be configured to assign static addresses as well as randomly assigned addresses. However, in cases where you don't have the DHCP service you will have to assign static IP addresses.

▶ Computer name—The system will automatically generate a unique computer name by appending a number to the previously set name, but to easily locate your Macs on the network, you will have to assign them all unique names.

▶ Host name—The Mac will automatically determine its host name, as long as it has an entry hosted on a DNS server. Otherwise, the host name will be generated automatically based on the computer name.

Because the host name is set automatically, you only have to set a unique IP address and computer name for your deployed systems. As you saw in the preceding section, the computer name can be easily set using the `systemsetup` command. However, if you don't have DHCP services, you can set TCP/IP settings manually using the `networksetup` command. The `networksetup` command options are clearly explained, and you can enter `networksetup -help` to see a list of all available options.

Managing Mac OS X network configuration is a little more difficult, though, because the system supports multiple network interfaces, and each interface can have a variety of settings. Thus, when using the network setup command you should first be absolutely sure that you know the exact names of the system interfaces. The following example shows how to find out the names using the network setup command.

```
sudo networksetup -listnetworkserviceorder
```

This command will return a list of the currently configured network interfaces, their given names, and the service order. Remember in Mac OS X the network service order applies to active network interfaces only, so although Bluetooth appears first in this list, it will be used only if a Bluetooth connection is established.

```
(1) Bluetooth
(Hardware Port: Bluetooth, Device: Bluetooth-Modem)
(2) FireWire
(Hardware Port: FireWire, Device: fw0)
(3) Ethernet
(Hardware Port: Ethernet, Device: en0)
(4) AirPort
(Hardware Port: AirPort, Device: en1)
```

The order and names shown here are the defaults for Mac OS X. In most cases only the Ethernet port will require a static configuration, but you can set any interface using the networksetup command. The following example configures the Ethernet interface with manual TCP/IP settings. The first line sets the primacy TCP/IP address information, which includes an IP address, followed by the subnet mask, and finally the router IP address. The next line sets the DNS server address, and the final line sets the default search domain.

```
sudo networksetup -setmanual "Ethernet" 10.1.17.2 255.255.0.0 10.1.0.1
sudo networksetup -setdnsservers "Ethernet" 10.1.0.1
sudo networksetup -setsearchdomains "Ethernet" pretendco.com
```

Configuring ARD Remote Management Settings

Ideally, you would configure remote management settings as part of your system image so you can easily access the ARD system. However, if you need to configure this service as part of your postimaging tasks, you can do so using the kickstart command. Using the kickstart command is a little different than using other commands because it is not part of the default command path. This means that you must enter the full path to

the kickstart command, which is /System/Library/CoreServices/RemoteManagement/
ARDAgent.app/Contents/Resources/kickstart. The kickstart command also does not
have a traditional command-line manual page entry, but its use is covered in the Remote
Desktop application's built-in help system.

> **MORE INFO** ▶ You can also access kickstart documentation online at http://docs.
> info.apple.com/article.html?path=RemoteDesktop/3.0/en/ARDC882.html.

The most common use for kickstart is to enable ARD remote management for a specific
local administrator account. The following example uses the kickstart command to activate the ARD service, enable all management options for the local administrative user ladmin, and then restart the ARD agent and menu item.

```
sudo /System/Library/CoreServices/RemoteManagement/ARDAgent.app/Contents/Resources/
kickstart -activate -configure -access -on -users ladmin -privs -all -restart -agent
-menu
```

TIP ▶ The Remote Desktop administrator application can create an installer that
can be used to set up and enable the Remote Management service on any client Mac.
From Remote Desktop select choose File > Create Client Installer from the menu bar.
This opens an assistant that will automatically create the installation package for you.

Configuration of Directory Services

If your Mac clients are bound to a network directory service, and if you are using authenticated binding like that used by Active Directory, you will have to bind each Mac separately
as a postimaging task. Every Mac OS X client uses a local Kerberos Key Distribution Center
(LKDC) to provide local authentication services and to identify each Mac when using
authenticated binding. This LKDC needs to be unique for each Mac client.

If you use System Image Utility (SIU) to create and deploy system images, you can take
advantage of the Apply System Configuration Settings action, as covered in Chapter 5,
"Deploying System Images." This action places a helper application in your system image
that will automatically bind the deployed system to your network directory services on
first startup. Further, this helper application is always placed in every system image built
by SIU to automatically reset the LKDC on first startup.

If, however, you plan to manually create your own images, then you will need to use several commands in a series of steps to configure each Mac's directory services. The following section explains the command-line tools that you would use for this task. These commands can be sent to clients from ARD or implemented into a first-time startup script.

> **MORE INFO ▶** Full coverage of directory service concepts is beyond the scope of this reference guide. To find out more please refer to *Apple Training Series: Mac OS X Directory Services v10.6* (Peachpit Press, 2010).

Resetting the LKDC

The first time a Mac OS X system is started, the LKDC is created with a unique identifier that is generated automatically. This LKDC provides unique authentication services for local file sharing and identification for authenticated binding. If you plan to use either feature, the LKDC configuration of your Mac must be unique.

This need for a unique configuration presents a problem if you're using a manually created cloned system image that started for the first time on another Mac. The LKDC information is retained as you deploy your cloned system image, and it must be reset as a postimaging task before you can perform any other directory service–related configuration.

> **NOTE ▶** Modular system images have no LKDC configuration because they have yet to be started.

If you are using a manually cloned system image, resetting the LKDC requires a few simple commands that you must run on each Mac, as shown in the following example. The first three commands remove all traces of the previously set LKDC, and the final command rebuilds a unique LKDC using a new automatically generated identifier.

```
sudo rm -fr /var/db/krb5kdc
sudo rm -fr /etc/krb5.keytab
sudo rm -fr /Library/System.keychain
sudo /usr/libexec/configureLocalKDC
```

> **TIP** ▶ A good time to remove the LKDC related files is when cleaning up your model system prior to creating a cloned system image. If you also remove the /var/db/.configureLocalKDC file from your model system, the LKDC will be automatically rebuilt the first time your restored system starts up.

As you can see, resetting the LKDC using this series of commands deletes the System keychain. This can be a problem if your system image relies on custom items saved inside the System keychain, like saved network authentication information, for example. If this is the case for your system image, you will have to use a different technique to reset the LKDC items inside the System keychain.

The LKDC uses multiple keys and certificates stored inside this keychain that are named "com.apple.kerberos.kdc" and "com.apple.systemdefault". There is no built-in Mac OS X command for removing individual items from a keychain. So the best solution is to simply deploy a System.keychain file that contains your necessary custom items, but not the aforementioned LKDC items. Then on first startup, the deployed systems will rebuild their LKDCs and populate the System keychain with the appropriate unique items.

Binding to Directory Service

Before you can bind to a directory service, Active Directory (AD) or Lightweight Directory Access Protocol (LDAP), you must first enable its respective directory service plug-ins. To enable these plug-ins at the command line you will use the `defaults` command to change the directory service configuration file, and then you will use the `killall` command to restart the `DirectoryService` process. The following series of commands demonstrates enabling both these services.

```
sudo defaults write "/Library/Preferences/DirectoryService/DirectoryService"
"Active Directory" "Active"
sudo defaults write "/Library/Preferences/DirectoryService/DirectoryService"
"LDAPv3" "Active"
sudo killall DirectoryService
```

The `dsconfigad` command is used to bind Mac OS X systems to an AD service. This command also has an excellent built-in manual page, or you can enter `dsconfigad` at the command line to view general usage. The following example shows how to use this command to initiate a basic AD binding. The first variable is the name of the local computer as it will be added to the AD domain; this variable is followed by the host name of the AD domain, then the name and password of the directory administrator who is allowed to add computer entries, and finally the name and password of the local administrative account.

```
dsconfigad -f -a MacTower3 -domain adforest.pretendco.com -u adadmin -p adsecret
-lu localadmin -lp localsecret
```

NOTE ▸ You don't have to use sudo to initiate this command; you're already providing authentication as part of the command arguments.

NOTE ▸ In Mac OS X, if you're going to bind to both AD and LDAP, you should always bind to AD first.

The dsconfigldap command is used to bind Mac OS X systems to an LDAP directory service. This command has an excellent built-in manual page, or you can enter dsconfigldap at the command line to view general usage.

Unlike Active Directory, Open Directory client can use an unauthenticated binding to the directory server. In this case, you will only need to supply the name of a directory server followed by a local admin username and password.

```
dsconfigldap -f -a server17.pretendco.com -l localadmin -q localsecret
```

An authenticated binding automatically adds a computer account to the network directory service; thus you must also enter authentication for a directory administrator that has the rights to create computer accounts. The following example shows how to use this command to initiate a basic authenticated binding. The first variable is the name of the local computer, as it will be added to the LDAP domain; this variable is followed by the host name of the LDAP server, then the name and password of the directory administrator who is allowed add computer entries, and finally the name and password of the local administrative account.

```
dsconfigldap -f -c MacTower3 -a server17.pretendco.com -u ldapadmin -p ldapsecret
-l localadmin -q localsecret
```

NOTE ▸ You don't have to use sudo to initiate this command; you're already providing authentication as part of the command arguments.

Setting the Authentication Search Path
In addition to binding your Mac client, to accept authentication information from a directory service you must modify the directory service authentication search path using the dscl command. The dscl command is the primary tool for interacting with the Mac OS X directory service system.

The following example shows what you would enter using `dscl` to add the previously bound directory servers to the authentication search path. The first `dscl` command creates the appropriate search policy entry. The second `dscl` command adds the AD server configured from the earlier example, and the final `dscl` command adds the LDAP server from the previous example.

```
sudo dscl /Search -create / SearchPolicy CSPSearchPath
sudo dscl /Search -append / CSPSearchPath Active\ Directory/adforest.pretendco.com
sudo dscl /Search -append / CSPSearchPath LDAPv3/server17.pretendco.com
```

TIP ▶ If you're not sure of the exact host names of your bound directory servers, you can enter `dscl localhost` to initiate interactive mode to navigate through the directory service configuration. Use `ls` and `cd` to navigate the directory service configuration, similar to the way you would navigate normally at the command line.

Configuring a Firmware Password

Another popular firmware configuration—and a necessity in secure environments—is the use of a firmware password to prevent unauthorized access to the different startup modes available on Mac computers. This configuration must be set separately for each Mac client, as firmware settings are saved to the hardware, not the system volume. On an individual Mac, you can enable and set this password protection using the Firmware Password Utility. This application is available on all Mac OS X installation media.

MORE INFO ▶ For more information about firmware password protection, refer to Knowledge Base document HT1352, "Setting up firmware password protection in Mac OS X."

For starters, the installation media is an incredibly inconvenient location if you're going to use this application on a regular basis. If you mount the Mac OS X Install DVD, you can use the following command to copy the Firmware Password Utility to your local Mac's /Applications/Utilities folder.

```
cp -R "/Volumes/Mac OS X  Install DVD/Applications/Utilities
/Firmware Password Utility.app" /Applications/Utilities/
```

Once the copy is made, simply double-click on the Firmware Password Utility to open it. In order to deploy a firmware password to multiple computers, you must first set it on a local Mac so you can retrieve it in a deployable form. Use the Firmware Password Utility on a local Mac to set the firmware password you wish to deploy. You can disable or change this password later once you have retrieved the password from your local Mac's firmware.

Once the firmware password is set, use the nvram command to retrieve an encoded version of the password. The following example shows the appropriate command and an example retrieved firmware password.

```
MyMac:~ michelle$ sudo nvram security-password
Password: (password not shown)
security-password    %cc%d8f%cf%92%99%c4%
```

NOTE ► This encoded firmware password only works on Intel-based Mac computers.

Now that you have the properly encoded version of the password, you can use the nvram command to set the password and enable firmware password protection. Assuming the same encoded password as the previous example, you would deploy the following two commands using ARD or a script on your Mac computers.

```
sudo nvram security-password=%cc%d8f%cf%92%99%c4%
sudo nvram security-mode=command
```

TIP ► To disable firmware password security from the command line, use sudo nvram -d security-mode. Note that this will still retain the password in firmware; it will simply disable the security mode that requires the password to modify startup.

Modifying Preference Configurations

Most Mac OS X settings, for both system and user resources, are saved to property list files. These property list files can be stored anywhere, but most reside in the Preferences folders throughout the system. Most system settings reside in the /Library/Preferences folder, and most user settings reside in each user's /Users/*username*/Library/Preferences folder. The naming convention for these files is a reverse URL scheme. For example, the Time Machine settings are saved in the file /Library/Preferences/com.apple.TimeMachine.plist.

Many of these preferences files can be included with your system image, but you may need to modify specific preferences as part of your postimaging tasks. The following section deals with the management and deployment of preferences after a system has been imaged.

Deploying Preferences

You can use a variety of methods to modify or set preferences for your deployed Macs:

▶ The best solution is to use a centralized directory service with managed preferences, as covered in Chapter 4, "Creating System Images." Instead of relying on local settings files, the Mac OS X client looks to a directory server for configuration information. As long as the clients are joined to a directory service hosting the managed preferences settings, you can manage the settings at the directory server instead of at each client. In this case, you wouldn't have to configure any postimaging settings except those necessary to bind the computers to the directory service, as covered in the previous section.

▶ A preference file can be replaced with an updated file as long as the replacement file is formatted properly, named properly, and in the correct location on the system volume. Preference files can be deployed using the same techniques as for any other files, covered in Chapter 2, "Deploying Individual Items and Containers," and Chapter 3, "Deploying with Installation Packages."

▶ For targeted preference changes, you can use the defaults command, covered in the next section. You can deploy changes using the defaults command as you would for any other command, by using ARD or an automated postimaging script.

NOTE ▶ Replacing a preference file or using the defaults command to modify a preference does not prevent a user from making future changes to those preferences. If you need to "lock down" preferences, you should implement managed preferences settings.

Modifying Preference Files

Most preferences are stored in a property list file, with a filename extension of ".plist".
Property list files come in two primary formats; XML-formatted plain text or XML binary.
There is a third legacy, text-based format that you may encounter as well, but the use of this
older format is quite rare. Plain text property list files can be edited with any text-editing
application or command. In general, most system preference files are still XML-formatted
plain text, thus making them easier to edit. However, many applications have moved to
binary property list files because they are faster. To modify a binary property list you will
have to use a dedicated editing tool.

Two Apple applications can modify property list preference files; Property List Editor,
installed as part of the Apple Xcode Tools suite, and Workgroup Manager, installed as part
of the Server Admin Tools suite. Workgroup Manager, as covered in Chapter 4, "Creating
System Images," is primarily used for modifying preferences to be deployed using
Mac OS X's managed preferences architecture. On the other hand, Property List Editor is
designed to edit local .plist files, but it provides the better interface of the two.

If you are just getting comfortable with modifying property list files, then Property List Editor
is the tool to start with. As you can see from the previous screen shot, preference files are made
up of key/value pairs. Knowing which property list and key/value are responsible for specific
settings requires knowledge obtained through research (this guide, for example) or experimen-
tation. Mac OS X uses so many different preference files and associated keys that it is beyond
the scope of this book to list all the available management options. Although most of the preference keys are undocumented, you can attempt to discover the keys by opening the preference
files in the Property List Editor application and exploring them.

> **TIP** If you're unsure of which file is used for a certain preference, a helpful
> third-party application is fseventer. This application will display all file system
> changes over time, so as you use the primary interface to modify a setting, fseventer
> will show you which preference files are being changed: www.fernlightning.com/
> doku.php?id=software:fseventer:start.

> **TIP** ▸ If you're unsure of which key/value pairs to modify in a preference file, make a backup of the preference file, modify the setting, and then use the FileMerge application to compare the two. FileMerge is included with the Xcode developer tools.

The downside to Property List Editor is that it's not easily automatable or deployable, unlike command-line tools. Mac OS X includes two command-line property list editing tools, `defaults` and `PlistBuddy`. Of the two, the `defaults` command, discussed in previous chapters as well, is the most commonly used tool for applying specific preference settings. The syntax for the `defaults` command is simple, as long as you know the exact preference setting that you want to modify.

At the command line, enter `defaults write` followed by the path or name of the preference file, then the specific setting key that you wish to change, and then the new value for the setting. The following example modifies the login window preference to show the Directory Service status instead of the computer's name.

```
sudo defaults write /Library/Preferences/com.apple.loginwindow AdminHostInfo DSStatus
```

Working with ByHost Preferences

Certain preferences, the ByHost preferences, are set on a per-computer basis and, by default, apply only to a specific computer. You can find these preferences in every user's home folder, specifically in the /Users/*username*/Library/Preferences/ByHost folder. The preference files in this folder are tied to a specific computer based on a unique identifier included as part of the preference file's name. For example, the screen saver settings for a specific Mac are saved in a preference file named com.apple.screensaver.89C53C04-06CF-5BF0-9751-C49D1C55CF3F.plist.

You can determine the unique identifier of a Mac from the hardware overview section of System Profiler or using the `ioreg` command. This command was demonstrated in the "Using the ARD Send UNIX Command" section earlier in this chapter, and it's also repeated in the following example. The following text is the exact command string that you would enter on each Mac to determine its unique identifier.

```
ioreg -rd1 -c IOPlatformExpertDevice | grep -E "(UUID)"
```

If you want to use a ByHost preference from one computer on another computer, you will need to rename the file using the appropriate identifier for the destination computer. Also, remember that these ByHost preferences are accessed separately for every user on the system; attempting to manage ByHost preferences by actually copying the files to your deployed systems, although possible, would be a huge headache.

Fortunately, if you're using Apple's management and deployment tools, these ByHost preferences issues can be remedied. When creating a cloned image using SIU, you can take advantage of the Apply System Configuration Settings action to reset any ByHost preferences that may be in your system image. However, this will not resolve issues with any ByHost preferences created after deploying the system. This is another reason to use the Mac OS X managed preferences architecture. When deploying settings using managed preferences, even if you import custom preferences using Workgroup Manager, the system will automatically set the appropriate ByHost names for managed preferences files.

A command-line alternative is to use the `defaults` command with the `-currentHost` option to modify ByHost preferences, but this still works only on a per-user basis. For example, the following `defaults` command will modify the screen saver preference so that the screen saver turns on after 10 minutes (600 seconds) of idle time, but only for the user account that runs the command.

```
defaults -currentHost write com.apple.screensaver idleTime 600
```

Because `defaults -currentHost` works only on a per-user basis, you would need to implement this as a login hook script, as detailed in the "Automating Configuration Tasks with `loginwindow`" section later in this chapter.

Configuring Postimaging Serialization Information

Many applications, from both Apple and third parties, require that a serial number or license code be entered to validate ownership of the product and acceptance of the license agreement. When deploying such applications, in many cases you can include the serial or license information as part of your system image. However, in some cases this may violate the license agreement or render the application unusable because the application will recognize other copies with the same serial number or license running on your network.

NOTE ▶ Do not violate license agreements.

Ideally, when deploying an application like this to multiple computers, you should acquire a multiuser or site-wide serial number or license code from the application vendor. You can then use a single number or code for all your systems and build that configuration in as part of your unified system image.

However, it may not be necessary to purchase licenses for every computer in your organization. If this is the case, you will have to manage the sterilization, or licensing, of these applications on a selective basis. Mac OS X does not include a built-in mechanism for managing this information. Thus, you're best served by implementing a third-party license management solution, as covered in Chapter 7, "System Maintenance."

Also, if you have a small deployment or only a few selective licensing issues to deal with, you can serialize these applications as a remote postimaging task. Each application handles serialization differently, which makes it difficult to apply this method in all cases. Generally, though, most serial numbers or license codes are saved in a configuration or preference file. For example, the QuickTime Pro license key is saved in the /Library/Preferences/com.apple.quicktime.plist file.

If you can locate the file responsible for storing the serial number or license code, you can deploy that file as you would any other file using the techniques covered in Chapter 2, "Deploying Individual Items and Containers." If the serial or license information is saved in a property list file, you can also use the `defaults` command remotely, as covered in the previous section of this chapter.

> **NOTE ▶** If you are unable to locate where the serialization information is saved, or if you are otherwise unable to manage the licensing of a particular product, you should contact the vendor to see if there is a suggested deployment methodology.

Automating Configuration Tasks with launchd

For many, the best solution for handling postimaging tasks is to implement a script containing your configuration steps. By scripting the appropriate postimaging tasks, you can guarantee a consistent configuration on all your deployed systems. Additionally, scripts can be set to run at specified times, like system startup or when a user logs in, further automating your deployment solution. If you implement these scripts as part of your system image, your postimaging tasks will automatically run without additional user action when the restored system is first started.

Because every deployment scenario is different, there is no best practice for developing a postimaging configuration script. You can, however, reference earlier sections in this chapter, which cover a variety of commands that can be used in a postimaging configuration script. The nuances of UNIX shell scripting are beyond the scope of this guide; the focus of this section is to show you how to enable Mac OS X to automatically run your scripts.

MORE INFO ▶ An introduction to the scripting technologies built in to Mac OS X can be found in *Apple Training Series: Mac OS X Support Essentials v10.6* (Peachpit Press, 2010).

The launchd process controls startup for all items in Mac OS X; it is quite literally the boss of Mac OS X. The first process to start is launchd, and then during system startup the launchd process looks to several specific folders for launchd property list configuration files. These files tell launchd exactly what to start up and when.

Understanding launchd Folders

The location of a launchd configuration file tells launchd who the process is running for. Case in point: when a user wants to start an application she opens the application, and when she is done with it, she quits the application or logs out. However, if a process is started automatically, then who starts it?

The launchd system defines a process automatically started on the behalf of a user as a *launch agent.* A launch agent is only allowed to be active during the time that a user is logged in to the system. The launchd system defines a process automatically started on behalf of the system (rather than the user) as a *launch daemon.* Launch daemons are allowed to run any time the system is running regardless of whether or not a user is logged in.

Launch agent folders:

▶ ~/Library/LaunchAgents/—Third-party agents for a specific user

▶ /Network/Library/LaunchAgents/—Third-party agents for all users as defined by administrators using a network automount

▶ /Library/LaunchAgents/—Third-party agents for all users as defined by administrators

▶ /System/Library/LaunchAgents/—Apple-supplied agents for all users

Launch daemon folders:

▶ /Library/LaunchDaemons/—Third-party daemons as defined by administrators

▶ /System/Library/LaunchDaemons/—Apple-supplied daemons

Thus, to start something automatically for any user when he is using the Mac, including as early as during user login, you would place a launchd configuration file in the /Library/LaunchAgents folder. On the other hand, to start something automatically any time the system is running, including as early as during the startup sequence, you would place a launchd configuration file in the /Library/LaunchDaemons folder.

Understanding launchd Configuration Files

The location of a launchd configuration file defines who the process is started for, while the settings in the configuration file define the what and the when. Specifically, launchd configuration files define what process or processes are set to run automatically and under what conditions they are to be started.

> **TIP** ▶ An alternative to manually configuring launchd configuration files, as covered here, is to use the third-party application Lingon. This graphical application provides an easy interface for editing existing launchd configurations or creating new ones: http://lingon.sourceforge.net.

Basic launchd Configuration

The launchd configuration file itself is nothing more than a plain text property list with the appropriate key/value pairs used by launchd. Thus, you can create and modify these files using your favorite text editor or Property List Editor. When creating a new launchd configuration, make sure to name the file using the default reverse URL scheme for property list files. For example, if your organization is Pretendco, an appropriate name for a launchd configuration file that starts a script called "jumpstart" would be com.pretendco.jumpstart.plist.

A launchd configuration file requires only two key/value pairs, Label and ProgramArguments. The Label value is used only for identification, and the ProgramArguments value is the exact path for the process or script you want to start. All other additional keys are used to define the conditions under which the specified item is to be started. For example, if you want the item to start as soon as possible, then you need to include the RunAtLoad key with its value set to "true".

The following text is an example launchd configuration file that automatically starts a script located at /Library/Scripts/jumpstart as soon as possible. Thus, if this launchd configuration file is placed in a launch agents folder, then it will run the script as soon as a user logs in. However, if this configuration is placed in a launch daemons folder, then it will run during system startup.

```xml
<?xml version="1.0" encoding="UTF-8"?>
<plist version="1.0">
<dict>
    <key>Label</key>
    <string>com.pretendco.jumpstart</string>
    <key>ProgramArguments</key>
```

```
    <array>
        <string>/Library/Scripts/jumpstart</string>
    </array>
    <key>RunAtLoad</key>
    <true/>
  </dict>
  </plist>
```

You can use this text nearly verbatim to create a `launchd` startup configuration for any script. You will need to change only the Label and ProgramArguments values to meet your needs and then place the configuration in the appropriate launch folder.

Advanced launchd configuration

The `launchd` system recognizes a variety of additional keys that allow you to define specific rules about when and how an item should be run. The most common addition to a user-created `launchd` item is the KeepAlive key, which in its simplest form can be set for "true" to always keep an item running. This key, though, is much more powerful when set with a dictionary, or collection, of other key/value criteria that can be used to limit when the item is run. Consider the following keys, which could be added to the previous example after the <true/> but before the </dict>.

```
    <key>KeepAlive</key>
    <dict>
        <key>NetworkState</key>
        <true/>
        <key>PathState</key>
        <dict>
            <key>/var/db/.AppleSetupDone</key>
            <true/>
            <key>/var/db/.PretendCoMaintenance</key>
            <false/>
        </dict>
    </dict>
```

In this example the KeepAlive dictionary includes the NetworkState key set to "true" indicating that the item should only run if the network is up. Further, the PathState key includes an additional dictionary of file conditions that must be met to run this item. Specifically, the /var/db/.AppleSetupDone file must exist, and the /var/db/.

PretendCoMaintenance file must not exist. The idea is that your custom script would create the .PretendCoMaintenance file as the last step before the script completes.

In other words, this KeepAlive dictionary is telling launchd to only run the item if the network is up, the Setup Assistant has completed, and the script hasn't been run. Once your script runs and creates the file, it essentially disables the launchd item. Then if you need to run the script again, simply delete the .PretendCoMaintenance file, and as long as the network is up, launchd will automatically run the script again.

Here are some other useful launchd configuration keys that you can add to automatically run a custom script or process:

▶ WorkingDirectory—Specify a folder to navigate into to before running the item

▶ EnvironmentVariables—Additional environment variables to be set before running the item

▶ UserName—Specifies the user to run the item as; default for launch daemons is root

▶ StartOnMount—Starts every time a new file system is mounted

▶ WatchPaths—Starts when a specific file is modified

▶ QueueDirectories—Starts when content is added to a specific folder

▶ StartInterval—Starts repeatedly on a timed interval

▶ StartCalendarInterval—Starts repeatedly on a specific calendar interval

MORE INFO ▶ The full list of launchd configuration file keys can be accessed at the command line by entering man launchd.plist.

Configuring an Automated Script with launchd

Before you configure launchd to automatically start your script, you need to place your script in the system and set appropriate permissions. The /Library/Scripts folder is a good location for your custom scripts. After it's in place, make sure the appropriate ownership and permissions are set for the script. If the script is to be a launch daemon that can change system settings, only allow execution of your script by the root user (chown root:wheel and chmod 750).

Also remember that if you want the script to run only at the very first startup, the last line of your script needs to disable the launchd configuration file. An easily scriptable method for this is to delete the launchd configuration file at the end of the script. An alternative method is to use the aforementioned KeepAlive and PathState keys in the launchd configuration file to watch for the existence of a "trigger" file. If the "trigger" file exists, the script doesn't run, so the last line of your script should be to create the "trigger" file.

Once your script is set, and you have created a launchd configuration file using the previous section's instructions, it's time to copy this file to the appropriate launchd folder, also covered previously. It's also a good idea to set ownership and permissions for the launchd configuration file to prevent users from editing it (chown root:admin and chmod 744).

The launchd folders are only consulted during system startup or user login. Thus, the easiest method to enable the automation is to simply restart the Mac. As an alternative you can use the launchctl command to force launchd to load your configuration without having to restart. Assuming the "com.pretendco.jumpstart.plist" from earlier was set as a launch daemon, the following command would immediately load the configuration

```
sudo launchctl load -w /Library/Preferences/com.pretendco.jumpstart.plist
```

> **MORE INFO** ▶ Using the -w flag with launchctl load will add the Disabled key, set for false, to your launchd configuration file. You can learn more about controlling the launchd service by referencing the manual page for the launchctl command.

Automating Configuration Tasks with loginwindow

In some cases you may want a certain configuration to occur when a user logs in or out of the system. As discussed earlier in this book, the loginwindow process handles all aspects of user login and logout. While you could configure a launch agent, as covered in the previous section, to run your script any time a user is logged in, only the loginwindow can be configured to run a script when a user logs out. You can easily modify the loginwindow configuration file using the defaults command, as shown here, to configure a login or logout script.

```
sudo defaults write com.apple.loginwindow LoginHook /Library/Scripts/loginscript
sudo defaults write com.apple.loginwindow LogoutHook /Library/Scripts/logoutscript
```

As you can see, the only value you need to specify is the exact path to the login or logout script. Again, make sure the ownership and permissions for any script files are set to allow execution only by the root user (chown root:wheel and chmod 750). When implemented, a login or logout script will run as root every single time any user logs in or out. Finally, loginwindow will pass the user's short name as the $1 variable if you need to have the script perform an action specific to the current user.

MORE INFO ▶ For more information about login hooks, refer to Knowledge Base document HT2420, "Mac OS X: Creating a login hook."

Understanding Automatic Server Setup

Mac OS X Server, in most cases, requires even greater postimaging configuration than Mac OS X on client computers. Seldom will you be deploying completely identical server systems. In fact, most server deployments start with a completely fresh installation of Mac OS X Server or an installation that has only system updates and no further configuration. Because nearly every server requires unique configuration, Mac OS X Server includes a more sophisticated setup assistant that allows you to automate the server setup process.

TIP ▶ Many of the techniques covered in the previous section for configuring Mac clients can also be used to configure Mac servers.

This section assumes that you already understand the general Mac OS X Server setup process, as covered in *Apple Training Series: Mac OS X Server Essentials v10.6* (Peachpit Press, 2010). Thus, this section does not focus on what your server settings should be or how to best configure a Mac OS X Server to meet your needs. Instead, this section discusses Mac OS X Server's automatic server setup system. With this system you can quickly deploy settings for multiple servers using an automatically discovered local configuration file.

Understanding Server Assistant

After an unconfigured copy of Mac OS X Server is installed or restored, the initial setup needs to be completed to enable use of the server. When an unconfigured Mac OS X Server system starts for the first time, the server setup system is started. The Server Assistant application is the primary interface for accessing the server setup system. In Mac OS X Server v10.6 the Server Assistant features are accessed from the Server menu of /Applications/Server/Server Admin.app. This application can also be installed as part of the Server Admin Tools v10.6 on any Mac OS X v10.6 computer.

MORE INFO ▶ The Server Admin Tools v10.6 installer can be found on the Mac OS X Server installation discs, or it can be downloaded from the Apple website, http://support.apple.com/kb/DL914.

As you can see from this menu, the Server Assistant allows you to remotely install or set up an unconfigured Mac OS X Server via another Mac computer. Alternately you can take advantage of the automatic server setup system to quickly deploy initial configuration settings to multiple servers. Using automatic server setup requires only basic initial setup because it's assumed that additional services will be configured individually later with customized settings.

The following initial basic server settings are required:

▶ Server system language and keyboard layout

▶ Mac OS X Server serial number and license information

▶ Time zone and network time

▶ Local administrator account configuration

▶ Network configuration and network naming

▶ Users and groups configuration, which may automatically set up an Open Directory Master

The following initial basic server settings are optional:

▶ Connect to a directory service

▶ Configure an Open Directory master

▶ Initial setup of services including file sharing, address book, calendar, instant messaging, mail and web

MORE INFO ▶ You can find more about the automatic server setup system in the Mac OS X Server Advanced Server Administration v10.6 guide, available at http://images.apple.com/server/macosx/docs/Advanced_Server_Admin_v10.6.pdf.

Understanding Automatic Server Setup

When a Mac OS X Server is waiting for initial setup, the server setup system will scan the root of all local volumes for a folder named Auto Server Setup. As new local volumes are mounted, the server setup system will scan those as well. This system is looking for two possible files in the Auto Server Setup folder; a server configuration profile and a passphrase file. If appropriate setup files are found in this folder, the server setup system will automatically configure the server based on the content of those files.

The first file is a server configuration profile property list file that contains all the required initial basic server settings. You can use any name you want for the profile so long as it ends with ".plist". The second file is an optional text file that contains only a single passphrase, which is used to decrypt an optionally encrypted server configuration profile. If you choose to use this file, its name must match the name of the configuration profile but end with ".pass" instead of ".plist".

Using a Server Setup Passphrase

If security is a concern in your environment, you will want to use an encrypted server configuration profile, as it contains your Mac OS X Server serial number and the password to the local administrator account. Keep the passphrase separate from the configuration and make the two available to the system only when needed.

For example, you can safely deploy an encrypted server configuration profile as part of your default server system image. When the Mac server starts up for the first time, it will automatically find the encrypted configuration file on the local hard drive, but it will wait for you to enter the passphrase to decrypt the file.

You can enter the passphrase manually using a keyboard attached to the server or remotely using Screen Sharing, ARD, or VNC. Alternately, you can carry a passphrase file on an external volume such as a key drive. As long as the passphrase file is in an Auto Server Setup folder on the root level of the key drive, the mere act of inserting the key drive will cause the server setup system to look for a passphrase file on that drive. As covered previously, the name of the passphrase file must match the name of the configuration profile.

Using Server Setup Profile Restrictions

Even if you have multiple Mac OS X Server computers to configure, each with its own unique settings, you can still use the automatic server setup system by creating multiple configurations, each saved with restrictions that limit the configuration to a specific Mac server. Thus, you could have a single volume that contains multiple server configurations.

When a new Mac server system starts up, the server setup system will scan all of the available configuration profiles and automatically pick a configuration for that Mac server based on the saved restrictions.

The following list presents the restriction conditions and the specific order in which the server setup system will search for these conditions:

▶ Built-in hardware serial number of the server—Use all uppercase letters and make sure to use all the characters: for example, *W88000AB1XY*.

▶ Ethernet (MAC) address of the first port on the server—Include the leading zeros but omit colons and always use lowercase letters: for example, *001a2b3c4d5f*.

▶ IP address of the server—This assumes the server has received an IP address from DHCP services: for example, *192.168.1.25*.

▶ Fully qualified DNS name of the server—This assumes that the server has an IP address and has resolved its DNS name: for example, *mainserver.pretendco.com*.

▶ None of the above—If nothing was set as a restriction, the profile will apply to any server it comes across.

If a server configuration profile contains multiple network connection services, Server Assistant tries to match the Ethernet (MAC) addresses. Failing that, it tries to match interface (BSD port) names. If a profile meets multiple conditions, it applies to a server that satisfies any of them.

> **NOTE** ▶ As of this writing the server setup profiles are created to only work with Mac OS X Server v10.6.0. This is courtesy of two key/value pairs found at the end of the property list file, maximumOSVersion and minimumOSVersion, which are both set for "10.6". Use a text editor or Property List Editor to change these values if you want to use this profile on newer versions of Mac OS X Server.

Using Automatic Server Setup

Assuming you have already appropriately planned your server configuration, creating and deploying an automatic server setup profile can be accomplished in a few steps:

1 On any Mac computer, open /Applications/Server/Server Admin.

2   Select Server > Create Auto Server Setup Profile from the menu bar to open the Server Setup Assistant application.

3   Complete each setup screen that appears by entering the appropriate server information for your server.

This process includes setup screens for Keyboard, Serial Number, Time Zone, Administrator Account, Network Interfaces, Network Names, Users and Groups, Directory Usage, and Services setup.

4   When you arrive at the Save Configuration screen select the encryption option from the pop-up menu. If you go with the default choice of Passphrase Encrypted you must enter a passphrase.

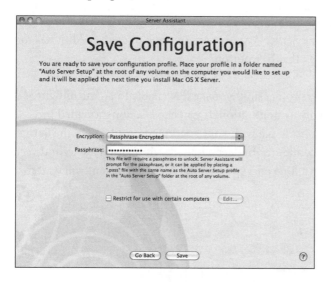

Remember, selecting None will create a plain-text setup profile that will clearly reveal your server's configuration including serial number and administrator password.

5   Optionally, to set restrictions for this configuration, select the checkbox and click the Edit button.

A new dialog will appear allowing you to set the restriction conditions. From the far-left pop-up menu select the condition type and to the right enter the condition value. Clicking the small plus button to the far right will add additional conditions. Click the OK button when you are done adding restrictions.

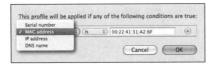

6   Once you are satisfied with your server profile, double-check your server configuration settings, and click the Save button to name and place the file.

> **TIP**   You can navigate back and forth through the Server Assistant screens to make corrections by using the Go Back and Continue buttons.

Again, you can use any name you want, so long as it ends with ".plist". Refer to the "Understanding Automatic Server Setup" section earlier in this chapter for information about the appropriate save locations.

7   At this point you can quit the Server Assistant or continue to create additional configuration profiles by clicking the Save button.

Again, to deploy the server setup profile, simply make it available to an unconfigured Mac OS X Server while waiting for configuration. If you chose a nonencrypted profile, or you are providing a passphrase file with your encrypted profile, then the Setup Assistant should automatically configure your server after waiting for a 30-second verification. Otherwise, if you are using a lone encrypted profile, Setup Assistant will wait for you to enter the passphrase.

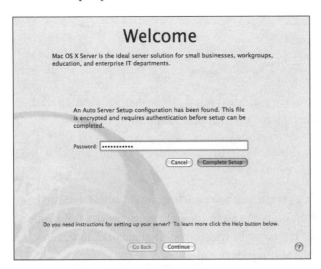

What You've Learned

▶ Some items must be configured uniquely for each Mac after you have deployed a unified system image, including network and firmware settings.

▶ ARD 3 can be used to configure nearly any system setting via the Send UNIX Command feature.

▶ Mac OS X includes a variety of easy-to-use UNIX commands for configuring system settings.

▶ You can automate any postimaging configuration script using custom `launchd` and `loginwindow` settings.

▶ Mac OS X Server includes an advanced server setup system that can be used to perform automatic server postimaging configuration.

References

You can check for new and updated Knowledge Base documents at www.apple.com/support.

Postimaging Considerations

▶ TS1245, "Mac OS X 10.5: Duplicate computer name alert when binding to Open Directory"

▶ HT1352, "Setting up firmware password protection in Mac OS X"

▶ HT2420, "Mac OS X: Creating a login hook"

Web Resources

▶ Apple Mac OS X Server Command-Line Administration guide, http://images.apple.com/server/macosx/docs/Command_Line_Admin_v10.6.pdf

▶ ARD `kickstart` command usage, http://docs.info.apple.com/article.html?path=RemoteDesktop/3.0/en/ARDC882.html

▶ fsevernter third-party file system observation tool, www.fernlightning.com/doku.php?id=software:fseventer:start

▶ Lingon `launchd` management tool, http://lingon.sourceforge.net

▶ Mac OS X Server Advanced Server Administration v10.6 guide, http://images.apple.com/server/macosx/docs/Advanced_Server_Admin_v10.6.pdf

▶ Apple Server Admin Tools v10.6, http://support.apple.com/kb/DL914

Review Quiz

1. What are some command-line tools that you can use to configure primary Mac OS X settings?

2. What are the command-line tools used for configuring Directory Service settings?

3. What is the default underlying format for many Mac OS X preference files?

4. What tools can be used to modify Mac OS X preference files?

5. What techniques can be used to automatically run scripts on Mac OS X?

6. What are the two primary types of launchd jobs? How are they configured?

7. To create a launchd configuration file that will run a job at startup, what are the three required keys in the configuration file?

8. How does starting a job automatically with loginwindow differ from starting a job automatically with a launch agent?

9. What basic server settings are required during the initial Mac OS X Server setup?

10. How can you automate the configuration of a newly installed Mac OS X Server system?

11. In what order does the Server Assistant search restriction settings in a server setup profile?

Answers

1. The systemsetup command can be used to set general system settings; the newtorksetup command can be used to set network configuration settings; the kickstart command can be used to set ARD settings; and the nvram command can be used to set firmware settings including the configuration of a firmware password.

2. The primary tool for interfacing with Directory Services is dscl. However, dsconfigad is used to configure Active Directory binding, and dsconfigldap is used to configure LDAP binding.

3. Mac OS X preference files primarily use XML-formatted key and value data stored in a text file format; however, they can also be stored in a binary file format.

4. The primary graphical tool for modifying preference files is Property List Editor, which is installed with the Xcode developer tools. The defaults command can also be used to modify preference files. Finally, any text-based preference file can be modified with any general text editor.

5. To automatically run UNIX scripts in Mac OS X, you can create a `launchd` configuration or you can modify the `loginwindow` preference to set login or logout hooks.

6. Launch agents run jobs on a per-user basis and are configured from files inside various Library/LaunchAgents/ folders. Launch daemons run jobs on a per-computer basis and are configured from files inside various Library/LaunchDaemons/ folders.

7. The three required keys in a `launchd` configuration file for a startup item are: `Label`, `ProgramArguments`, and `RunAtLoad`.

8. Jobs started by `loginwindow` only run during user login or logout. Launch agents, on the other hand, can run at any time the user is logged into the system.

9. The basic settings required during initial Mac OS X Server setup are keyboard, serial number, time zone, administrator account, network, network names, users and groups configuration, directory services (varies based on previous selections), and services (varies based on previous selections).

10. You can automate the setup of Mac OS X Server systems by creating an auto server setup profile. To create the profile, from Server Admin select Server > Create Auto Server Setup Profile and then walk through the Server Assistant screens until you can save the profile. Once you've created the profile, save it to a folder called Auto Server Setup on the root of any volume that you can connect to the server awaiting setup.

11. The Server Assistant searches restriction settings in the following order: hardware serial number, MAC address, IP address, DNS name (fully qualified), and finally, no restrictions set.

7

Chapter Files	Deployment Planning Template.pdf, available at www.peachpit.com/acsa.deployment
Time	This chapter takes approximately 3 hours to complete.
Goals	Investigate system maintenance concepts to keep your deployed systems working properly
	Learn to use Apple tools for system maintenance tasks
	Configure the Apple Software Update service to provide local Apple update services
	Explore third-party options for system maintenance tasks

Chapter **7**

System Maintenance

Even after a successful rollout of new systems, the administrator's job isn't done—system deployment is an ongoing task. The pace of computer technology is relentless, especially when it comes to software. It's not uncommon for Apple to release an average of one software update every week, and updates to third-party software will need to be deployed as well. Further, new software may periodically need to be deployed, and it may also require deployment of configuration changes. Finally, all these changes to deployed systems will need to be monitored to ensure consistency. All of these system maintenance tasks are necessary to keep your deployed computers running smoothly.

This chapter discusses how to most effectively maintain systems once they have been deployed. You will be introduced to both Apple techniques and third-party tools for accomplishing these maintenance tasks. Specific attention will be paid to Apple Remote Desktop (ARD) and the Apple Software Update service so that you learn how to use these tools to maintain your Mac OS X computers.

Understanding System Maintenance Concepts

System maintenance can be divided into three basic categories: remote administration and system monitoring, asset and license management, and software additions and maintenance.

Remote Administration and System Monitoring

Even if all your computers are using similar configurations, you may still have to "reach out and touch" them to perform administrative functions.

Tools that provide remote administration functionality allow you to perform maintenance tasks remotely on multiple computers simultaneously, enabling you to complete tasks much more quickly than if you had to manually work at each deployed system.

TIP ▶ Mac OS X v10.6 includes limited remote administration capabilities through the built-in screen sharing feature accessible from both the Finder and iChat.

These tools usually also provide system monitoring mechanisms that allow you to observe system changes. In some cases this may mean remotely monitoring the system's display, but it can also mean gathering usage or error data over time so you can track patterns and potential issues.

ARD is the primary tool for providing this type of functionality for Mac OS X systems. You should already be familiar with ARD concepts, as in nearly every chapter of this book you have seen how ARD can be used to accelerate administrative and deployment tasks. In this chapter you will learn about the system maintenance–related capabilities of ARD.

Asset and License Management

Computer hardware and software are valuable assets and should be accounted for on a regular basis. This task is complicated for software because it can be deleted or copied (which in itself can be a form of stealing) with relative ease.

Asset Tracking

Asset tracking refers to monitoring important elements of your deployed system's hardware and software. For hardware, asset tracking involves tracking the location of the devices, such as computers, as well as tracking such elements as serial numbers, organization-specific asset numbers, component specifications, and upgraded components.

Software tracking involves monitoring the software titles installed and also the software versions and modification dates, to ensure that applications are up-to-date. Tracking software usage statistics is also important as it indicates how users are spending their time on the computers and can help you determine the value of specific software titles. For example, if you have deployed an expensive third-party tool but no one is using it, you probably shouldn't spend any more money on the tool.

ARD easily meets most hardware and software asset-tracking needs for Mac OS X clients. Using ARD for asset tracking is covered in Chapter 6, "Postimaging Deployment Considerations."

License Tracking and Enforcement

License tracking monitors the serial number or license codes of installed software. Your deployment may require dedicated license management tools to ensure compliance with software vendor agreements.

In many cases software vendors embed some form of license enforcement technology in their products to prevent users from running unlicensed copies of the software. Most of these solutions either scan the local network or consult with a centralized database to ensure that no other unlicensed copies are running on another computer. Because each vendor handles license enforcement differently, or in some cases not at all, license tracking may be difficult for you as an administrator to manage.

However, as mentioned in Chapter 6, "Postimaging Deployment Considerations," the easiest way to avoid having to manage licenses is to acquire multiuser or sitewide licenses from software vendors. These licenses make deployment and management much easier by offering a single serial number or license code that can be used for all your systems.

If this is not an option due to fiscal or technological limitations, you will be tasked with having to manage license enforcement for your systems. Apple does not produce any tool that can be used to track or enforce third-party software licenses. For this job check out the tools covered in the "Third-Party System Maintenance Tools" section later in this chapter.

Software Additions and Maintenance

After spending a significant amount of time building a unified system image that helps ensure consistent software across all your computers, it would be careless to give up that control after the systems have been deployed. Thus, after the initial deployment, if you intend to keep the systems uniform, you must implement a plan that ensures that the software across all your computers remains similar as new software is deployed. This plan should also include processes for handling problems when new items have negative effects and for integrating new items into your system images.

Software Update Planning

Software bugs are always being fixed, and new features are always being introduced, so it's a fair bet that at any moment at least one piece of software you're using is in need of an update. The frequency of software updates necessitates techniques to deploy those updates as efficiently as possible.

Thus, many software titles, including those from Apple, include built-in update mechanisms that the user can initiate or agree to initiate when reminded by the update software. However, if your goal is uniformity, these auto-updaters are not an ideal deployment solution; you simply cannot rely on your users to implement the appropriate updates. Further, without proper testing there is no way to guarantee that a new update won't negatively affect your systems.

TIP ▶ If you plan to manage software updates, you will need to disable third-party update mechanisms either locally at each client or via network filters. Check with the software developer for a recommended method.

For Apple software updates, you can take advantage of the built-in Apple Software Update mechanism and still maintain control over which updates are made available by configuring an Apple Software Update server. This topic is detailed in the "Configuring Apple Software Update Service" section later in this chapter. Third-party updates are best handled by manually acquiring the necessary updates, often from the software developer's website, and then deploying these updates as you would a software addition.

Software Addition Planning

The methods for managing software additions vary based on deployment needs, and it's possible you will rely on multiple methods, depending on the scope of the additional software. Further, many of the same techniques used to manage software additions can be used to manage software updates and even software settings, which rely on configuration files that can be easily replaced.

Methods for deploying software additions to existing systems are covered throughout this book:

▶ The methods covered in Chapter 2, "Deploying Individual Items and Containers," are best for software additions or simple changes. For example, if you needed to add an application that is installed from a single package icon, like the Firefox web browser, these methods would be appropriate. They are also appropriate for configuration changes, as you may be able to simply distribute a new preference file, as is the case with most Apple software.

▶ The methods covered in Chapter 5, "Deploying System Images," are suitable for any software additions but may be overkill for simple changes. These methods work best for software that's already distributed in the form of an installation package, like all Apple software.

▶ The methods covered in Chapters 2 and 3 rely on the administrator to manage software additions and updates. This task may become difficult to manage if you require frequent changes or if you have multiple system types that receive different collections of software. In these cases you may be best served by investing in a third-party software management suite, as covered in the "Third-Party System Maintenance Tools" section later in this chapter.

Testing and Rollback Planning

It's important to consider exactly how you will resolve any problems that may occur due to a bad software update or addition. The best solution is, of course, to avoid the issue entirely by not deploying the problematic software in the first place. This is where appropriate software testing comes into play. One option is to test new software in a closed environment by deploying it to a specific test computer. Or you could deploy the new software to a small group of trusted "beta users." Though more involved, this method will always yield more thorough test results than in a closed environment.

Even with good testing, bugs may slip through, and if the problem is serious enough you may have to resort to a rollback scenario. The term *rollback* refers to a process of returning the systems back to their previous state before the change occurred. Mac OS X has no built-in architecture for removing bad software or easily rolling the entire system back to a previous state.

> **NOTE ▶** Time Machine, though incredibly useful as a data backup solution, does not provide an ideal restoration mechanism for multiple systems.

Using Apple-only tools leaves you with just two possible rollback options. The first is to manually locate and remove the problematic items. Deploying the removal of an item is best handled by an automated script or by sending the appropriate removal commands via ARD, thus providing quick and uniform resolution.

The second Apple-only rollback option is to restore from your latest working system image. The effectiveness of this method is highly dependent on the age of your system image. Obviously an older image may require that previous updates and additions be reapplied as well. Keeping your system image up-to-date is an important software maintenance issue, which is covered in the next section.

The effectiveness of restoring a system image is also dependent on how you have chosen to handle user home folders. If the users' home folders are stored separate from the system volume or are synced to a home folder server, you can safely reimage each computer's entire system volume. On the other hand, if users' home folders are saved only to the local system volumes, you will have to perform a much slower file-level restore to preserve the users' home folders. Further, you will need to ensure proper backups of all your users' home folders should anything go wrong during the reimaging process.

As you can see, attempting to roll back your deployed systems using Apple-only tools can be quite involved. For this reason several of the tools covered in the "Third-Party System Maintenance Tools" section later in this chapter feature automated software rollback functionality, which makes managing this process much easier.

Future Image Modification

Keeping your system image(s) up-to-date is another important system maintenance task. Because updating and testing a system image can take quite a bit of time, in most cases administrators choose "milestone" events to trigger the creation of a new system image. In some cases a new system image is created and deployed at the time doing so is most convenient, such as the start of a new semester or business season. In other cases a new system image may be required because of the release of significant software or the purchase of computers.

The problem with delaying the update of your system image is that deploying that update will require increasingly more postimaging software updates as your system ages. For example, if your system image is ten months old, and you have to replace a system drive in a Mac, not only would you have to restore the system to that Mac, but you would also have to install all the required updates and changes from the last ten months.

In an ideal world, your system image would update in unison with your deployed software updates and additions. As covered in Chapter 4, "Creating System Images," the type of system image you choose to create will directly affect your ability to update the image. Cloned system images are generally much more difficult to update, thus leading to the typical administrator's practice of waiting until it's most convenient or absolutely required to update the system image.

The modular system image build process, on the other hand, lends itself to frequent updates. In fact, an automated modular build tool, such as SIU, could build multiple updated system images in a single day with very little user interaction. Simply adding the updated installation packages to the modular build process ensures that a newly built modular system image will also contain those updates. Furthermore, you can build a new modular system image using the exact same installation packages as you used to install software updates or additions to your currently deployed computers.

Firmware Considerations

Every Mac computer includes firmware, which is software built into the hardware that controls the hardware at a very low level or when the operating system is unavailable. Intel-based Macs use Extensible Firmware Interface (EFI) technology. The firmware's most important job is to initiate the startup process by loading the core system components. For instance, firmware enables the startup modes that allow you to select an alternate system volume, modifying the Mac OS X startup process and enabling target disk mode. Apple occasionally issues updates to a specific Mac model's firmware. These updates are acquired similarly to other Apple software updates by either visiting the Apple support website or using the Apple Software Update mechanism. The firmware updater is an application that you can deploy as you would any other item. However, a firmware update requires you to manually shut down and restart the Mac in a special mode by holding down the power button until you hear a long tone. This task cannot be automated and must be handled manually for each Mac requiring a firmware update.

MORE INFO ▶ Firmware updates for recent Mac models are listed at the Apple support website. Firmware updates for Intel-based Macs can be found in Knowledge Base document HT1237, "EFI and SMC firmware updates for Intel-based Macs," and for PowerPC-based Macs in document HT1395, "Mac OS X: Available firmware updates."

Using an ARD Task Server

The ARD Task Server is designed to act as an intermediary between the Remote Desktop administrator application and the Mac clients that are being managed. Task Server is included with every installation of the Remote Desktop administrator application. Even if you are only using a single copy of Remote Desktop, that application is interfacing with the local Task Server to initiate connections to the clients.

If you have access to multiple copies of the Remote Desktop application, you can set up a remote Task Server, thus separating the two components onto individual computers. This provides several advantages:

▶ Enhanced installation package deployment—This allows administrators to initiate an installation package deployment from the Remote Desktop application, perhaps on a portable computer that may be removed from the network or on a slow network connection. The Task Server computer will receive the installation packages and then will deploy them to the managed clients. The Task Server also can cache packages and wait for any unreachable managed clients to become available to complete the process.

▶ Enhanced report-generating capabilities—By using a dedicated Task Server, you can schedule system reporting, including the ongoing tracking of user and application use. Further, client reports will be stored on the Task Server, so administrators can access this information even when managed clients are unreachable.

▶ Better response when using multiple Remote Desktop administrator applications—The use of a dedicated Task Server is highly recommended if multiple administrators will be using the Remote Desktop application simultaneously. When a dedicated Task Server isn't used, each instance of the Remote Desktop administrator application is its own Task Server. This creates a problem because managed clients are temporarily "bound" to a Task Server while a task is active, and they will not communicate with other Task Servers until the task is complete. Thus, later administrators will not have access to managed clients that are bound to the first administrator's instance of Remote Desktop.

It's important to remember that, aside from these three Task Server functions, the Remote Desktop administrator application is still responsible for executing most of the remote management features. For example, if you copy individual files using ARD to your managed clients, the copy task originates from the administrative Mac and is not handled by the remote Task Server.

Configuring a Remote ARD Task Server

Setting up a dedicated remote ARD Task Server takes just a few minutes:

1   Install and configure the Apple Remote Desktop administrator application on at least two separate Macs.

     This configuration process was covered previously in Chapter 2, "Deploying Individual Items and Containers."

     One Mac will be the Task Server and should always remain on and connected to the network. Any additional Macs with the Remote Desktop application can be used for standard remote administration functions.

2   On the Task Server, open the Remote Desktop application, and then open its preferences by choosing Remote Desktop > Preferences.

3 In the toolbar, click the Task Server button to reveal the Task Server settings.

By default, every instance of Remote Desktop is running its own Task Server.

4 Enable the "Allow remote connections to this server" option to allow this Mac to act as a Task Server for other Remote Desktop applications.

It's recommended that you deselect the automatic computer settings at the bottom; these settings are best handled on an individual client basis.

5 You can quit the Remote Desktop application and even log out of the server now. The Task Server will remain running as long as the server is on.

6 On your administrative computer(s), open the Remote Desktop application, and then open its preferences by choosing Remote Desktop > Preferences.

7 In the toolbar, click the Task Server button to reveal the Task Server settings.

Again, by default, every instance of Remote Desktop is running its own Task Server.

8 Click the "Use remote Task Server" button, and then enter the IP address of the dedicated remote Task Server.

You can also drag the Task Server from a computer list in the main Remote Desktop window to the address field.

Again, it's recommended that you deselect the automatic computer settings at the bottom; these settings are best handled on an individual client basis.

9   Close the Remote Desktop preferences window, and the administrator Mac will now check with the dedicated Task Server to establish any future managed client connections. Also, all your managed clients, even the ones you are managing from your administrative Mac, will automatically register with the dedicated Task Server.

10   You can verify which Task Server a managed Mac is using by opening up the Client Info window and selecting the Administrators tab.

By default simply double-clicking on a Mac in any computer list will open the Client Info Window, but you can also access it by choosing File > Get Info or pressing the Command+I keyboard shortcut.

NOTE ▶ If you're going to have multiple administrators using Remote Desktop, they should all be configured to use the same remote Task Server. If you do not do this, administrators who are not connected to the Task Server will not be able to establish a reliable connection to the managed clients.

Using ARD to Create Reports

ARD features a powerful reporting mechanism that can be used to track Mac hardware and software assets. Data can be collected for more than 200 attributes and is stored in a PostgreSQL database. This allows an administrator using Remote Desktop to quickly build detailed reports about all her managed clients.

The Remote Desktop application includes easy access for 14 report types: remote Spotlight search, file search, software version, software difference, application usage, user history, system overview, storage, network interface, PCI card, memory, USB devices, FireWire devices, and network performance. However, those familiar with SQL can build any custom reports that they desire by directly accessing the ARD database, as covered on the Apple website http://developer.apple.com/appleapplications/ardsql.html.

Managing Automatic Data Collection and Uploading

Tracking and creating reports with ARD can cause quite a performance hit to your managed clients. You can minimize this problem by fine-tuning the way that ARD report data is collected for your managed clients.

One way to manage performance is to adjust ongoing data-collection options. Two ARD reports—application user data and user accounting data—require that the client perform continuous data collection, adding significant overhead. The data collection for the reports can be enabled on a per-client basis. Although these two reports can be extremely useful, because of the performance cost they should be enabled only if necessary.

Another way to manage data collection is to have the data automatically collected and uploaded to a dedicated Task Server on a scheduled basis. Configuration of a dedicated Task Server was covered previously in the "Using an ARD Task Server" section of this chapter. Once the Task Server is configured, data collection can be scheduled, on a per-client basis, to occur only during nonpeak times so as not to interfere with the user's work. Further, when you need to create a new report in Remote Desktop, instead of collecting the data from each client separately, the data is collected from the Task Server, not only decreasing client overhead but also increasing report creation performance.

To manage automatic data collection and uploading:

1 Open the Remote Desktop administrator application, and then authenticate if necessary.

2 In the sidebar, locate and select the target Macs that you will be managing.

3 Choose File > Get Info, or use press Command+I, to open the Client Info window.

4 If you selected multiple Macs, skip to step 5. If you selected a single Mac client, in the Info window click the Data Settings tab, and then click the Edit button.

From the Info window, you can manage the data-collection options. You will be presented with slightly different windows, depending on whether you selected a single Mac or multiple Macs.

5 Choose which ongoing data-collection items you want to use from the Data Collection area:

▶ Collecting application usage data will allow you to monitor usage statistics for each application, including the duration of time open for each application.

▶ Collecting user accounting data will allow you to monitor the exact times each user has been logged in to the selected client.

6   Configure the automatic upload schedule from the Data Upload Schedule area:

▶   Select the appropriate days of the week and time for the data collection and upload. Ideally this should be a time when users are not logged in to the Macs.

▶   Select the items you want to include with each data collection from the Upload section. The more items you choose, the longer the collection will take and the more space will be used on the Task Server.

7   After you have made your selections, click Done or Apply to send the data collection settings to the Macs.

Creating Reports

Once you have set up a dedicated Task Server, as covered previously in the "Using an ARD Task Server" section of this chapter, and set up automatic data-collection settings, creating reports with ARD is fast and easy. It's not required that you set up a dedicated Task Server or automatic data collection, but doing so increases the amount of data you can collect and decreases the amount of time needed to collect all data.

To create a report in ARD:

1   Open the Remote Desktop application, and then authenticate if necessary.

2   In the sidebar, locate and select the target Mac(s) for which you want to create a report.

3   In the toolbar, click the Reports button.

This opens an untitled reports window that defaults to a System Overview report.

4   Choose the type of report you want to create from the pop-up menu in the reports window.

TIP You can also create a specific report from the Reports menu.

5   Select your reporting options from the top half of the reports window.

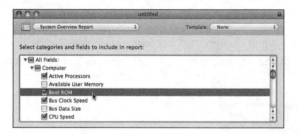

The figure shows the default System Overview report. Each of the 14 report types has a unique interface that reflects the type of data collected. You should explore each report option to see the variety of available data.

6   Optionally you can select to rebuild the report data. Selecting this option will bypass any report data cached on the Task Server and force the selected clients to collect fresh data for the report. This may be necessary if you suspect that the data is out of date or otherwise inaccurate.

7 Check the status of any selected Macs at the bottom of the reports window.

If you're not using a Task Server to cache report data, or if you're rebuilding the data for the report, this report will not complete on any Macs that are in sleep mode or otherwise unresponsive. To resolve unreachable connections, don't close the copy window. Instead, return to the main Remote Desktop window and attempt to wake or reconnect to the unreachable Macs.

8 Once you are satisfied with the report settings, click Generate Report.

You automatically return to the Active Tasks list, where you can view the progress of the task. If the report progress appears to stall, you may have experienced a network interruption. If so, click the Cancel button to the right of the progress bar to stop the report. You can easily reattempt the install by accessing it from the History list.

The report results window opens when the report collection is complete. In the results window, you can browse through the report results and click Print or Export to save the report information.

Don't forget about the Schedule and Save buttons at the bottom of the ARD reports window, which are two important time-saving features. The Save button allows you to place a shortcut of this task in the Remote Desktop sidebar; the Schedule button is covered in the next section.

Using ARD to Schedule Tasks

Nearly every ARD task window has a Schedule button in the lower-left corner. This button allows you to set a task to occur once or repeatedly in the future, thus enabling you to easily schedule recurring maintenance tasks. For example, you could have ARD automatically send and execute a UNIX maintenance script every night or create a usage report once a week.

Note, though, these two caveats when using the ARD scheduling system:

▶ A scheduled item will run only if the Remote Desktop application is open on the administrator's Mac. If the Mac goes into sleep mode, or Remote Desktop is not open for any other reason, the scheduled task will not complete. To remedy this problem, schedule the tasks to run from an open instance of the Remote Desktop application on a Mac that is never turned off, such as the Task Server.

▶ A scheduled task, like any task, will fail if the client Macs are unreachable during the execution of the task. The only exceptions are tasks to install packages or create reports using a dedicated Task Server. The Remote Desktop application must be open to start the task, but because the task is run from the Task Server, even if clients aren't immediately available the task will eventually complete.

To schedule an ARD task:

1 Open the Remote Desktop application, and then authenticate if necessary.

2 In the sidebar, locate and select the target Macs for which you want to create a scheduled task.

3 Open and configure a task. Almost any task can be scheduled, with the only exceptions being direct remote screen monitoring and control tasks.

4 After you have configured the task, click the Schedule button.

5 Set the schedule settings from the schedule dialog that appears, and then click OK.

You can choose to schedule the task just once, or you can have it repeat on nearly any schedule.

6   Check the Schedule button at the bottom of the task window, and then click Save.

7   Give the task an appropriate name so you can easily identify it in the Remote Desktop sidebar, and then click Save.

Upon returning to the main Remote Desktop window, you will see the newly scheduled task in the sidebar, as indicated by the task's name and the clock icon. Select the task to view the current status of the selected client Macs. You can run the task immediately by clicking the play button to the far right. Further, you can edit the task by double-clicking it, or you can delete the task by pressing the Delete key.

Configuring ARD Directory Service Integration

Aside from Apple's system deployment technology, this guide has spent a great deal of time focusing on two other primary Apple management technologies; directory service–based preference management and ARD. These two provide a powerful combination of policy management and system administration functionality. With the latest version of ARD, version 3.3, Apple included enhanced integration between these two technologies.

One of these improvements is the ability in Remote Desktop to select computers from a computer list hosted on a Mac OS X Open Directory server. This feature works as long as the Mac you are running Remote Desktop from is bound to the directory server. If this is the case, within the Scanner list you can select Directory Server from the sources menu and then select computers from any computer lists hosted on the bound server.

Another type of integration allows you to use directory service groups and preference management information to control ARD access privileges. Normally, you would configure these privileges separately on each ARD client from either the Sharing preferences or using the kickstart command. However, this method doesn't provide an easily scalable solution for configuring a large number of ARD administrative users. A better solution is to enable and configure directory-based ARD administration settings, which allows you to define ARD management privileges from your network directory service.

NOTE ▶ The techniques discussed here assume your administration and client Macs are bound to your network directory service and that you have knowledge of how to configure advanced preference management features, as covered in Chapter 4, "Creating System Images."

Enable Directory-Based ARD Access Privileges

By default ARD is not configured to use directory-based ARD administration privileges. Thus, you must first enable this feature on all ARD client computers. As a testament to the flexibility of ARD, there are a variety of methods for deploying this ARD client setting (and others) to multiple Macs.

▶ Change Client Settings assistant—If you are already using ARD to manage the Macs, you can perform an across-the-board change to the ARD client settings. In Remote Desktop select the Mac clients you wish to change and then select Manage > Change Client Setting from the menu bar. This will open an assistant that will step you through a variety of ARD client settings, including the ability to enable directory-based administration.

▶ Create Client Installer assistant—This assistant is nearly identical to the Change Client Settings assistant, but instead of immediately applying the settings, it instead creates an installation package that can be applied to the client Macs. This is a good solution if you are building new system images, as you can easily integrate the resulting installer into your system build workflow. This assistant can also be reached in Remote Desktop by selecting File > Create Client Installer.

▶ Using the `kickstart` command—If you prefer to adjust your ARD client configuration via the command line or a script, then you can use the `kickstart` command to enable directory-based administration. The following command shows the appropriate syntax to enable this feature.

```
sudo /System/Library/CoreServices/RemoteManagement/ARDAgent.app/Contents
/Resources/kickstart -configure -clientopts -setdirlogins -dirlogins yes
```

▶ Using custom managed preferences—If you are taking advantage of the Mac OS X managed preference architecture then you can use it to enable directory-based ARD administration for current and future Macs. Using the Details section of the Preferences pane in Workgroup Manager, import the ARD preference manifests by selecting the Remote Desktop application (do not import your own settings). This will import three preference manifests, including the com.apple.RemoteManagement preference, which contains a Boolean (true/false) key for enabling directory-based ARD administration.

Manage Directory-Based ARD Access Privileges

Once you have enabled directory-based ARD administration on your Mac clients, you can apply access privileges based on information accessed from directory services. ARD access privileges are defined using one of four privilege keys; ard_admin, ard_interact, ard_manage, and ard_reports. The following table shows the specific ARD features that are tied to each privilege key.

Management Privilege	ard_admin	ard_reports	ard_manage	ard_interact
Generate reports	●	●	●	
Open and quit applications	●		●	
Change settings	●		●	
Copy items	●		●	
Delete and replace items	●		●	
Send messages	●		●	●
Restart and shut down	●		●	
Control	●			●
Observe	●			●
Show being observed	●			●

You will use these privilege keys to manage ARD access. Again showing ARD's flexibility, there are three different methods for applying access privileges from directory services.

▶ Use local groups—This method is used if you are unable to create and manage groups at the network directory level. Instead you create local groups using the ARD privilege key names; com.apple.local.ard_admin, com.apple.local.ard_interact, com.apple.local. ard_manage, and com.apple.local.ard_reports. Using Workgroup Manager to create these local groups, you then populate the group's membership with the users and groups who are allowed to have the associated ARD privileges.

▶ Use network groups—This method involves creating and populating groups created on your network directory service; ard_admin, ard_interact, ard_manage, ard_reports. Again, you populate the group's membership with the users and groups who are allowed to have the associated ARD privileges. These groups can be created on any network directory service so long as the "short" group name matches the ARD privilege key.

▶ Use custom managed preferences—This involves creating a custom managed preferences entry using the Inspector interface of Workgroup Manager. As this book went to press, managing ARD access privileges was not part of the collection of ARD-related preference manifests. Thus, to use this implementation you must manually edit an entry's MCXSettings attribute. This is beyond the scope of this reference guide, but you can find out more from Apple's ARD Administrator Guide v3.3 (see the "Web Resources" section at the end of this chapter).

Automating System Maintenance Scripts

Mac OS X includes a predefined set of daily, weekly, and monthly periodic maintenance scripts. These scripts perform a variety of recommended maintenance tasks. By default the daily scripts run every day at 3:15 a.m., the weekly scripts run every Saturday at 3:15 a.m., and the monthly scripts run on the first day of the month at 3:30 a.m.

> **NOTE** ▶ Unlike older versions of Mac OS X, the periodic scripts will always be run even if the computer is off or asleep at the time the script is scheduled to run. Instead, the scripts will be run when the computer starts up or wakes from sleep.

You can also modify the periodic schedule to better suit your needs. Like all items that automatically run on Mac OS X, these periodic scripts are handled by launchd. In the /System/Library/LaunchDaemons/ folder you will find a set of three com.apple.periodic property list files that control when `launchd` runs the various periodic maintenance scripts. These items are protected by root permissions, but as an administrator you can easily modify these files using any text editor, Property List Editor, or the third-party tool Lingon.

> **MORE INFO** ▸ Creating and modifying launch daemons was covered previously in Chapter 6, "Postimaging Deployment Considerations."

You can also add to the existing periodic maintenance scripts. These scripts are located in one of three folders: /etc/periodic/daily, /etc/periodic/weekly, and /etc/periodic/monthly. It's Modifying the existing periodic maintenance scripts is not recommended because these items are set by Apple to ensure proper execution. Each folder can contain as many scripts as you need. The scripts are run in an order based on their names, with each script having a name that starts with a three-digit number. The default system script names start with 100 and go to 999. Any custom maintenance script you add should have a name that starts with a number that falls either before or after this range so as not to interrupt any system scripts.

Configuring Apple Software Update Service

With Mac OS X Server you have the option of mirroring the Apple Software Update servers with your own local Software Update server. Mirroring has two advantages. First, you can save Internet bandwidth. All of your client computers will retrieve their software updates from the Software Update server on your local network rather than over the Internet.

The second advantage is that you can control which updates are downloaded and which are available to your users. This can be particularly useful when a software update might be incompatible with some of the software you're using, thus giving you time to test the software update before making it available to your client Macs.

In this section you will learn how to set up a local Software Update server using a Mac OS X Server. After setup you will configure your client Macs to use this server instead of the default Apple server. Finally, you will experiment with some advanced Software Update service configurations and learn how to troubleshoot this system.

> **MORE INFO** ▶ A great deal of Software Update service information is presented here, but you can also download the Apple System Imaging and Software Update Administration guide at http://images.apple.com/server/macosx/docs/System_Imaging_and_SW_Update_Admin_v10.6.pdf.

General Software Update Service Configuration

These instructions assume that you have already installed the server system software, completed the initial server setup, and properly set up the network configuration. They also assume that the server has access to the Internet so it can download the updates from the Apple primary Software Update servers.

Like all other Mac OS X Server services, the Software Update service is configured from the Server Admin application. Server Admin is located in the /Applications/Server folder on your Mac OS X Server v10.6 computer. This application can also be installed as part of the Server Admin Tools v10.6 on any Mac OS X v10.6 computer.

> **MORE INFO** ▶ To learn more about basic Mac OS X Server v10.6 configuration, please refer to *Apple Training Series: Mac OS X Server Essentials v10.6* (Peachpit Press, 2010).

Configuring the Software Update service on a Mac OS X Server is relatively easy. First you must configure a few general Software Update service settings and enable the service.

> **NOTE** ▶ Make sure you have enough free space on your server to store all the available updates. If you choose to automatically download all the updates, you should actively monitor the server's available disk space. Redirecting the storage for the Software Update service to another volume as described in the instructions below will help keep the boot volume clear. As this book went to press, the current Apple Software Update library was around 60 GB.

NOTE ▶ The Software Update service will only work for the version of the operating system installed on the server and older versions. In other words, the Software Update service on a Mac OS X Server v10.5 will only handle updates for Mac OS X v10.5 or earlier computers, and will not handle the updates for a Mac OS X v10.6 computer.

To configure Software Update service general settings:

1   Open /Applications/Server/Server Admin, and then connect to your server.

2   If the Software Update service isn't visible from the left column, add it:

▶   Click the Add (+) button in the lower-left corner, and then choose Add Service from the pop-up menu.

▶   In the Services pane that appears, select the Software Update checkbox to enable it for configuration, and then click Save.

3   Select the Software Update service from the left column, and then click the Settings button in the toolbar.

4   Click the General tab to reveal the primary Software Update service settings.

5 Select the Software Update service options that are appropriate to your situation. The options need to be configured only if you want a custom configuration.

▶ You can choose to limit the bandwidth from your local Software Update server to the client Macs.

▶ You can select an alternate location for storing the downloaded software update packages. The default location is the /var/db/swupd/ folder, which is indeed on the system volume. Redirecting this is a key feature if you have an Xserve with a smaller system drive.

▶ You can select a different port to provide the updates, but in most cases the default port is acceptable.

▶ By default, no updates are downloaded, and you have to manually choose to download the updates. Or you can choose to automatically download "all" or "all new" updates from Apple to your local Software Update server. This feature is convenient, but it takes a very long time to download all the updates and requires quite a bit of storage space. Further note that by enabling "all" updates even older Apple updates are downloaded, which in many cases are not necessary.

▶ By default no downloaded updates are made available to your local network, and you have to manually choose to make updates available. This is ideal for an environment where you need to control the updates. Or you can choose to automatically enable any update that has been copied to your Software Update server. If you choose this option and the previous option, your local Software Update server will essentially mirror the Apple Software Update servers.

▶ By default, older updates are not deleted from your Software Update server. Or you can choose to have older updates automatically deleted. Unless you need to keep older updates available for a specific reason, this feature should be enabled. Note that even if you don't select this option, Apple still has the ability to resend updates if it finds reason to remove them.

6 Click Save after you have made your general Software Update service selections.

7 Click the Start Software Update button to enable the service.

Regardless of your selections, the Software Update service will first download a full catalog of available updates from the Apple Software Update servers. Depending on the speed of your Internet connection, this step could take up to an hour. Once the update catalog has been downloaded, if you chose to have updates automatically downloaded, the Software Update service will immediately start to download individual updates. Depending on your Internet connection speed, automatically downloading all the Apple updates could take several hours or even a few days.

> **TIP** Even though the Server Admin interface may be unresponsive, you can verify that the Software Update service is active by opening /Utilities/Activity Monitor and verifying that the swupd_syncd process is open and using CPU resources.

> **TIP** If you are on a slow Internet connection but have access to a server that has a fast Internet connection, you can prime the Software Update service on the server with the slower connection by copying the updates from the server with the fast connection via an external disk drive.

Managing Software Updates

Once the Software Update service has downloaded the catalog of available updates, you can start to manage the updates from Server Admin. Keep in mind that if you chose to automatically download updates, you will be unable to manage these updates until all the update files are downloaded. This is because once the Software Update service is given a list of items to download, it will ignore any configuration changes until it completes the download task.

To manually manage software updates:

1 Open Server Admin, and then connect to your server.

2 Select the Server Admin service from the left column, and then click the Settings button in the toolbar.

3   Click the Updates tab to view the current catalog of updates.

The listing will show the update's Name, Version, Size, and release date along with the current status of the update.

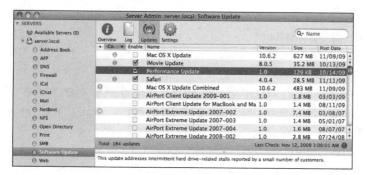

4   Select an update from the list to view its release notes at the bottom of the window. This information will help you identify which software updates are appropriate for your systems.

To the left of the update's name, you'll notice the Software Update status indicators. In the first column from the left, a circle with a triangle indicates that the update requires a restart, and an exclamation point indicates that the update is currently unavailable. In the figure, the update is being downloaded.

TIP If you know that a new update is available, but it's not showing in the Updates list, click the refresh button to the right of the Last Check time to force an update of the list. Again, it may take several minutes for the updated list to refresh.

5   If you're manually managing update downloads, select an update or a list of updates and click the Copy Now button to add those updates to the download queue.

TIP The Choose Version button allows you to select a specific version if multiple updates are being offered.

A gray dot immediately appears in the Copied column, indicating that the updates are in the queue to be downloaded. Once the updates have fully downloaded, they will appear with a blue dot in this column. If Server Admin appears to stall while the updates are downloading, refresh Server Admin's connection by selecting View > Refresh from the menu bar.

6   If you're manually managing update availability, select the checkbox in the Enable column for the updates that you want to make available to your network. Click Save after you have selected the appropriate updates.

Once your local Software Update server is configured to your satisfaction, you should test it using a small group of deployed systems.

Configuring Clients for Your Software Update Service

Just because you have set up a local Software Update server does not mean that client Macs are prepared to use it. By default, the Software Update application on all Mac OS X computers looks to http://swscan.apple.com for Apple updates. Thus, for your deployed Macs to use a local Software Update server you must reconfigure the client's Software Update application settings. This can be accomplished using managed preferences or by modifying a local configuration file.

> **TIP** You can completely disable Software Update access by forcing your client systems to use a nonexistent server source. Using 127.0.0.1, for example, will prevent your clients from finding any updates.

Configuring Software Update Server Source

The best method for configuring Software Update to use your server is to use managed preferences. If this is the case, in Workgroup Manager simply select a computer account or computer list to manage and choose the Software Update managed preference. As you can see in the following screen shot, all you have to do is add the URL to your local Software Update service.

NOTE ▶ At the time of this writing, the URL for the Software Update server depends on the version of Mac OS X in use. Mac OS X v10.4 uses http://server:8088/index. sucatalog, Mac OS X 10.5 uses http://server:8088/index-leopard.merged-1.sucatalog, and Mac OS X 10.6 uses http://server.example.com:8088/index-leopard-snowleopard. merged-1.sucatalog.

The Software Update application uses a preference list configuration file located at /Library/Preferences/com.apple.SofwareUpdate.plist. This property list file, like any other, can be modified with the Property List Editor or the `defaults` command. When it comes to quickly deploying a new local setting, the best solution is to use the command-line method. For example, if your local Software Update server's host name is "sus.pretendco. com," you would only need to enter the following command to configure a client Mac to use your server.

```
sudo defaults write /Library/Preferences/com.apple.SoftwareUpdate CatalogURL
"http://servern.pretendco.com:8088/"
```

As you learned in Chapter 6, "Postimaging Deployment Considerations," you can quickly deploy this command to multiple systems using the ARD Send UNIX Command task. Or you could make this configuration part of your standard system image.

Configuring Software Update Schedule

By default, Software Update is configured to check for updates once a week. You can adjust this stetting or completely disable it, thus only allowing manual updates. It can be changed locally on the Mac from the Software Update preferences, but this is clearly not an efficient deployment method. Again, in this case you can deploy this setting using managed preferences or locally using the command line. However, because the Software Update schedule is a ByHost preference, there are few extra steps you will have to take to manage this item.

NOTE ▶ Only administrative users are allowed to install using Software Update, so disabling the schedule may be a moot point if most of your users log in with standard accounts.

To adjust the Software Update schedule using managed preferences, you should first manually configure the settings you want on a client Mac from the Software Update preferences. This will allow you to easily import the preference without having to manually adjust the key/value pairs. Now, on this client Mac use the Details section of Workgroup Manager to import the ~/Library/Preferences/com.apple.scheduler.UUID.plist preference file. When importing this preference you must select the Often and ByHost options.

This example screen shot reveals that the schedule setting is actually set to repeat in the distant future, whereas it might as well be "off". This will set the Software Update schedule every time a user logs in. To prevent further schedule changes you should also disable the user's access to the Software Update Preference pane.

As an alternative to using managed preferences you can use the `softwareupdate` command to disable the schedule. Simply entering `softwareupdate --schedule off` at the command line will disable the Software Update schedule, but only for that user. Thus, for this to remain an effective tool, you will have to include this command string as a startup launch agent so that every time a user logs in to the Mac the schedule will be set to off. Keep in mind, though, this command does not disable the user's ability to access the Software Update preferences.

Finally, if you need to manually initiate the Software Update process, you can also use the `softwareupdate` command. Specifically, enter `sudo softwareupdate -i -a` to install all available updates. Again, this type of command is best deployed using the Send UNIX Command task of ARD as covered in Chapter 6, "Postimaging Deployment Considerations."

Blocking Access to the Apple Servers

If giving users access to the main Apple Software Update servers is a concern, you may want to block the service outright on your entire network.

The Apple Software Update servers can be reached at http://swscan.apple.com. Apple chose to use the default port 80 for this service to make it easily reachable from anywhere on the Internet. Unfortunately, this means that unless you want to block all web traffic, you cannot simply configure your firewall to block port 80. A network administrator must instead configure your network systems to block access to that domain name in order to prevent Mac clients from reaching the default Apple Software Update servers.

> **NOTE** ▶ Don't inadvertently block access to the Apple server for your Software Update server.

Using Cascading Software Update Servers

Configuring a single local Apple Software update server as covered earlier fits the needs of most deployment scenarios for a single location. However, if your deployment spans multiple locations you may need to set up multiple Software Update servers. You would also need to set up multiple servers if you require different sets of available updates. Although you could set up multiple independent Software Update servers, Software Update offers a cascading configuration option that may suit your situation better.

> **NOTE** ▶ When setting up multiple Software Update servers, you must manually configure your client Macs to use the appropriate server.

If you set up cascading Software Update servers, your primary Software Update server is the only server that needs to access the main servers. Any secondary servers you require can simply point to your primary Software Update server.

This cascading configuration provides two benefits. First, the secondary servers can provide a further limited set of updates; for example, in an educational environment, administrators can have access to the primary Software Update server, and faculty and staff can have access to only the secondary servers. Second, the secondary servers will not need access to the Internet, as they will receive all their updates from your primary Software Update server. This setup not only conserves your Internet bandwidth, it also allows you to place secondary servers in secured environments that don't have access to the Internet.

Configure Cascading Software Update Servers

The setup of cascading Software Update servers requires modification of only a single configuration property list on any secondary servers. The /etc/swupd/swupd.plist configuration file contains a single key that directs the Software Update service to the location of the primary server that it's retrieving updates from. By default, this key directs the server to look at the main Software Update service.

Here's how to set up a secondary Software Update server:

1   Configure the General settings as covered in the "Configuring Clients for Your Software Update Service" section earlier in this chapter, but *do not* start the Software Update service. Before you start the service for the first time, you must change the default primary server to point to your primary Software Update server.

2   Edit the /etc/swupd/swupd.plist file manually instead of using the `defaults` command. Open this file with your favorite text editor or Property List Editor, and then change the value for the metaIndexURL key to the URL for your primary Software Update server.

For example, if your primary Software Update server's host name is sus.pretendco. com, you would need to change this:

```
<key>metaIndexURL</key>
<string>http://swscan.apple.com/content/meta/mirror-config-1.plist</string>
```

to this:

```
<key>metaIndexURL</key>
<string>http://sus.pretendco.com:8088/catalogs.sucatalog</string>
```

3   Once you have modified the configuration file, start the Software Update service as you would normally.

Once the secondary Software Update server has downloaded the new catalog from your primary server, you'll see that the secondary server has access only to the updates you choose to make available from the primary server.

Using a Test Software Update Server

Setting up a test Software Update server is an excellent way to deploy new updates to a limited number of test systems. You can set up an independent test server, or you can use the advanced configurations covered previously to configure a test Software Update server.

If you have set up cascading or duplicate Software Update servers, your primary server can act as a test server. The configuration is simple.

1   Allow the additional updates on your primary server, and set only your test clients and secondary servers to access the primary server.

2   Configure your secondary servers with a more limited list of updates, and then set all normal clients to receive updates from the secondary servers.

3   Once you have tested and confirmed that an update is valid, make that update accessible on your secondary servers as well as the primary one.

Troubleshooting the Software Update Service

Here are some troubleshooting options for your local Software Update server:

▶ As always, human errors are prime suspects when problems occur. Ensure proper Software Update configuration in Server Admin. Double-check your Software Update server settings. Verify that the appropriate updates are downloaded and enabled.

▶ From another computer, open a browser and verify that you can access these URLs (assuming the server name is "sus.pretendco.com"): http://sus.pretendco.com:8088/index.sucatalog, http://sus.pretendco.com:8088/index-leopard.merged-1.sucatalog, http://sus.pretendco.com:8088/index-leopard-snowleopard.merged-1.sucatalog. These URLs represent what Mac OS X v10.4, v10.5, and v10.6 look to for software updates, respectively.

▶ Double-check the server's network configuration. This includes making sure the firewall isn't blocking access to the Software Update port, which is 8088 by default.

▶ Double-check the configuration of the client Mac. Make sure the CatalogURL key in the /Library/Preferences/com.apple.SoftwareUpdate.plist file points to your local Software Update server.

▶ Make sure the Software Update server can access the main servers or another computer running Software Update server. To verify access to the Apple servers, enter the following URL in the Safari browser on your Software Update server: http://swscan.apple.com/content/catalogs/others/index-snowleopard.merged-1.sucatalog. Your server must be able to access this file in order to download the Apple updates.

▶ If the Updates list in Server Admin appears unresponsive, the Software Update service is likely synchronizing the catalog or downloading updates. You can verify this by checking to see if the proper services are running.

▶ Ensure that the Software Update services are running. It's easiest to use the Activity Monitor application on the Software Update server. If the server is synchronizing the catalog or downloading updates, you should see the swupd-syncd process running. This process runs only when needed, however, so you may not see it. You can also check for the httpd process running as user _softwareupdate, which should always be running when the Software Update service is active, to reshare updates to your clients.

▶ If all else fails, you can rebuild the Software Update server. To do this, stop the Software Update service and delete all the items inside the /etc/swupd folder and the updates storage folder, which defaults to /var/db/swupd/html. Then reconfigure and restart the Software Update service, and it will rebuild the catalog and redownload the updates.

Third-Party System Maintenance Tools

Although Apple provides tools for many system maintenance functions, for most medium-sized to large deployments, the Apple tools are not appropriate. Fortunately, a wide array of third-party system maintenance tools are available. Some tools provide specific functionality; others provide a full suite of system maintenance features.

> **MORE INFO** ▶ Website links to all the third-party tools discussed here are available at the end of this chapter in the "Web Resources" section.

Remote Administration Tools

Remote administration tools provide remote management and system monitoring functions. The most popular of these tools are based on the VNC remote-control standard (as is the ARD screen sharing function). Simply searching the web for "VNC" will yield several free and commercial tools. The tools mentioned here—LanSchool, NetSupport Manager, and Timbuktu Pro by Netopia—go beyond screen sharing, providing additional remote administration functionality similar to ARD.

LanSchool

LanSchool is a commercial remote administration solution geared toward the needs of an educational environment. In addition to remote screen sharing, this product provides an easy-to-use interface with tools designed specifically for instructors and teachers to manage a computer classroom environment. NetSupport Manager supports Windows, various thin clients, and Mac clients.

NetSupport Manager

NetSupport Manager is a commercial remote administration solution geared toward the needs of a technical support professional. In addition to remote screen sharing, this product provides remote hardware and software asset reporting and remote diagnostics. NetSupport Manager supports Windows, Linux, and Mac clients.

Timbuktu Pro by Netopia

Timbuktu Pro is a commercial remote administration solution that supports both Windows and Mac clients. This product also features some remote management features such as remote file copy. One of Timbuktu's outstanding features is the ability to easily reach clients that are, from a network perspective, quite distant, including the ability to automatically discover a client's network location through routers and firewalls. Recently this tool has been integrated with Skype to allow live conferencing.

Asset and License Management Tools

Asset and license management tools provide various combinations of asset tracking, license tracking, and license enforcement. These tools are especially welcome, as Apple currently provides no license management solution for Mac OS X.

Altiris Asset Management Solution

The Altiris Asset Management Solution is a popular commercial asset-tracking and management tool. This product works with a wide range of platforms, including mobile handheld devices. The primary advantage to this solution is that it features advanced accounting functionality that ties in to other Altiris enterprise solutions.

Asset Trustee by FileWave

Asset Trustee can track hardware, software, and license assets for both Windows and Mac clients. This product uses a client-side push mechanism to save report data to a centralized database, so even if clients are unavailable, the asset database still can be accessed.

K2 by Sassafras

The K2 KeyAuditor and KeyServer provide the only Windows- and Mac-compatible license tracking and enforcement solution. This product provides live tracking of used and unused software licenses and also provides a policy-based license enforcement mechanism that works with many third-party products.

License enforcement allows you to minimize software licensing costs by purchasing fewer licenses. The KeyServer acts as a central control point for all software licenses; the KeyServer can automatically distribute or revoke a limited set of licenses based on policies set by the administrator, mitigating the need for a license for every single client.

Along with these advanced license management features, the K2 suite provides a range of general asset-tracking features, including hundreds of built-in reports covering deployment, hardware and software inventory, software usage, and license compliance.

Recon Suite by JAMF

Recon is a commercial asset-tracking tool that works with both Windows and Mac clients. Recon is a subset of the Casper suite by JAMF and integrates with the JAMF Software Server (JSS), and even though Recon is available as a standalone solution, its true advantage is that it integrates with the rest of the Casper system maintenance suite. The Casper Suite is covered later in the "System Management Suites" section of this chapter.

Software Additions and Maintenance Tools

Software additions and maintenance tools focus on managing software additions and updates. They can help you maintain uniformity across your systems, or if you have a wide variety of installed software they can help you manage the differences between your systems.

Deep Freeze by Faronics

Deep Freeze ensures that your Mac clients are identical after every restart. It allows your users to make nearly any changes they want to the system, but after each startup, the Deep Freeze system completely restores the Mac to a predefined system configuration. This restore information is saved in a hidden volume on the system drive, so no additional network services are required. Deep Freeze works with both Windows virtualization tools and Boot Camp and can be administered via ARD or LANDesk.

Puppet by Reductive Labs

The open-source Puppet offers highly flexible, granular deployment for software and configuration. Puppet was designed for servers but can be used with a variety of platforms.

Puppet is a powerful and flexible solution that, with some work, allows you to define nearly any desired configuration. However, Puppet also has a very steep learning curve, and you must be comfortable with scripting languages.

Radmind by UMICH

Radmind is an open-source file system administration tool that works on various UNIX systems, but it also sports a graphical interface for Mac OS X. Radmind allows you to create specific Mac OS X system configurations, and then distribute those configurations to other Macs via a Radmind server. Further, you can build a base system, and then add specific sets of files on top of that system.

Radmind also keeps track of every item that is part of the file system. This allows Radmind to detect differences between a Mac computer's current system and the desired system configuration. Further, an administrator can have Radmind make repairs.

System Management Suites

If you're looking for a single source for a wide range of system management features, system management suites are your best bets.

Casper Suite by JAMF

The Casper Suite provides system imaging, inventory management, patch management, software distribution, remote control, settings management, and license management capabilities all in a single suite of tools. The Casper Suite is preferred by some Mac administrators because it's a Mac-only product.

KACE Systems Management

KACE provides a suite of system deployment and maintenance tools built around specially designed hardware appliances. The KACE solutions support system deployment, discovery and inventory, software distribution, asset management, security audit and enforcement, and help desk features. KACE supports Windows, Linux, and Mac clients.

FileWave Suite

The FileWave suite is an automated software distribution and management system that lets you manage deployment of software additions and updates, configuration changes, and entire systems all from a centralized database. FileWave can also roll back your clients to a previous state. FileWave works with Windows, Linux, and Mac clients.

LANDesk Suite

The LANDesk Suite Mac Agent provides system deployment, software distribution, configuration management, asset tracking, software license monitoring, and remote control capabilities all in a single suite of tools. LANDesk works with both Windows and Mac clients.

LANrev Suite

The LANrev Suite provides software distribution, license management, patch management, remote management, asset tracking, and disk imaging capabilities all in a single suite of tools. LANrev works with both Windows and Mac clients.

What You've Learned

▶ Many tasks are involved in keeping systems properly maintained after deployment. Apple provides ARD and the Software Update service to help with system maintenance tasks, but there are also many third-party alternatives.

▶ ARD features an advanced reporting mechanism that can be used to track hardware and software assets.

▶ ARD features a scheduling component that can be used to automatically run system maintenance tasks.

▶ The Mac OS X Software Update server can be configured to fully mirror the Apple Software Update servers or can be modified to host only a limited set of applicable updates.

References

You can check for new and updated Knowledge Base documents at www.apple.com/support.

Troubleshooting ARD and Software Update

▶ TA24108, "Remote Desktop stops responding at the Task Server pane of the Setup Assistant"

▶ TA24198, "Remote Desktop 3.0: Some reports appear blank or respond with an error message"

▶ HT3923, "Mac OS X Server v10.4 or later: Requirements for Software Update Service"

▶ HT3765, "Mac OS X Server v10.5, v10.6: How to cascade Software Update Servers from a central Software Update Server"

Web Resources

▶ Accessing the ARD 3 SQL database, http://developer.apple.com/appleapplications/ardsql.html

▶ ARD Administrator Guide v3.3, http://images.apple.com/remotedesktop/pdf/ARD_Admin_Guide_v3.3.pdf

▶ Apple System Imaging and Software Update Administration guide, http://images.apple.com/server/macosx/docs/System_Imaging_and_SW_Update_Admin_v10.6.pdf

▶ Apple Server Admin Tools v10.6 download, http://support.apple.com/kb/DL914

▶ LanSchool—remote classroom management, www.lanschool.com

▶ Net Support Manager—remote administration tool, www.netsupportmanager.com/mac.asp

▶ Timbuktu Pro by Netopia—remote administration tool, www.netopia.com/software/products/tb2

▶ Altiris Asset Management Solution, www.altiris.com

▶ Asset Trustee by FileWave—asset management tool, www.filewave.com/products/assettrustee

- ▶ K2 suite by Sassafras—asset and license management tool, www.sassafras.com

- ▶ Recon suite by JAMF Software—asset management tool, www.jamfsoftware.com/products/recon-suite

- ▶ Deep Freeze by Faronics—software maintenance tool, www.faronics.com/html/DFMac.asp

- ▶ Puppet by Reductive Labs—software and configuration maintenance tool, http://reductivelabs.com

- ▶ Radmind by the University of Michigan—software maintenance and configuration suite, http://rsug.itd.umich.edu/software/radmind

- ▶ Casper Suite by JAMF Software—system management suite, www.jamfsoftware.com/products/casper_suite

- ▶ FileWave—system management suite, www.filewave.com/products/filewave

- ▶ KACE—system management suite, both software and hardware appliance solutions, www.kace.com

- ▶ LANdesk—system management suite, www.landesk.com/products/ldms/mac/index.aspx

- ▶ LANrev—system management suite, www.lanrev.com/product/overview.html

Review Quiz

1. What are the three primary concepts that you should consider as part of a complete system maintenance plan?

2. What service does the ARD Task Server provide?

3. What three methods can you use to manage ARD access privileges with Directory Services?

4. Where can you place UNIX scripts to run automatically on a periodic basis?

5. How do you configure a Mac OS X client to use a custom Software Update server?

6. What should be blocked to prevent access to the main Software Update servers?

7. To set up cascading Software Update servers, what file should you update on a secondary server to retrieve updates from another primary Software Update server?

8. Where are the updates stored on a Software Update server?

9. What processes are used to provide the Software Update service?

Answers

1. The three primary system maintenance tasks that you should consider are remote administration and system monitoring, asset and license management, and software additions and maintenance.

2. The ARD Task Server acts as an intermediary between the Remote Desktop administrator application and the managed clients. You can set up a remote Task Server to provide enhanced installation package deployment, enhanced report-generating capabilities, and better response when using multiple Remote Desktop administrator applications.

3. The three methods for managing ARD access privileges with Directory Services are: using local group names with predefined ARD privilege keys, using network-based group names with predefined ARD privilege keys, and using custom managed preferences with ARD privilege keys.

4. You can place custom UNIX scripts to perform system maintenance tasks in the /etc/periodic/daily, /etc/periodic/weekly, and /etc/periodic/monthly folders.

5. To configure a Mac OS X client to use a custom Software Update server, you must modify the CatalogURL key in the /Library/Preferences/com.apple.SoftwareUpdate.plist file. This can be done using the `defaults` command or managed preference settings.

6. To prevent Macs from accessing the main Software Update servers, you must block access at the network level to http://swscan.apple.com or set a fake Software Update server address.

7. To set up cascading Software Update servers, on any secondary server you must modify the `metaIndexURL` key in the /etc/swupd/swupd.plist file.

8. On a Software Update server, the default location for downloaded updates is the /var/db/swupd/ folder.

9. On a Software Update server, the `swupd-syncd` process synchronizes the catalog and downloads the updates, and the `http` process owned by "_softwareupdate" reshares the updates to your Mac clients.

Index